(Out)Classed Women

Recent Titles in
Contributions in Women's Studies

(Out)Classed Women

Contemporary Chicana Writers on Inequitable Gendered Power Relations

Phillipa Kafka

Contributions in Women's Studies, Number 184

GREENWOOD PRESS
Westport, Connecticut • London

Library of Congress Cataloging-in-Publication Data

Kafka, Phillipa, 1933–
    (Out)classed women : contemporary Chicana writers on inequitable gendered power
relations / Phillipa Kafka.
      p.   cm.—(Contributions in women's studies, ISSN 0147–104X ; no. 184)
      Includes bibliographical references and index.
      ISBN 0–313–31123–4 (alk. paper)
      1. American literature—Mexican American authors—History and criticism. 2. American
literature—Women authors—History and criticism. 3. American literature—20th
century—History and criticism. 4. Women and literature—United States—20th
century—History and criticism. 5. Power (Social sciences) in literature. 6. Sexism in
literature. 7. Sex role in literature. 8. Feminism in literature. 9. Mexican American
women in literature. I. Title: Outclassed women. II. Title: Out classed women. III. Title.
IV. Series.
PS153.M4 K34   2000
810.9′352042′0896872—dc21   00–023948

British Library Cataloguing in Publication Data is available.

Library of Congress Catalog Card Number: 00–023948
ISBN: 0–313–31123–4
ISSN: 0147–104X

First published in 2000

Greenwood Press, 88 Post Road West, Westport, CT 06881
An imprint of Greenwood Publishing Group, Inc.
www.greenwood.com

Printed in the United States of America

The paper used in this book complies with the
Permanent Paper Standard issued by the National
Information Standards Organization (Z39.48–1984).

10 9 8 7 6 5 4 3 2 1

To
Celene Krauss
and
Ed Weil
For the Way We Were

And to
Olavi K. Koskinen
For the Way We Were,
Are, and Always Will Be

Contents

Preface

DEFINITION OF THE TERM "CHICANA"

In terms of language, Gloria Anzaldúa claims that although the Spanish of Chicanas is as varied "linguistically as it is regionally" (1993c, 294), Chicanas who speak only English or only Spanish are as much Chicanas as those who speak several variants of Spanish. Chicanas from the southwest are no more or less authentic than Chicanas from any other geographic area in the country. In other words the term Chicana does not necessarily imply the necessity of a linguistic connection to the Spanish language so much as to a given ancestry and perspective.

Denise Segura defines the term Chicana entirely through ancestry, as signifying birth in the United States with Mexican ancestry and the identification of oneself as such. Of all those men and women who identify themselves as Spanish by origin, more than sixty percent are Mexican by origin (1986, 61).

Vicki Ruíz defines the term Chicana as encompassing second-and-third generation Mexican American women (1993, 123). Irene Blea defines Chicana "as a Mexican American female, a minority female" subject to oppression by race and sex. She also notes that scholars rarely include in their analyses class issues in relation to Chicanas (1991, xi). This is an omission that I correct in this work.

However, in her otherwise penetrating analysis Blea accuses the United States of having an "internal colonial model." Only within the United States are minorities such as Chicanas unwillingly controlled systematically by oppression and treated as Third World populations. Coded discourse is used to indicate their inferiority, such as with derogatory stereotyping. She defines a colony as internal if one group is supposed to enjoy equal status legally with any and all other groups, but is discriminated against and subordinated to second class status (1991, 139). But by failing to differentiate Chicana experiences from those of

Chicanos under the colonizers, Blea makes Chicanas invisible. Either Blea views Chicana experiences as interchangeable with those of Chicanos, as on a level with Chicanos in terms of inferior class status relative to the colonizers, or she is excluding Chicanas from her definition. She also does not distinguish Chicanos from Chicanas on the basis of class. In fact, Chicanas are first subordinated to Chicanos, and then both Chicanos and Chicanas are subordinated to the colonizers. Although Chicanos are subordinated once, Chicanas are subordinated on three levels–once to their Chicano men, a second time to Anglo men who rule the culture, and a third time to the Anglo women who have internalized Anglo men's values.

Vicki Ruíz places the term Chicana at the end of more than three chronological divisions of Mexicans and Mexican Americans by categories by generation. A first generation in the United States is called Mexicano, a second generation, Mexican American, and the third generation and beyond, Chicana. She uses this categorization on the grounds that it emphasizes cultural changes over time and place, as well as cultural continuity or "cultural coalescence," as she calls it. Through an ongoing process of creating culture by picking, borrowing, retaining, and creating "distinctive cultural forms," Mexican/Mexican American culture is far from being one "single hermetic" culture. Rather, it is characterized by a diversity of cultures impacted by generational changes, gender and class differences, regional variations, and diversity of individual experiences. For individuals are not only passively influenced by external forces, but they also react to them and consciously choose how and in what ways they are going to attempt to perpetuate their culture's values onto succeeding generations (1995, 72).

Blea further defines Chicanas "as Spanish, Mexican, Hispanic, Chicano, and Latino females." Certain women are referred to as Chicanas just as certain men are referred to as Chicanos, to indicate that they object to discrimination by the United States against Mexican Americans historically and in the present. Blea views as Hispanic anyone who speaks the Spanish language and is from a Spanish culture. She also includes Mexicans and Mexican Americans in the term Latino on the grounds that if members of this group wish to call themselves Chicanos or Chicanas, they may do so (1991, xii). Here, again, she subsumes Chicanas and makes them invisible when she lists only Chicanos as being Hispanic and also when she subsumes both Latinas and Latinos under the masculine rubric of Latino should they wish to call themselves Chicanos and Chicanas.

Elisa Facio, who also defines Mexican Americans or Chicanos as a subset of Latinos omits Chicanas entirely from her definition. Blea's Hispanics and Facio's Latinos are listed identically as from Central America, Latin America, Cuba, and Puerto Rico, and as including Chicanos. Facio does not include Spanish Europeans in her definition of Latinos as Blea does, but Facio also emphasizes Latinos' great diversity in geography and culture (1996, 8), as does Asunción Horno-Delgado. Unlike Facio, however, she also notes educational and class differences (1989, 8).

Previously, Hispanic, not Latino, was the blanket term within which Chicanos/as were considered a subset. Latinos were also previously generally defined as a separate group in a parallel manner to Chicanos, also under the main category of Hispanics. However, the term Latinos/as is becoming the preferred alternative definition to the term Hispanic used as an inclusive term. On the grounds that if contemporary Hispanic writers align themselves with and are influenced by previous generations of women who were "storytellers" of "oral histories," or if they were activists in earlier movements such as the Civil Rights, or gay or women's rights, or La Raza, or Latin American movements, Horno-Delgado calls them Latinas and claims these origins for "a Latina literature" (1989, 8–10). On this basis, regardless of the differences between Chicana and Latina literature, she expands the term Latina philosophically to include Chicanas and Puertorriqueñas, as well as any other women writers who identify and align with those movements in "struggle" (1989, 6, 11).

I am in accord with this perspective, which is beginning to prevail in influential quarters.[1] I am also grateful for it, if only because it includes critics such as myself on the basis of our identification with Chicanas and with their struggle. Most importantly, I define "Chicana" as Guillermo Hernández does, by expanding his definitions for the term "Chicanos" to include Chicanas. He sees "diverse interpretations," although he himself only uses his third one:

(1) [P]olitically, to refer to individuals who identify with the political ideology arising during the 1960s; (2) culturally, alluding to individuals of Mexican ancestry but who are either unfamiliar or uncomfortable with Mexican cultural codes–a usage that differentiates them from "Mexicanos" or "Latinos"; (3) historically, an ample meaning that subsumes a wide variety of perspectives, that is, it refers to the full range of historical experiences of the people of Mexican descent living or having lived in the territories that are now considered the United States. (1991, 118)

The following text is devoted only to an analysis of those contemporary female writers whose ancestors were "Indian and indigenous on this continent, Spanish, and then Mexican" and who live in the United States. I define these writers as Chicanas and restrict my discussion to their works in terms of their responses to inequitable gendered power relations. I rarely make cross-references to Latina critics and writers, except where parallels are so strong as to demand them, as, for example, when I link the Puertorriqueña Carmen Valle's "Diary Entry #1" with the Tejana Chicana Sandra Cisneros's "Woman Hollering Creek."

ORGANIZATION AND STRUCTURE OF THIS TEXT

I analyzed representative samplings of contemporary Chicana authors and critics by topic within and across various Chicana texts and looked for patterns that exposed "broad recurring themes" (Ferdman and Cortes 1995, 254). I always attempted to bear in mind that how women are represented was not merely the result of an author's "individual consciousness," but was also a part of a "larger, historically specific discursive setting" (Kutzinski 1993, 213).

In my introduction, I discuss both my findings and my aims in writing this text. I then divide my work into two parts. The first part deals with the major themes and concerns of Chicana writers and critics in relation to the problems caused by inequitable gendered power relations. In the second part, I discuss the Chicana writers' and critics' proposed solutions. Finally, in an Afterword, I explore the relationship between Chicanas and other women writers and critics of color to the "mainstream" feminist movement and Jewish feminists.

NOTE

1. See for example, the current catalog of Arte Publico Press, "the oldest and largest publisher of U.S. Hispanic literature" which now publishes in accordance with Horno-Delgado's broad parameters.

Introduction

CHICANAS' MAJOR CONCERNS AND THEMES

Peter McLaren justly complains that the problem with mainstream critics is that they are for the most part "unwittingly implicated in the reproductions of systems of class, race, and gender oppression" (1996, 158). Although this could be the problem with other critics, as well, contemporary Chicana critics generally make a conscious attempt to read Chicana authors from the lens of a mutual concern about women's relationship to "the materiality of oppression and its operation in structural and institutional spaces" (Walters 1996, 860). They also read Chicana authors in order to "inquire into the power relations requiring such suppression" (Ebert 1991, 889).

Chicana critics also consider the so-called privacy of the home and the family as intrinsic elements of the cultural institutions of capitalism that replicate how those institutions operate. In this manner unequal gendered power relations are reinforced and perpetuated (de la Torre and Pesquera 1993, 10). Are they so intent on critiquing the system of their colonizing oppressors that they forget that it is not unique in the world; that all other systems are sexist? Be this as it may, there can be no doubt that critical discussion of the works of Chicana authors focuses on the multitude of ways in which Chicana authors expose the pervasiveness of inequitable gendered power relations. They focus on Chicano and Anglo-American institutional systems and attempt to propose solutions to improve this situation in those cultures.

They are far from content in wallowing in complaints about the various areas of their victimization, wherever they turn. Chicana critics do not view Chicana authors' diverse suggestions for improvement in terms of the flaws and shortcomings of their faulty characters merely as individual appeals to modify behavior. Nor do they view Chicana literature as escape mechanisms that substitute for the need to focus on affecting and changing "material reality"

(Peck 1994, 108). These critics view Chicana authors as dislodging individualistic solutions from the primacy that they have traditionally held in mainstream literature. They adamantly refuse to valorize private solutions characteristic of the heroic, individualistic model of traditional Anglo mainstream literature. Instead the Chicana critics view Chicana writers as calling for "solutions that are collective and political," not "individual and psychological" (Peck 1994, 110). They view Chicana writers as attempting to frame their characters' problems so as to convey them as primarily the results of social issues, as situating their characters and their major concerns "in a sociohistocial context."

Most importantly, the topic of my text, inequitable gendered power relations in a variety of venues such as "inequitable access to political-economic wealth and power," is perceived by Chicana critics not only as the byproduct of racism and sexism, but also as the byproduct of class oppression. Janice Peck goes so far as to note an attempt to dislodge the traditional perception of racism as a problem to be dealt with in terms of individuals: their "individual rights, attitudes, and behavior." Instead racism should be viewed as "a history of structural inequalities in the American political-economic system" (1994, 112). Suzanna Danuta Walters, however, does include what Peck fails to note. American history also points to links between sexism and "class oppression" which feminists deplore as two intrinsic systems within global systems of "patriarchal, capitalist, racist regimes" (1996, 865).

Chicana critics also view Chicana authors as depicting their characters as indoctrinated into an "organization of human life . . . that has become normative" for women (Levinson 1995, 125). Furthermore, Hispanics in general, according to many critics, come from a *"power distance"* model created when traditional mainstream "culture-specific" values differentiate between Hispanics and non-Hispanics (Rosenfeld and Culbertson 1995, 221). "Cultures high on power distance [such as Hispanic cultures] place a great emphasis on power and status differences, show respect and deference for those in power, and tend to be conforming and obedient to authority" (Rosenfeld and Culbertson 1995, 221).[1] "Normative" or "naturalized" divisions of "social classes" become "realities" to most Hispanics. Class divisions are perceived as such, because they are "shared by the majority of social agents." Thus "a common and sensible world" is produced, a world of common sense (Leps citing and translating Bourdieu 546, 1995, 179–180).

According to Bernardo M. Ferdman and Angelica C. Cortes who did a survey covering forty countries, there are four major patterns traceable in Hispanics throughout diverse "national value systems": *power distance, uncertainty avoidance, individualism/collectivism,* and *masculinity/femininity.* On the basis of this work, Hispanics in the United States, as well as in Latin-American societies, have been described as being more collectivist than Anglos. The group is emphasized over the individual, the need for consensus is greater, and interpersonal behavior is stressed over task achievements (1995, 248).

For example, Ferdman and Cortes cite the tendency of Hispanics to emphasize dignified and respectful, "positive" rather than "negative" treatment in "interpersonal relations." They also claim that Latin American cultures are "high-context" cultures; i.e., that the communication they prefer is informal, grounded in trusted personal relationships rather than "formal" and "impersonal" relationships and communication. Hispanics avoid "uncertainty"and prefer those in power and authority to be distant, "with a clear delineation of formal rules, and relatively autocratic, paternalistic leadership styles" (1995, 248). They also claim that both Hispanic men and women maintained the same preferences and avoidances.

The findings of this survey are contrary to the findings of Chicana critics in relation to Chicana authors' rebellion against Chicano and Anglo male power and authority over Chicanas. Chicana critics and writers expose Chicano and Anglo cultures as irrational in controlling and constraining women, thereby perpetuating women's subordination as a "category" in status and class as compared with their menfolk. Walters defines this notion of power and authority as constructing women "in power relations" (1996, 851). For men, according to Chicana writers and critics, power and authority is a different experience than for women. Power and authority is a direct exercise, a possibility for themselves involving their own subjectivity. Thus their concern about how power and authority are wielded is not so much over women as subjects who handle the power and authority, but over women as objects of that power and authority. As Marjorie Levinson notes, women's "subordination" to men as the holders of power and authority in all cultures is the result of "economies of subjectivization and of value, economies entailed by the qualitative and philosophically founding distinction between subjects and objects" (1995, 115).

Similarly, Judith Butler sees such Othering constructions as "identity categories" that cut both ways because as "instruments of regulatory regimes" they are used as "the normalizing categories of oppressive structures." When they are opposed, as is the case with Chicana writers, they can be used by rebels as "the rallying points for a liberatory contestation of that very oppression" (1990, 13–14).

Margarita Zamora is even more specific in her assessment of the source of differential class rankings for Chicanas. She conveniently ignores the presence of differential class rankings in extant Indian populations. Instead Zamora traces such rankings to gender differences conceived of by western white males in "Columbian New-World hermeneutics" and even further back, thousands of years, in "Aristotelian notions of difference" (1991, 140).

Coupled with Columbus's comparisons of the Indians to beasts, they complete the triad which according to Aristotle constituted the category of natural servant or slave–animal, women, and deficient men. . . . The similarities between the Aristotelian natural slave and the larger Columbian portrait of the Indians are obvious. In both cases inferiority is expressed as *lacking*, especially in the areas of intellectual and moral capacity. Superiority is conceived as *possession* of a full complement of the attributes that constitute humanness in its highest form. In the Columbian texts as well as in Aristotle's

Politics, domination is presented as a philanthropical and paternalistic act: the "haves" (read fully human elite males or citizens) supplement the deficiency in the "have nots," or natural slaves, through paternalistic intervention. They thus allow the natural slaves to lead better lives. Inferiority, then, means to lack, while superiority means to have, but it especially means to be able to supplement a deficiency in others, to complete, to fill an empty space. (1990–1991, 141)

In contrast, Gloria Anzaldúa supplements Zamora's "deficiency" theory by passionately and directly exposing to shame and blame those responsible for gender oppression. Courageously including her own culture, this great critic indicts "male culture" for brainwashing Chicanas into believing that treachery flowed into their veins at birth from their maternal line only, from their female Indian foremother. Here she is striking back at the centuries of masculinist discourse that conceptualized Malinche as a traitor. This served the purpose of men very well, because as a result of such training women of color have been colonized and enslaved mentally as well as physically by Spanish and Anglo invaders for more than 500 years. Anzaldúa adds that the lot of women before the Spanish conquest over indigenous Indian culture in Mexico was by no means an enviable one, either. So no matter which men ruled throughout all these centuries, women were kept silent and invisible, although many times they did wish to have a voice and to "openly rebel against their oppression." Unfortunately "the odds" in the form of total male supremacy were too heavily weighted against them and still are (1987, 22–23).

Emma Pérez, a Chicana historian, deplores Anzaldúa's sweeping condemnations of patriarchal hegemony precisely because they are sweeping, but perhaps in reality because they included Indian ancestors in her critique. Pérez vigorously agrees with Anzaldúa that ruling male elites are the ultimate source of inequitable gendered power relations. However, she excludes her own Indian and Mexican ancestors, as well as contemporary Chicanos, in her definition of ruling male elites as confined entirely to middle-and upper-class white men who have situated themselves over all women, especially women of color, politically, socially, racially, and sexually. And men of color did not do so? For as long as history has been recorded, she firmly maintains, white men have *man*ipulated their class status and power for their own benefit against all women so that they are always in power over women, always controlling and constraining them (1993, 61). And men of color did not do so?

In addition to Chicana critics' vewing Chicana writers as questioning the oppression of women by men in their cultures, they see these writers as focusing especially on "how and WHERE men's dominance is constructed and maintained." Out of all the multitude of "arenas and practices of [male] domination" over women, an overwhelming number of Chicana writers view "women's conceptual location" as forcibly situated by men in constrained home spaces, involving only "certain forms of family life" (Resnik 1996, 965). And through it all, in every era and in every aspect of patriarchal cultures and institutions, many Chicana writers see women as silenced, without recourse. Alcalá's view, as expressed through one of her characters, is common: "I will study my lessons; God told her just what to say: Thou shalt not think. Thou shalt not be free. Thou shalt not seek happiness in this land of strangers, for their ways are not ours. Thou shalt not cry out, for mine is the Power" (1992, 41).

Some writers and critics, such as Yvonne Yarbro-Bejarano, are somewhat more sanguine. She agrees with postmodern critics that the subject has contingency and is influenced from diverse sources. Nevertheless, she believes that the subject can still be self-reflexive about the messages coming at her from all sides, still can choose a position from which to theorize her experiences in her environment, and can then choose how to conduct herself (1994, 5–28). Others see such an easy solution as simplistic because of the binary nature of Chicana subjectivity. Angie Chabran Dernersesian perceives this split as occurring twice over time (1993, 34–71). Therefore Yarbro-Bejarano does not sufficiently separate a first stage, where most Chicana writers situate their characters, from a second stage where Chicana writers consistently situate their solutions. Chicana writers do not necessarily reflect their characters or even themselves as yet having achieved a second stage.

According to Dernersesian, in the first stage Chicanas are either not included or considered when groups are characterized, or else the systems that produce gender differences use only masculine definitions for locating and identifying subjects. In a second and preferred stage, Chicanas subvert and displace masculine discursive models by creating their own alternative definitions. Chicana writers depict their characters as having voices both as individuals and as a group. These female characters define themselves and their own subjectivity and situatedness. They do not accept male definitions and discourse for women in relation to themselves and other Chicanas (1993, 39). Readers will see Dernersesian's analysis verified in my analysis of Chicana texts, even when paradoxically Chicana writers do depict characters as victims of their masculinist culture. In so doing, Chicana writers are consciously exposing the errors of any Chicanas who believe the lies that entrap them.

Chicana critics and writers also ask whether in view of the awesome global power and continuity of the patriarchal machine over aeons, women can ever hope to join together and fight a revolution that will achieve success. The solution Pérez offers is to reject what she deplores as the destructive patterns to which women are addicted that are present in all power relations. The steps that she believes are vital for women to follow in order to bring about the desired change are difficult to take. They involve behavior modification. Women need to first cast off the complex patterns of sexism, racism, class elitism, and homophobia that we have all inherited and internalized to the point of addiction. If we hope to train future generations to successfully live free from addiction to our culture's pervasive masculinist discourse, which she believes is sourced by capitalism, we must start doing so immediately. Painstakingly, one woman at a time, we must heal ourselves. Only then can women as a group collectively be cured of these addictions. Expressing the communitarian values that feminists valorize, she calls for the group to take responsibility for individual women within the group at the same time as individual women are responsible to the group collectively (1993, 69).

It is unclear whether she is addressing only Chicanas in Chicano culture, or Chicanas in Anglo culture, or all women globally. In any case, I perceive the Chicana and her collective as contained within another, greater collective–a system of collectives, in fact–which comprises a global system beginning with Chicano patriarchal culture and extending out into a global patriarchal culture. All these are addictive, and all these have to be healed, from individual boy to individual man, to groups of men, as well, not only by women, in order for the global patriarchal system to achieve transformation.

When Neil Armstrong landed on the moon, exulting that he had taken one small step for mankind, he lost an opportunity to express a truly global vision. He addressed the world once again in such a way as to perpetuate the masculinist discourse that has made half of humanity invisible for so long. Perhaps Col. Armstrong was acculturated to the mythology of the moon as female and that of "the man IN the moon." At the point he actually touched down on the moon, he may have believed what he said. Certainly he came from the same perspective as that of the European explorers when they landed on the American continent. Like them, he (a white, Western, Anglo), a generic man in his eyes and those of most "First World men," was taking possession of, conquering a virgin territory in the name of *his* civilization, "mankind." At any rate, far from exhilirating millions of his female listeners, his omission disappointed, depressed, and offended them. Dernersesian satirically puns off Armstrong's trivializing sexist exultation when she defines her solution for women to overcome their global addiction to masculinist discourse as also "only one small step" (1993, 66).

Pérez includes Chicana writers as assisting in the struggle to change patriarchal society through emphasis on the demeaning ways in which that society engenders Chicanas. Simply to be born females serves as a rationale for their culture to automatically situate them as inferiors symbolically. She views as the single most imperative motive behind Chicana writers' creativity the gender asymmetrical relationship thus created through social symbolism inimical to healthy female subjectivity. It is this drive that causes Chicanas to become self-reflexive, to find and define their own subjectivity (1993, 66). This process arouses and stimulates their creativity to seek and find expression in a variety of forms, including literature and art.

Ultimately, therefore, Chicana concerns about the various forms of oppression to which they are subjected serve, in Herrera-Sobek's and Helena María Viramontes's view, as "primary vectors" (1988a, 10) which provide the structure for their works. Other ethnic literature reveals this characteristic, yet Herrera-Sobek and Viramontes consider it as unique to Chicana writing.

Herrera-Sobek views the most crucial components of Chicana literature as pragmatism, combined with concern for social issues (1988b, 172). Her pride in these attributes of Chicana literature flies in the face of all that the established traditional literary canon values. Traditional scholars have traditionally refused to admit that critical interpretation can ever be based on anything other than an individual's situatedness in the culture. Whatever is defined as political, social, and aesthetic shifts meaning depending on individual interpreters' situatedness according to the "relations in which they are involved" (Fiske 1996, 204). Oh, but even if it is impossible to ever be abstract or objective, everyone should at least pretend to sound that way. If not, heaven forfend, critics, philosophes, intellectuals, and cutting-edge thinkers such as traditional scholars and professors might sink to sounding emotional, and subjective, the way inferiors such as women and Others do habitually, which has traditionally branded them as inferior thinkers.

Therefore because political and social concerns based on their situatedness in the culture are paramount in many Chicana works, many traditional, mainstream white elitist critics claim (I suspect without reading their work) that they find both Chicana criticism and Chicana literature inferior. That is, when they deign to acknowledge that such criticism and literature does exist. Such a sweeping dismissal results from the traditional critics' unexamined belief system based on their elitist acculturation and training. If any literature is overtly and primarily political, as is Chicana writing and criticism, then it is deemed unworthy of serious attention and consideration and dismissed. The grounds given are that "minority" literature, which includes Chicana literature, lacks "aesthetic" elements that ought to be primary over political elements. Unless, of course, the author is a dead male, already canonized, generally a white European, like the great satirist Jonathan Swift. His oeuvre was almost entirely given over to politics, as was his life. In order to attain advancement, given his not altogether promising situation in life, he did the best he could. Garbing himself in the robes of an Anglican clergyman, he eventually became the dean of St. Patrick's Cathedral in Dublin, although he had hoped and indeed deserved greater reward. He played politics in order to be given a secure sinecure within the mechanism of one of the English State's most powerful institutions—religion. His celebrated, impassioned arguments against the English oppression of the Irish people had to be couched in anonymous rhetoric because a price was put on his head by the English government. It had no clue that he was the guerrilla in their midst.

Traditionalist mainstream critics fail to examine their training, to comprehend that their own supposed aesthetic is always and currently situated politically and socially in an elite hierarchical, patriarchal global value system that runs all cultures. It is impossible for human beings not to be situated somewhere. Without a conscious examination of where we find ourselves, how we have been produced as scholars by the system, we will replicate what we have been trained to valorize as natural—the abstract, objective, godlike distance, the rational voice. This is humanly impossible. They are always and can never be other than postures or acts. Hererra-Sobek and Viramontes, uniting on this point with most feminists, demand that the elitism that disguises the racist, sexist, and classist perspectives of the traditionalists and their canon be addressed and condemned. I for one also condemn the perpetuation of traditional parochial and exclusionary thinking on innocent, trusting younger generations of students who come under their influence.

Chicana critics and writers also depict Chicanas as molded and influenced by their immediate female kin, to a large extent their grandmothers and mothers. They tend to live in female-only or female-dominated homes. Men are depicted for the most part either unsympathetically–as oppressive, dictatorial, violent, and abusive to their women–or as absent.

Another hallmark of Chicana writing, according to Yvonne Yarbro-Bejarano, is that they do not tend to make any character's voice privileged over any other character's voice. Rather they create a sense of collaborating community through the inclusion of many individual voices about the experiences of Chicanas in an oppressive culture (1988, 134–143). It is true that readers find in Chicana literature a multiplicity of voices, each with her own separate perspective, each supposedly contained or held without being made wrong. Nevertheless, a commonly held message lurks under the surface, either in the author's own voice, or in her persona, and in a narrator who pulls the various voices together into a symphonic whole. Furthermore, when they are not doing so directly, as is most frequently the case, contemporary Chicana authors expose their thematic message for decoding through the deployment of some privileged passage, or tone, or individual voice.

As an "affirmation of individual and collective identity," Tey Diana Rebolledo and Eliana Rivero claim that for the most part Chicana writers practice what linguists define as code switching: that is, using two languages. Further they believe that code switching should be noticed by critics and readers who would understand Chicana literature (1993, 76). I would add, once again, that code switching is not unique to Chicana writers, but is a characteristic common to most ethnic writers.

Rebolledo and Rivero also contend that the majority of elements common today in Chicana literature were present in the earliest writings. They list these elements as the primacy of the family, the necessity to preserve traditions, and the use of folklore. They also include depictions of alternative healing practices such as those of curanderas and brujas (1993, 39).

Blea isolates certain major elements in Chicana culture that I would argue are also elements in the work of Chicana writers and critics. She notes, as have other observers, the intense indoctrination of Chicanas into concepts such as honoring and respecting authority figures and elders, and familism. Blea also notes as important thematic elements "the environment, community, and language" (1991, 78). But her terminology is so abstract that readers cannot grasp what specifically she has in mind when she refers to these elements as coming to light in studies of Chicanas of all ages in the form of values that shape the lives of the elderly. Further elements Blea observes as common in Chicana works are an emphasis on cleanliness, marriage, the need for learning, respectful treatment of elders, an emphasis on religious and spiritual experiences, male-female relationships, the observation of important holidays, and the necessity of improvement in conditions in their society (1991, 122).

In my reading I also found other elements characteristic of Chicana works. These are expressed most often in the form of an "irreverence toward the myths of religion and marriage," or what Jamaica Kincaid calls western and gender-based "fixtures of [masculine] fantasy . . . subject to the subliminal mechanisms of social control" (Cited in Kutzinski 1993, 213).

Anzaldúa also provides an excellent synopsis of elements in their works that are common to many Chicana writers and critics. Like Cherríe Moraga and many others, Anzaldúa refuses to buy into the myths of Chicano culture about women. One of the few Chicanas to openly do so, she admits being repelled by Chicano machismo. She considers machismo a caricature of reality; that it demeans Chicanas by conceiving of them "como burras" [like burros] (1987, 21) because Chicanas retain their dignity even in the face of such humiliations. She especially despises the claim by men that women are most virtuous as their servants. For these reasons Anzaldúa refuses to valorize the culture which has done injury to her while claiming to be protective of Chicanas. She then commands her compliant gatekeeper sister Chicanas not to impose their masculinist belief systems and values on her. She insists, instead, upon getting). a reckoning from all three cultures in which Chicanas are enculturated–the Indian, the white, the Mexican cultures, all in her view badly flawed (1987, 21–22). Her highly influential term, the "Borderlands," eponymous with the title of her work, is her term for where women are currently situated in these three cultures, out on the perimeters of society–in its borderlands [or in my term "outcast/classed"]–by the males who rule these cultures. In order to end this marginalization, Anzaldúa advises us that we must learn to "live *sin fronteras* [without borders]/ be a crossroads" (1987, 195), in spite of how liminally men would place women, how marginalized we are.[2]

According to Adela de la Torre and Beátriz M. Pesquera, most contemporary Chicana writers' major concerns and themes focus on the ideological manipulation of Chicanas into political and sexual domination and exploitation, or as I put it, into inequitable gendered power relations (1993, 7).[3] De la Torre and Pesquera also explore Chicano culture's enforcement of familism in their analysis of all its diverse manifestations of inequitable gendered power relations. As Judith Resnik astutely perceives, the problem of familism arises from "power and subordination–not families" (1996, 965). Constraining elements manipulate the concept of family until it becomes familism.

Because Chicana critics and writers are acutely conscious of the complex of cultural constructions that create male and female identities, they seek to upset normalizing, naturalizing separate female existences in all cultural institutions, not only in marriage and religion. They envision a different world in which diverse forms of love and family structure are commonplace. They are antagonistic to the Catholic Church and would subvert and destroy it; they would rewrite traditional myths and folklore, especially for the young and for other women. When I analyze the revamped myths of Chicana writers, readers will note with much pleasure that their efforts to rewrite "the plots of patriarchal culture" (López Springfield 1994, 701) have been successful.

The evils resulting from gender oppression remain constant, before and after the colonizers. Nevertheless, some Chicana critics and writers also castigate the psychic "dismemberment" (Anzaldúa 1987, 251) of Chicanas that they blame on the evils wrought by the European Spanish and Anglo racist and sexist colonizers.

Chicana critics and writers also tend to focus on the patterns exposed in dysfunctional relationships between men and women as significant and originary sites of inequitable gendered power relations (García 1986, 24). Such relations are complex, but always result in the lowering of women's class status throughout all institutions of the social fabric. De la Torre and Pesquera claim that gender inequalitiy is indigenous to the capitalist society and strengthens and perpetuates the structural organization of all its institutions (1993, 10). Gender inequality within patriarchy flourishes everywhere, even within the so-called "private" domain in the outside world. And even if a culture is not capitalist, even if it does not function as part of a global system of capitalism, still a global culture of patriarchy pervades all our institutions, not just those of the capitalist system. The capitalist system is indeed patriarchal and hierarchical, but so are all other systems. Gender inequality exists within all systems and the globe itself, in every culture.

In this text, readers will see Chicana critics and writers critiquing a variety of patriarchal institutions. This is a focus common to all feminist writers, not only Chicana writers, because it is patriarchy, not capitalism or communism or fascism, or any other "ism" that has given birth to feminism. The goddess Athene in Greek mythology is conceived by her male creators as emerging at birth full grown, not from her mother's womb, but from her father Zeus's brow. To no feminist's surprise, she has no mother, denied an experience common to all human beings ever born. That is the beauty of imagining gods and goddesses, the ability, at least in imagination, to have life created without mothers. What more appropriate way of being born for a female godhead who represents wisdom, an attribute only males are capable of, than to be birthed by the chief god himself? Despite this ridiculous misogynist male fantasy, only once in human history has a father ever unilaterally succeeded in giving birth–and that is patriarchy–to a daughter–and that is the feminist movement.

Chicana critics' and writers' strongest antagonism, and with good reason, is felt against the legalized, socially sanctioned, religious institution of marriage. In fiery words, Anzaldúa excoriates the institution of marriage as having "silenced, gagged, caged, bound [women] into servitude" (1987, 22). Even in more measured tones and language, other Chicana writers and critics agree. In fact, describing and analyzing this particular example of inequitable gendered power relations between men and women provides Chicana authors with a fulfilling mechanism for venting their outrage to some degree in creative ways through the use of direct, raw, hard-hitting, violent imagery.

Rather than "sanitizing" (1996, 1086) their feminine psyches, as Janice Haaken puts it, many Chicana writers use violent imagery that helps foster a sense of healthy self-identity in the face of a culture that forbids females from displaying outrage at the outrageous treatment of them. Extending Haaken's observations to Chicana works, they can be defined as in the genre of "revenge narratives . . . that . . . unmask patriarchy–lays it bare–in a way that avenges at least some of the wrongs done to women in its name" (Vélez 1989, 2). But patriarchy is difficult to expose, to uncover, because it is sophisticated in both structure and ideology. Women have never been consciously and consistently trained as a group from infancy onward to recognize and to learn its strategies, techniques, its devious ways. They have had to learn about it the hard way, as individuals, across cultures, or as members of small guerrilla bands confronting a culture, a society, an entire world that would ostracize them.

Cynthia Orozco sees the only antidote to this hitherto successful division and conquest of women as feminism (1986, 11-18). Diana Vélez has studied patriarchy and isolated what she believes to be the crucial component of patriarchal structures as the "division of labor by sex" (1989, 4). From this division the patriarchy constructs an ideology of complex, artificial models that naturalize gender division so as to situate male identities as superior and dominant. Female identities are then created to complement what is considered masculine so as to be inferior and subordinate to male identities. In this theory of constructed identities, however, Vélez fails to note how this division is achieved, that masculinist discourse serves to naturalize those given masculine and feminine identities or subjectivities whose divisive source she isolates.

Above all else, Chicana critics and writers write "from the perspective of the oppressed classes: workers, peasants, women" (Vélez 1989, 4). Anzaldúa also sees inequitable gendered power relations as sourced by class inequities. All of us on the planet are connected, although we imagine otherwise. If we were not connected, then we would not all be on this planet together. She believes that a "false" class system was constructed to make human beings imagine that we are not connected. This system is characterized by artificial hierarchical binaries such as rich/poor, colored/white, tall/short. Cutting to the root of the problem in her inimitably direct way, she sees all such distinctions as "bull" because all humans "eat and shit in the same manner" (1981c, 228). Until she finds a human being whose blood is not red and whose food intake does not end in waste matter, who never cries and never sleeps, then she might consider such a person better than other human beings. Moreover she reserves the right not to make such an unexamined assumption of superiority based on such differences, if indeed she did find such a person.

MY AIMS

My aims throughout this text are to perform an inquiry through the writings of selected contemporary Chicana writers and critics "into the power relations requiring [women's] suppression" (Ebert 1991, 889). In the course of this inquiry, I focus on the use of inequitable gendered power relations "to explain the societal positions" (García 1986, 24) of all women, not only Chicanas. This is begun, reinforced, and perpetuated through patriarchal deployment of "sociosexual racial power as a form of survival" (Rebolledo and Rivero 1993,

26). Carlos G. Velez-I agrees, viewing the situation as curiously paradoxical. All "nation-states" use rhetorical claims of equitable treatment for all their citizenry. But they assign the "rights and duties" of their citizens in relation to "preconceived" notions about various "subcultural" (1995, 184) ethnicities that somehow mirror only the values of that one group that holds all the power over all other groups. No reader should have any difficulty in guessing the identity of the dominant group. Here I would expand Rebolledo and Rivera's and Velez-I's observations to point out that the distribution of "rights and duties" is done in societies, not only according to the dominant power's notions of ethnicity and race, but according to their notions of gender, as well.

Further, Velez-I reasons that the dominant group perpetuates its power over the subordinate group as an inferior group (or lowering them in class compared with the ruling group). This demotion is justified by the group in power on the grounds of difference–namely, that they subordinate ethnic/racial groups because the have different (i.e., inferior) ways of doing things, different political and economic positions, different spiritual beliefs and ideologies, different value systems, and express themselves differently. That is, according to the dominant group's standards these groups display inappropriate, unsuitable behavior (1995, 184). In terms of why women would then be subordinated as a group, Velez-I's paradox obviously does not hold, although it could justify women's stratification within the subordinate groups to which they belong.

What Chicana critics rarely take into account, but what Chicana authors notice and stress, is that a critical mass of "gatekeeping" women collude with their cultural training. Without collusion by male-identified women, none of the systems that now run societies could have maintained themselves in configurations of male supremacy–in the dominance of patriarchy and its ideologies. Gatekeepers illustrate Blea's astute observation that "the oppressed will oppress themselves once they have internalized dominant values" (1991, 146). This is the case because patriarchal ideologies dominate over all others even when "interpellated by a series of different, competing, and overlapping ideologies, including class and non-class ideologies" (R. Sanchez 1990, 5).

In the following analysis of Chicana writers and critics, I pursue a class-based exploration of gendered power relations as reflected in Chicana texts in order to examine how those relations work both in the Chicano community and the larger world. Skeptical of such efforts, Jinhua Emma Teng inquires as to the fruitfulness of gender "as a category of analysis" in view of the fact that gender is "a relational term." Instead, she recommends that we situate analyses of gender "within a framework of other social relations." Otherwise, she claims, "without consideration of class, ethnicity, age, and other factors" we could become as "one-sided" as the sweeping "studies of 'women'" (1996, 142) favored by second-wave feminists (such as myself). Clearly such thinking situates Teng as in accord with those who would replace "Women's Studies" with "Gender Studies." The second wave response, as well as that of other feminists who do not agree with her, is that we will no longer be feminists when there is no longer a patriarchy.

She charges that such broad perspectives were ironically limited only to our own kind, presumably white, middle class, heterosexist. This "cheap shot" is common and convenient on the part of some women of color feminists, young feminist historians, posteminists and antifeminists. So repeated in so many venues is this charge that it is fast becoming an integral mantra of an unexamined belief system hardening into a defining, essentialist summation of second-wave feminists. Today it seems accepted in all quarters as historical reality. Second wavers, however, have begun to respond to this charge, as I do in my conclusion to this text.

Teng does qualify her critique of the sweeping rather than particularist critiques of patriarchy characteristic of second wavers. If feminist critics enter into "endless particularizing," she cautions, specifically in relation to "working-class women [and] rural women" we might be prone to the "pitfalls of essentialism" which can result in "the ghettoization that so often flaws multiculturalism" (1996, 142–143). First Teng accuses second wavers of essentialism in our sweeping condemnations of patriarchy, and then condemns as essentialist "particularization" characteristic of Afracentric and other women of color critics.

I reiterate as strongly as I can that in my view there is indeed an all-encompassing enemy out there. And why shouldn't we take a broad view, as broad as we humanly can, when patriarchy is a conspiracy so immense as to be global? Essentialism is necessary in combating patriarchy, because our theory has to be large enough and sweeping enough to describe and critique its enormity of dimensions, encompassing the globe and all cultures. I also contend that gender, like race, *is* a class issue, or rather, that being de-, dis-, or outclassed as women *per se*, globally, is an issue so far more neglected than noted, with only a few exceptions.[4]

From my reading and analysis of Chicana writers, I have observed, as Segura does, that race and gender are linked to class. According to women's class at birth, their access to opportunities in life varies. Because Chicanas are racially and ethnically minorities and considered as such, they therefore begin life ranked low in class status, a radically different situation in life than that of most Euro-Americans, regardless of gender. Before any improvement in the quality of life for Chicanas can be devised and implemented, this fundamental chasm between Chicanas and the rest of the population needs to be noted and evaluated (1995a, 133).

Segura, like Vélez, concentrates on locating the source of women's inferior status and class and bringing an end to it. She finds it residing in a blanket system of male "privilege" that must somehow be wrested away from them everywhere–at home and in the workplace. The crucial link between these two areas of women's lives needs to be noted by us because throughout "all classes and racial groups of women . . . all men gain by female subordination" (1995a, 129). Sadly for Segura's hopes, the results of the socialist Algerian struggle against the French are typical of many for women in cultures that pride themselves on successful class struggle. Success did not put an end to the practice of inequitable social stratification by gender for women. Segura argues that patriarchy precedes capitalism, that it is in fact "its organizing principle" (1995a, 129). I would add that patriarchy is also the organizing principle for and precedes every other "ism, " whether socialism or capitalism.

In the course of identifying the major concerns and themes of Chicana writers and critics, I first noticed that the topic of gendered power relations was paramount. Men and women are classified so that men and women dominate and control and are dominated and controlled in terms of their gender, regardless of their stratification within the subordinate groups to which they belonged. This led to my undertaking an analysis of inequitable power relations on the basis of gender as the primary factor in cultural allocations of class rankings. I focus specifically on Chicano culture because I discovered in my reading of Chicana writers and critics that gender differentiation alone, regardless of race and ethnicity, was sufficient to exclude or "outclass" women from status and ranking by class. I discovered that "outclassing" of women extended *beyond* and *beneath* issues of race and ethnicity. Regardless of the race and ethnicity of Chicanas, as females they were assigned no class ranking or status in their culture *except* that as females they bore a relationship to males. Chicanas as females were assigned class rankings only in relation to males. Chicanas were therefore situated outside of their culture's system of class rankings and status. As Velez-I puts it (without reference to gender), when in the colonizers' belief system the rankings they have imposed on the conquered are due to "cultural differences," and when that mind-set also forms an integral part of the culture's institutions, then the colonizers will enslave and exploit the colonized. They will do this by situating their inferiors in and restricting them to a "structurally asymmetrical and subordinate status" (1995, 185), or what I call inequitable power relations–and when applied to women specifically, inequitable gendered power relations.

Above and beyond, or, rather, beneath everything else, "*class*, as opposed to culture" is the means by which the "triple oppression [of Chicanas] is organized and expressed" (Segura 1986, 61). The subordinating of Chicanas by class at birth places them in inferior positions structurally in the culture in relation to all whites and to all Chicana men in a multitude of arenas. These "stratifications" (Segura 1995a, 130, 111) begin in the home, then extend out to discriminatory treatment in school, and then on into the workplace through lower levels of employment and income rates.

In this text and in my title, I follow Blea's description of inequitable gendered power relations as resulting in class "inequality" (1991, 57). According to Blea, Chicana scholars situate the root cause of this problem in an advanced capitalist society, in combinations of elements of that society, how class is structured and functions. These scholars perceive that capitalism and male dominance in the capitalist culture contribute to the control of women. Men within this capitalist culture and through its very existence dominate and oppress women to their advantage. However, men in all other cultural forms globally– whether socialist or communist, fascist or monarchist, Muslims or Orthodox Jews, or American capitalist materialists–use their cultures' structures, as well, to dominate and oppress women. Therefore men are the root cause of the problem, regardless of the kind of hierarchical structure they create. However, men are raised by women in all cultures, and in all cultures women perpetuate the systems prevalent in those cultures. Therefore women who perpetuate women's oppression share responsibility with men for the ongoing oppression of women. For this reason it is necessary for Chicanas to confront and rebel against male oppression in a patriarchal system whose "mechanisms" through which men control all institutions in that system are "sexism and racism" (Sosa Riddell 1995, 405).

Clara Lomas cites history as exposing the drawbacks to this successful system of inequitable gendered power relations, drawbacks never publicized or taught to women. For example, confining women to unpaid labor within the home has had powerful negative results on them such as "alienation, economic dependency, and domestic slavery" (1986, 198). These conditions in the home provide major thematic patterns in the writing of Chicanas in their depictions of women's oppression.

Segura dreams of bringing "an end to unequal power relations in society." As the result of their power, men have expanded their range of free choices by freely expanding constraining items for women as contained within their "definition of gender." Somehow gender content expansion narrows the range of free choices for women, always to their disadvantage, but never to men's. Greedy opportunists revel in their discovery and celebration of endless myriad variations of essentialist gender differences and grow wealthy and famous in the process. Their shameful agenda feeds on the patriarchy's delighted celebration of anyone who reinforces the perpetuation of inequitable gendered power relations.

The placement of males on Mars and women on Venus, gender distinctions between right brain side and left brain side usage, and the effects of estrogen and testosterone are all examples of discoveries of gender binaries. All are designed to perpetuate the patriarchy and reinforce gender differences in order to benefit the patriarchy and its masculinist discourse. These exciting finds about innate gender differences somehow all only valorize female passivity and nurturing and only reinforce male displays of conflictual conduct for power and control, their "innate, inborn drive" to war with one another, to mark out turf. The media and all the lords of the institutions that create culture exult in and publicize every sign of difference that enables them to deploy masculinist discourse as signifiers of male superiority to women. The purpose behind all their unpacking of layers of incontrovertible proof of women's inferiority to men serves only to reinforce patriarchal systems of power relations so that "gender inequality" pervades Chicano and all other cultures to the point where it " transcends class" (Segura 1986, 48).

Unlike Segura, I see gender inequality as not transcending class, but providing yet another class category within each class or throughout all classes in Chicano culture and all other cultures. Thus its lowest class category falls so low as to be underclassed in every instance. For whether we place emphasis on race, on class, on gender, or attempt to work on all three strands simultaneously, all are based on "ideological constructs, or processes of signification" (Peck 1994, 122). These form international patterns economically and politically in terms of the history of the development of capitalism, as well as other less prevalent patriarchal "isms," as I have previously argued. Inherent in this history "are relations of domination and subordination" (Peck 1994, 122). These relations not only form between men of different cultures, but within the same cultures, whereas in all cultures all men dominate all women.

All the Chicana authors in this text share Anzaldúa's feminist perspective. But by no means do all of the Chicana critics (such as Moraga and Anzaldúa) face inward as well as outward in their anger against the oppression of Chicanas. Too often, after they have declared themselves Chicana "or *mestiza*" deliberately and consciously both to themselves and others, when they have published their declarations of identity, they nevertheless confront varying fragments of cultural messages, codes, and indoctrination inscribed deep within their psyches, and all at odds, conflicting (Yarbro-Bejarano 1988, 140).

Chicana feminist critics see Chicana writers as characteristically viewing Chicana experience as that of working class women of color within Chicano culture. In turn, Chicano culture is within the dominant culture. A major element, therefore, of Chicana criticism and writing is devoted by necessity to an analysis of how the diverse aspects of Chicanas gendered, raced, acculturated, and class identities form, combine, and clash. Of necessity, therefore, Chicana texts are primarily devoted to battling against the "objectification" (Yarbro-Bejarano 1988, 140, 141) of Chicanas through the cultural imposition of constraining gender roles, as well as simultaneous exploitation racially and economically.

According to Blea, many contemporary Chicana feminist scholars analyze the implications of cultural control in terms of race, ethnicity, class, and gender issues. They view race as "a genetic variable" and ethnicity as "a cultural and social variable." Gender is "another genetic variable" and class is "a cultural or social variable" which, when combined together form "a complex of patterns" that cause only Chicanas to be "disadvantaged" (1991, 3–4). This claim is a debatable or extreme one, which other Chicanas and even mainstream women would dispute. It is not borne out either by statistics, anecdotal evidence, or in literature by ethnic and women of color writers. Regardless of class, across many cultures globally, women actually experience being "disadvantaged" by class, if nothing else, because of inequitable gendered power relations, even when they are born into the upper classes.

There are more areas for identification of similar "disadvantaged" situations for women globally than taking an extreme "centric" and ethnic working-class perspective would warrant. Reading across the races, ethnicities, and cultures, reading transnationally, exposes broad patterns of oppression against all women. Nevertheless Blea's analysis of the sad history of the relationship between the Anglo feminists and women of color feminists in her first chapter on major elements in scholarship by Chicanas is indeed hard-hitting and often on target. Take for example when she complains that mainstream women for the most part have never apologized or attempted to right wrongs against women of color, or to understand women of color. This is the case because Anglo women belong to the men who comprise the power structure that dominates over all women. The basic difference she observes between Chicanas and Anglo women is that the former group of women long for a better system, whereas the latter group is content with the system and only wants power for their own group only within that system.

Blea here makes the distinction between mainstream and other feminist women most commonly made by Chicana critics. Racism, sexism, and classism built into the capitalist system form the dividing lines between Anglo feminists and "feminist of color." Interestingly she omits ethnic feminists like myself who also feel this division, although we are not necessarily of color. Also the phrase "feminists of color," which Blea uses, or "women of color" has come under criticism by some African American female critics. They argue that both phrases code white women as having no color, as if they were the standard and norm, and therefore women of colors other than white were aberrations. In addition, sexism and classism are not confined to the capitalist system, but universal to all cultures, including African, Asian, and Middle Eastern. They all practice inequitable gendered power relations, sexism, on their own women, although men of color rule these cultures.

Similarly but with one crucial difference to Blea, I see these Chicana writers' works, not so much as stemming from a coalescence or intersection of issues of gender, race, culture, and class. I see them also as critiques of class rankings of women according to gender and race "under patriarchal, racist regimes" (Walters 1996, 865). I would add that the assumption made by Walters and many other critics that patriarchy and racism are characteristics only of capitalist regimes is flawed. Patriarchy and racism are found in all regimes, as is sexism. In this text I am doing precisely what Jennifer Russell suggests needs to be done in an interview, namely that women (and men) need to talk about class more among themselves, across groupings, around the world:

A lot of people argue that we can't speak of "woman" in essentialist terms, that we have to account for class differences. I'm asking, "What do you mean by that? Are we talking about differences in mere income and occupation, is that what we mean when we're talking about class?" We need to talk about the concept of class in a way that does not focus merely on income and occupation, especially in the American experience, which is too fluid. *We have to think about class as a form of social positioning* [emphasis mine]. (1996, 32)

Blea lists certain normative cultural oppressive patterns against which Chicanas have to struggle in order to change traditional gender roles: how women are socialized, the current limitations that circumscribe their lives because of their gender, sexism as functioning like racism, and abuse (1991, 9). But she does not relate both racism and sexism to the class setup of gendered power relations. She does trace the devaluing of women by society as the cause of their oppression, both socially and physically, again without linking devaluing with declassing, although devaluing permeates all classes of women.

She does see abuse, however, as symptomatic of discrimination on a sexual basis which privileges males. If so, then what is the devaluing of women as opposed to the overvaluing of men, if not inequitable gendered power relations in terms of class? She concludes that both racism and sexism are due partly to how the genders are socialized. For this reason, dividing by gender becomes naturalized and therefore desirable (1991, 121). As Marie-Christine Leps puts it, "The habitus we find in our cultures perpetuates and reinforces the assumption that previously decreed, regulated, and common practices of 'relations of domination and resistance' are 'natural rather than social,' i.e., socially constructed" (1995, 180). This "habitus" perpetuates and reinforces in succeeding generations of men and women "a passive consumption of hegemonic truths rather than an active participation in their determination or contestation" (1995, 182).

In this text, then, I explore how inequitable gendered power relations determine the classes of women, or, rather, their lack of class, as represented in the works of selected contemporary Chicana writers. As I have shown, critics do see Chicanas as classed, no matter in which group Chicanas attempt to include themselves. In contrast, I see Chicanas (and by extension, all other women) as declassed, "un"classed, or "beneath" the class system of rankings in their culture, a patriarchal culture, and, by extension, in all patriarchal cultures. Chicanas are "outclassed" from within the existing structure of class systems. My aim, therefore, is to analyze what Chicana works reveal about gendered power relations in patriarchal culture in terms of (de)class(ify)ing women, or excluding them from the cultural institutions, or (under)class(ify)ing women, making women into an underclass.

De la Torre and Pesquera claim that Chicana writers are not only "questioning and restructuring feminist and national discourses." They are beginning to incorporate into their work themes involving class issues and "new forms of identity" that have hitherto been ignored in both Chicano and Chicana art forms. "[W]ithin a colonial dialectic, the authors expose the gender inequitable power relations of the culture, as well as their 'resistance'" (1993, 3, 6) to their colonizers. Like de la Torre and Pesquera and most other Chicana feminists, Walters and other mainstream feminists also confine their scope to those cultures where only white men rule. But they expand their theory to include women of all races and classes as still always enmeshed in inequitable gendered power relations in subordinate positions to white men in all cultures where white men rule (Walters 1996, 851). Such Chicana and mainstream feminist theories are confined entirely to white male rulers and colonizers. I would expand their perspective to include all known cultures globally in history and currently. Except for rare instances in time and place, women and whatever groups are Other have been and are always placed in subordinate positions in terms of class compared with those in power who are always males.

Such feminists are not sweeping enough in their condemnation of the global rule of white men. I see all men of every culture for the most part ruling over all women. In many cases, of course, white men rule over men of color, but in cultures where men of color rule, they also situate women exactly as white men do, as subordinate and inferior to themselves. In cultures where men of color rule, women of color are situated in subordinate positions in real life, as well as in the text. It should be apparent, then, that everywhere on the planet, in every culture, "lines of power" extend from rulers, colonizers, oppressors of all kinds into the "lives of gendered, raced, ethnic subjects" (Walters 1996, 863). Not only are women declassified globally. Everywhere and in every culture, every community, every nation, state, city, town, village, and in the countryside, women's subordination to men is taken as a given, "invisible . . . 'at the center of the world,' while appearing 'hidden . . . incognito'" (Lane 1994, 36). It is routine, every day of women's lives, "a ubiquity," naturalized, normalized, like breathing, even to vigilant feminists who are committed to continually observe the culture. Even we are still daily surprised by ever new manifestations of inequitable gendered power relations, like weeds abundantly and endlessly sprouting in the rocky garden of equality we have been endeavoring so hard to cultivate.

According to Velez-I the only means by which subordinate groups would be allowed to enjoy acceptance is if they would mainstream themselves by acculturating and assimilating. Obviously, he is not speaking to women and Others who cannot do so by appearance. Certainly this is impossible for women who will not and cannot disguise themselves as men. There are, however, women gatekeepers, the gender equivalent of "oreos," who have internalized masculinist values, despite their outward appearance. Their headsets are so constructed that they go through life with external female corporeal materialities. However, they have internalized male psyches, attitudes, perceptions, values, judgments, and prejudices to the point where they impose them on succeeding generations, as is amply revealed in this work and as I discuss at length elsewhere.[5]

Ruth Behar, who identifies herself as a "US Latina," a Cubana critic, valorizes Chicana writers and other women writers of color because they have the courage, unlike mainstream feminists, to refuse "to separate creative writing from critical writing." They practice "writing personally in the academy" and outside of it. By doing so, they challenge "the politics of exclusionary theoretical languages" which she perceives as "characteristic of Anglo feminist writing until the recent move toward autobiographical criticism." In declaring her preference for the personal voice, as well as the intellectual and political voice, Behar takes the opportunity to castigate mainstream ("Anglo American") feminist writers (1993, 17). She deplores their reinforcing and perpetuating traditional masculinist discourse and lauds Chicana feminist writers for being the ones who rebelled against this form of patriarchy in literature. As a student, from the 1940s to the 1960s, it was impressed upon me very strongly in college and graduate school that I must never use the first person singular in my papers, only the impersonal word "it" followed by an abstraction, such as "it would appear that."

To make matters worse, when second wavers attempted to enter the academy in the seventies, and to write and publish our papers, our theses, our books, we came up against influential female academics in high places who abhorred feminists. They agreed wholeheartedly with and colluded with the male professors who vastly outnumbered and outranked females. In addition, I experienced mainstream feminists adamantly insisting upon the masculinist perspective and discourse they were taught. They too prevented other feminists from getting published and their messages from getting heard because they found any use of the personal and feminist revisions of masculinist generic discourse offensive, embarrassing, and "trivial." I myself fought pitched battles alone against these three groups of academics in my department and my university for twenty-five years over every attempt of mine to substitute terms like "humanity" or "humankind" for the so-called "generic" "man" or "mankind," or "staff the tables" for "man the tables." For this reason Behar is anachronistic, because many second wavers like myself had no other choice but to retreat into silence if we wished to remain in academia and at least influence our own students in the privacy of our own classrooms. Most second-wave feminists hired in the sixties, seventies, and eighties did not survive academia if our feminism surfaced in any way. We were fired before reaching tenure.

Our struggles, our voices, cursed and ostracized as we were, paved the way for succeeding generations of feminists of all colors and both sexes, as well as gays and lesbians to theorize, to write, and to speak out from within academia. Our daily crucifixions for attempting to do so, our sacrifices, our sufferings enabled the current generation to scale the ivy towers of academia, to survive and succeed, although still against opposition. In our day most of us were the equivalent of the Japanese kamikaze pilots who dived and died, not for any emperor, but for a vision of true equality for all. I was one of the few second wavers to receive tenure in the academy, and then only because the president's wife had by chance been my student. She threatened to divorce him if he fired me, as he had fully intended to do. So, originally trained to specialize in traditional English literature and then in American literature, I became the pioneer in the academic wilderness, my new specialization in ethnic studies demeaned and unwanted. I was excoriated for my feminism and ignored, without promotion, until the next generation came along. Fresh and new, and reinventing the wheel without being aware of it, they demanded that the canon be expanded to include "minorities." Already there, long awaiting them, finally in the right place at the right time, I was swept along in the wave known as "multiculturalism." I then achieved great success–at the very end of my long career.

I also want to address Behar's dismissal of the use of citations by scholars as "ransacking [the writing] for juicy quote-unquotes to use in a prefab theoretical scheme" (1993, 17). It is ironic that Behar, while blaming traditional critics for intolerance toward other values than theirs, does not have tolerance for different ways of approaching writing and criticism than those she prefers and forwards. I would have hoped that she would not have assumed that the use of "juicy quote-unquotes" defines critics who choose this method as critics "who . . . appropriate" rather than as critics who "facilitate the appreciation of literary texts." She equates citation with appropriation, thereby precluding the existence of other reasons for citing "juicy quote-unquotes." How about because we want to do honor to those we cite, because something they write is written well? I cite if in my opinion another writer has a particularly insightful and brilliant perception that reinforces and influences my thinking. I also use citation when I wish to disagree with other writers, such as Behar, for purposes of pinpointing and illustrating for readers exactly what statements I am debating.

I also cite in order to dialogue with my colleagues, by weaving my thoughts in with theirs in a community formed of written words. We are separated geographically, by age differences, and on the surface by a diversity of race/ethnicity and life experiences. Yet I always feel a pleasurable sense of excitement whenever I come across a passage in a work of literature or literary criticism that resonates strongly for me; that matches what I myself have already experienced, thought, and written about. Whenever I find such passages in my research and cite them, it feels as if I am not an isolated individual laboring alone at the computer for months and years at a time to publish my message. I feel, instead, like one of a large chorus of feminist voices, mainstream, ethnic, and women of color in the United States, as well as around the world. Each time I find and use "juicy quote-unquotes," there is re-created within me the precious experience that I originally had as a second waver, of finally belonging somewhere; of being a member of a group of like-minded thinkers that I have rarely felt in my professional and personal life otherwise.

For me, the addition of citations adds an invaluable dimension to scholarship, as does the judicious use of relevant autobiographical material. Why can't the two co-exist? Isn't the simultaneous inclusion of paradox, ambiguity, ambivalence, and difference part of our feminist theory, pedagogy, and practice? In spite of many artificial barriers created between women and women (and men and women) by social constructs, we can nevertheless each strive to bridge them.

Finally, I also aim to bring the literature and criticism of contemporary Chicana writers to the attention of mainstream and feminist and other ethnic and women of color critics and writers, to assist in the project of integrating Chicana writers into the literary canon and curriculum. Although I analyze the works of several Chicana critics and writers in this text, I have primarily emphasized the work of Roberta Fernández and Sandra Cisneros. The diversity of the problems and the solutions that many critics consider as characteristic of Chicana writing is most succinctly and powerfully illustrated by these two authors. They explore the historical conditions for Chicanas. They are conscious of and denounce the unjustified sufferings Chicanas have endured in specific and allegorical ways. They have the courage to deplore the external cultural, as well as familial forces that constrain Chicanas. They situate themselves politically as feminist Chicanas. By doing so, they convey hope to their readers that Chicanas can improve their lot through solidarity with other Chicanas, as well as with other feminists through active participation in efforts to bring about change in their own culture's patriarchy, as well as in the global patriarchy.

NOTES

1. Ferdman and Cortes define the term Hispanic as incorporating "people with a multiplicity of backgrounds and ethnic experiences, encompassing Mexican Americans, Puerto Ricans, Cubans, Dominicans, and Central and South Americans" (1995, 247). This text deals only with Mexican American or Chicana writers under the rubric "Chicana." Elsewhere, I analyze the work of Puerto Rican, Cuban, and Dominican writers, for example, under the rubric "Latina."

2. See Phillipa Kafka, preface and conclusion to *(Un)Doing the Missionary Position: Gender Asymmetry in Contemporary Asian American Women's Writings* (Westport, CT: Greenwood Press, 1997).

3. Blea makes eloquent arguments relating to violence against Chicanas, especially in discourse, such as when Anglos joke about them. They complain about the violence of American society and place especial emphasis on violent "incidents such as muggings, shootings, and murder," as well as on violence in the media. Ironically, they do not include in their definitions of or discussions about violence "ethics and morals," how too many Anglos use language discourse "to demean and discredit minoritiesand women." Anglos do not realize that discrimination "begins at the cognitive level with thoughts and ideas transmitted first by means of language, then into behavior" (1991, 61).

4. Such as Zillah Eisenstein, the well-known Marxist feminist, who also argues that women form a sexual class.

5. See Phillipa Kafka, *"Saddling La Gringa": Gatekeeping in Contemporary Latina Writers* (Westport, CT: Greenwood Press, 2000).

Part I

Chicana Writers' Major Concerns and Themes

Chapter 1

Catholicism and Religious Mythologies

Antonia Castañeda situates the source for current gendered inequitable power relations as the European colonizers' project to convert the Indians to Christianity. The colonizers' primary goal was to restructure existing gender relations so as to create inequitable gendered power relations, or what she calls "gender stratification" (1993, 29). Second, within a patriarchal concept of family values and organization the colonizers subordinated women to men primarily through normalizing harsh legal and religious rules and regulations, such as depriving them of recourse to divorce. Again, most cultures, not only European culture, have the same characteristics.

In her poem "Theatre," Bernice Zamora maintains that the Catholic Church makes participation impossible for women. It decrees against full sexual expression for women in binary terms. For males sexual expression is always moral and sanctioned, considered "male play" (1995, 37–38), for females, always immoral and forbidden. Here Zamora, like many other Chicana writers, attacks Catholicism as an arbitrary male enclave and sees its transformation and destabilization as a solution. Denise Chávez accuses the representatives of religion of perpetuating mindlessness in their pedagogical methods and of elitist distancing of themselves by class ranking and privilege from their worldly charges:

I served my need to serve a handsome Christ without understanding Old Testament Covenants, altared symbols, or ancient religions of early, early Americans. By instruction, I served those generations of teachers who tested the truth of religious theories not at all, teachers who, when inclined to generosity with Biblical promptings of THE WORD, made it available jab by syllabic jab, whole constructs be damned, and by the grace of the Christian God "be thankful the sun shines on you at all, child," I recall a Bishop saying to us beggars of confirmation. And so indeed, by the grace of administers of grace, I breathe slowly and in time to a time unrecorded, a time of creaturehood. . . . Thinking for myself is a new experience. (1992, 51)

Anzaldúa also charges the Catholic Church with failure to make her daily conduct and spiritual experiences meaningful. She expands her critique of the Catholic Church to include other religious institutions on the grounds that they somehow deprive Chicanas of a natural, spontaneous, pleasurable life-affirming existence (1987, 37). However, she does not detail the specifics of her charges. Or as Demetria Martínez puts it in "Power": "at 20 you killed him [God]" (1995, 49). But by the age of thirty, she has finally come to terms. The scars of uprooting the incompatible training inscribed in her are healing. Now, in contrast, she can "bury" the cruel training "like [an] umbilical cord," enjoy her morning coffee, a new book, listen to the "language of trees" (1995, 49). Clearly religion and spirituality in the form of Catholicism have been institutionalized in Chicana culture in a way that many Chicana feminists view as destructive.

In the wonderful cuento, "Flora's Complaint," in *Mrs. Vargas and the Dead Naturalist*, Kathleen Alcalá attacks Chicano cultural constraints as hellish for females. Instead of directly attacking the religious and ethical arguments that situate females in hell during their lives, she satirically describes their situation as though from within the perspective of a self-righteous woman who has internalized Catholicism as a means to dominate others. With the greatest hypocritical cruelty imaginable, Flora uses the Catholic-based cultural prescriptions for women for her own ego aggrandizement. This cuento contains the most powerfully written negative depiction of a mother and grandmother I have encountered. The process of reading "Flora's Complaint" is painful in the extreme, even while one laughs.

A gatekeeper to end all gatekeepers, Flora ends up in hell. But long before she does, a huge black swan that smells "burnt" becomes a fixture in her back garden. For many years, Flora complains about her hard life to this swan— actually exposing her sins to this emissary from hell that listens and records everything.

According to Flora, her children are not at all grateful to her for all the trouble she has gone through in raising them. She argues that although she did all she humanly could to raise them decently, to obey the law like a good citizen, not one of them grew up according to her expectations. She excoriates her daughters for having married ill-mannered husbands who are disrespectful of "their elders," namely, Flora herself.

As for her sons' wives, they morally disgust her. She defines them all as "fallen women" because they use cosmetics and allow Flora's granddaughters to wear jeans and play games with boys. Instead her daughters-in-law should be teaching their little girls household duties such as cooking and preparing them to care for children by playing with dolls. Further these women are materialistic and consumerist. To Flora's moral horror, their only interest in life is amassing material possessions, at least in their mother-in-law's opinion. Whenever they don't give her what she wants, she complains that they don't give her anything worthwhile "after all I've done for them" (1992, 119).

As for Flora's daughters, they were always worthless. In order to assure them a proper upbringing, she watched them with utmost care, not to protect them from harm, but to be able to punish them if "they used slang or acted like boys." She is outraged that they still had the nerve to complain when she fed their brothers more than she fed them. Boys, in her opinion, needed to "grow up stronger."

She claims that she indoctrinated her daughters to be "simple" and "pious" in "spirit" because men want only "submissive," "feminine" wives (1992, 119). For this reason, Flora cannot fathom why they all wanted to leave her, why, "instead of praying in their spare time and embroidering pillowcases for their dowries, they bit their nails and pulled out their eyelashes." She is mystified as to why they claimed she was purposely punishing and hurting them. Flora maintains staunchly that her daughters should have realized that she only did it "for their own good" and blames them for not "having the decency to cover up the bruises" (1992, 120).

She is also embarrassed about the fact that one of her daughters is unmarried and lives alone. She cannot comprehend why her daughter was "upset" one night after Flora called the police when her daughter didn't answer the phone at ten at night. She questions the kind of woman this daughter is because normal, "decent" women stay home after that time.

Even her former pastor remonstrates with Flora, but to no avail. Insulted, she leaves for another church because

He actually had the nerve to take me aside and say that some of the women, he wouldn't give me their names, had complained because I suggested that they hadn't been married nine months before their first babies were born. How dare they say anything to him, when I was just letting them know that other Christians were watching them? He said that it wasn't any of my business. If he had done his job, I wouldn't have to count. (1992, 120)

As though her priest was to blame for what she considers his inappropriate accusations, Flora admits to the reader that she has indeed abused her children. He "had the nerve to suggest that I had. . . . improperly touched some of the children. Who does he think he is? And who could have told him?" (1992, 120–121).

The priest responds with compassion and firmness. First he tells her the truth–that she is sick spiritually–and then he advises her to seek help. Flora, sadly, deludes herself into thinking that her perspective on her conduct is correct: she lives and acts on a higher spiritual plane than the priest. She conceives of herself as having lived a life devoted to carrying out "God's will," although only in a private capacity. She deplores her limitations to the domestic sphere and would expand her activities so that she could enforce "God's will" with the sanction of an official governmental title, not just those of mother and grandmother. Inquisitor perhaps? Then she would be able to "make people obey the laws of God. . . . Sometimes . . . it's hard to see the justice in life. But I know that God has a plan" (1992, 121) she states complacently with total self-righteousness. Indeed, ironically, Flora is going "to see the justice in life," but only after life, when, instead of going to heaven, as she so firmly believes, she finds herself in hell.

When she dies, her children gather around her deathbed. In an almost unbearably smug parting speech, she boasts about her goodness, that she has "lived a good life" because she has never drunk alcohol or smoked, never gone to a place where there is "immoral dancing," or played cards. She has never used slang, or cursed, or committed adultery. But she has experienced dreadful suffering because "of the pain of raising ungrateful children."

She believes that it is this suffering that is going to get her into heaven: "I count each hardship as a star in my crown. On Judgment Day, which is soon if we can tell by the state of the world, the gold will be separated from the dross, and I will receive my just reward. As will you" (1992, 122). She then glares at every one of her children and refuses to die until the last of her children, a daughter, finally arrives. Flora sits up in bed in order to point at her and scream: "That dress is too short!" Then she dies.

Rebolledo and Rivero state that Denise Chávez's work "captures the orality of women's voices" (1993, 29), as well as their humor. These qualities are illustrated in Chávez's story "Saints," where the narrator's heretical grandmother uses a sardonic tone in describing nuns' prayers. This earthy grandmother maintains that God "is grateful" to nuns for having "dedicated their lives to God." Then she jokes about their dedication as having an effect on God. As a result, "little by little the nuns are making God a nicer man" (1992, 49). If women do not have the calling to be nuns, then they are, as depicted, "Woman. Wife. Mother. Martyr" (1992, 50).

The narrator's grandmother then gives her "spiritual" advice from her vast store of personal experience:

Every woman wishes she could become a nun. You don't know what I mean yet, *m''ija*, may the Blessed Mother, she was a woman too, don't forget that, so she knows what I'm talking about, may she spare you a drunken man late at night smelling of *chicharrones* [pork chitlings] and *tequila*, worse yet, of frijoles [beans] and beer. ¡Dios mío el gas! (1992, 44)

In "'Mericans" in *Woman Hollering Creek*, Sandra Cisneros describes an "awful" grandmother who is praying at the altar in a church to divine providence, making promises and expressing gratitude to God on behalf of her daughter who does go to mass, as well as her male relatives who do not. This woman is so self-righteous that she thinks she has the power of the Virgin of Guadalupe to mediate between humans and Christ.

That Cisneros titles another story in *Woman Hollering Creek* "One Holy Night" about a Chicana girl bearing an "illegitimate" child is significant also, because of its inevitable, heretical identification of the young narrator with the Virgin Mary. As for the "illegitmate" child in the young girl's womb, it is the offspring of a mass murderer. The girl, however, conflates its birth with the infant Jesus's birth. By doing so, Cisneros is here repudiating patriarchal religious and gendered power relations that classify certain individuals in the highest class possible–as worthy of going to heaven. Other individuals are classified as "illegitimate," as declassed, and consequently devalued as human detritus–if their parents are not married in the Catholic Church before their children's birth.

Cisneros here links culturally despised female sexuality and its inevitable aftermath with a universally revered religious mythology. She succeeds in this by maintaining that sexuality is as "holy" as the asexual myth about Mary's conception of Jesus. Cisneros courageously views the masculinist patriarchal religious construct for women as detrimental to the reality of women and how they procreate. Further she views it as a sinister weapon deployed in religiously gendered inequitable power relations to constrain women unnaturally from full and free enjoyment of their sexuality.

According to Adelaide Del Castillo, man is the arbiter of inequitable gendered power relations. He dictates and determines what it is to be female, without regard to the validity of his views. Del Castillo attributes this arrogance to an "ego-testicle" perspective. As for female virginity, she is just as hard-hitting, rejecting the outlandish but traditional culturally inscribed notion that women are somehow naturally abstemious sexually. The concept of "virginity" is a creation of men rather than women's real sense of themselves if they had not been intensely socialized into making an issue of it. In reality, what is most natural between the sexes is to copulate. Because one of our major biological drives is to procreate our species, the desire to have sex is natural to women, not an avoidance of it. Women would not be negative about it, unless they were ruthlessly taught to act that way (1995, 22–23). Cisneros, through her cuentos in *Woman Hollering Creek*, argues that another factor that would make women negative about sex, besides training, would be if their experiences of sex were negative–if they were abused, raped, treated with violence, and made subject to incest and murder.

Chapter 2

Gatekeeping and Familism

Erlinda Gonzales-Berry sees grandmothers as mediators between Chicana mothers and daughters, as a kind of buffer between the two when Chicana mothers abuse their daughters. She claims that this is rare, though, with white women, because white mothers and daughters "often have conflictual relationships" (1995, 124). Her claim is irrational on two counts. Chicana grandmothers are mothers to their Chicana daughters and Gonzales-Berry claims that Chicana mothers abuse their daughters. So how can Chicana grandmothers be mediators when they themselves have been guilty of abusing their daughters who are, in turn, mothers to the daughters *they* abuse? Second, how are white women different from Chicanas, if Chicanas and white women both abuse their daughters?

It would appear that Gonzales-Berry is more interested in distinguishing Chicanas from white women in order to cast Chicanas in a more favorable light as mothers. Her most powerful argument is that white women fight "often" with their daughters, but when Chicanas do so, grandmothers immediately step in to mediate with them. Apparently Chicana grandmothers are on the spot, always available, always hovering nearby to prevent any conflict from arising. They have no lives of their own. In contrast, as everyone knows, white grandmothers are in nursing homes, or doing aerobics in retirement communities, or sightseeing around the world in Elderhostels. At any rate, Gonzales-Berry's claim regarding Chicana grandmothers is not borne out in the texts analyzed in this work. Relations between the generations there are depicted as varied and diverse, and Chicana grandmothers are not by any means always sympathetically portrayed. Further, in just as much literature by white women where grandmothers are depicted, they are depicted similarly as mediators between generations.

Nevertheless, surprisingly, a common element in all the authors I analyze in this text, as well as in ethnic literature, in general, is an indictment of many senior women characters as cultural collaborationists in Chicana and other Latina cultures. They are the group that perpetuates the patriarchal rules and regulations with the most dedication and the most fervor, acting as its custodians or gatekeepers, like vigilant watchdogs. Understandably, Chicana authors are riddled with ambivalence about these foremother characters who are simultaneously nurturers to their female children, as well as their cultural censors and guides into the prison house of adult womanhood in a dystopic patriarchy. Because of their connection to future generations, these older women play a crucial role in perpetuating the culture. They form loyal cadres of volunteers who train children to be obedient to all the interconnected institutions of traditional patriarchy. Conscientiously, they pour the young into cultural molds, teaching them to be terrified of breaking the rules on pain of religious, legal, political, economic, educational, social, cultural, community and family ostracism, and even death.

Perhaps the single most critiqued source of inequitable gendered power relations and gendered success models for women in the works of contemporary Chicana writers is familism, as buttressed by religious and secular law, as well as social customs which devolve from them in both Mexico and the United States. Eliana Ortega, for example, notes Puerto Rican women writers' battles against the Latina culture's harsh demands on every woman who becomes a mother (and therefore on every girl). This is the case because indoctrination has to be successful before the girl becomes a marriageable woman, so that she learns to conduct herself at all times passively, submissively, in a servile manner to men, and always remain silent in their presence.

The grandmother figure lives forever as "an intermediary for men but never as an active agent of her own life or that of her descendants" (1989, 127–128). Ortega could just as well be summarizing the responses of Chicana writers to their culture's inequitable gendered power relations in terms of women's roles, especially and primarily that of mother. Like Puerto Rican and other Latina writers, one of the Chicana writers' major goals in relation to the sacred cow of motherhood, as well as other constraining female roles in the masculinist discourse of patriarchy, is to divest these roles of their resonance by various means (Ortega 1989, 129).

Chicana writers undertake this daunting task in a variety of ways, for example, by adding a feminist dimension and complexity to culturally essentialized paeans to Chicana mothers and grandmothers. Whenever such characters appear in the works of Chicana writers, some Chicana, Latina, and many mainstream critics tend to react on the basis of unwarranted assumptions that these characters will fit the culturally decreed stereotypes for mothers and grandmothers and gloss over the authors' actual depictions of these characters. Ortega deplores such unthinking valorizations as "deforming myths" (1989, 129) about older women imposed by the culture's rulers on its citizenry. Generation after generation, primarily through the assistance of a group known as the family, upon which the young are dependent, mothers assault their young charges, as they were assaulted, with what the culture decrees as appropriate conduct for women. These mothers in the role of gatekeepers of the culture do this in order to keep the succeeding generations from breaking the rules of the hegemony by teaching little girls how to become women in the culture.

Another negative discursive and highly popular scare tactic is the strategic deployment of the term "emasculation" by white male rulers against Chicanos and men of color. This term has repulsive and frightening connotations because it is based on historical and contemporary reality, but it becomes overdetermined when used by Chicanos to "blackmale" Chicanas, to emotionally reinforce the loyalties of Chicanas and women of color to their oppressed men. Chicanas and other women of color would be naïve and gullible, they thunder, to be tempted to join mainstream feminists and therefore assist the oppressors against their men. At the very sound of the word, even when "emasculation" is not Chicanas' intention, but, rather, to protest their men's oppression of them, many other Chicanas and women of color are immediately silenced, shamed at the thought of being disloyal and treacherous to their own kind. They are then easily persuaded to fall back into line behind their men.

Such discursive emotional appeals are based on unexamined assumptions, as well as fact. The men who use them on their women to keep them from protesting gendered inequitable power relations are knowingly conflating gender categories. Susan Z. Andrade gives the example of numbers of "male cultural critics" who consciously define colonialism only as "emasculation . . . of male natives." She requests us to examine the term emasculation as the feminization of men of color on the grounds that it is a discursive "pejorative" move to codify "femininity" as the deplorable situation in which poor mistreated and abused men of color find themselves. Simultaneously such a term ignores the fact that "female natives" equally experience "gendered and racial violence" (1994, 209).

Similarly but to a different conclusion, one that appeases Chicano sexism, Blea traces as the sources for that sexism, not that Chicanos are patriarchal themselves, but that they are emasculated by the dominant Anglo colonizers' cultural attitudes and perspectives. First, Anglo men deny Chicano men what are universally deemed to be codified signs of masculine value which ensure a sense of meaningful existence for males in terms of status in the culture: "power, money, and control of resources." The human need for power then forces Chicanos to exert power wherever it is possible for them to do so. Because this is denied Chicanos by Anglo culture, Chicanos then exert what power and control they can over any Chicanas within their domain.

Blea therefore urges both Chicanos and Chicanas to acknowledge that any difficulties between them are entirely due to Anglo racist and sexist oppression. Once they realize the source of that oppression, Chicanos and Chicanas should do all they can together to put an end to the cycles of abuse they experience because of the Anglo patriarchal regime. If both Chicanos and Chicanas would shore themselves up with "self-esteem, love of one another, and a high value for family," she is convinced that they would never accede to or maintain "abusive relationships" (1991, 139).

First, Chicanas and Chicanos must agree with her perception of the basic problem of gendered inequitable relations in Chicano culture. They must agree that it is due to the emasculation of Chicanos by Anglos: that by depriving them of the ability to support themselves and their families, Anglos deprive Chicanos of a positive image of themselves. Blea includes sexism as part of the problem. Like Andrade she elides over the problem as due to the unmanning of Chicanos, as if Chicanas are not oppressed as women by Anglo men and women *and* by their own men, even when there has been no contact with Anglos, even before the Anglos, even before the conquistadors conquistadors. The Indians and Spanish were sexist, and Chicanos are the descendants of these highly macho cultures. True, Anglos oppressed them and oppress them today, but Chicano culture was and is a sexist culture, notwithstanding. Since when does oppression or any other group give Chicanos or Chicanas, or any other group, including women, license to turn around and oppress those within their domain? Feminists globally call for the end of oppression wherever it exists and not just an end to oppression against themselves alone, so that they can then oppress Others in turn, as many centrics claim.

Chicana writers' concerns about traditional concepts of marriage and the family, including the public's general lack of self-reflexivity about these sacred cows, are concerns common to feminists in all cultures globally, not only ethnic and women of color feminists in the United States. In this regard, most of the Chicana writers analyzed in this text, such as Cisneros, Chávez, and Zamora, reveal an embittered attitude toward the Catholic Church. They accuse this institution of keeping women's inferior position securely in place. They also accuse Chicanas themselves, such as Alcalá's Flora or Cisneros's fanatically religious grandmother, of maintaining and perpetuating inequitable gendered power relations. Their attitudes are complex, as I have pointed out. They portray such women as strengthening and perpetuating familism and in so doing also serving as gatekeepers who perpetuate traditional Chicano culture (Ruíz 1993, 115).

Herrera-Sobek sees two reasons for Cisneros's critique of so many older women: First, Cisneros objects to their keeping silent. She also rages against older women's collusion with the culture by disseminating and perpetuating its construction of "a fairy-tale-like mist" (1988b, 178) about men's various relationships to women, including violent ones like rape: of glamorizing and idealizing them, making even rape seem romantic. Grandmothers, like Michele's in Cisneros's "'Merican" and "One Holy Night" in *Woman Hollering Creek*, are only two grandmother gatekeepers among many depicted in Chicana literature. In addition, the community of women surrounding the granddaughter in "One Holy Night" spies on her at every opportunity and reports on her every movement. In doing so, they act as surrogate gatekeepers for the grandmother, so that the culture's messages are continuously reinforced. Instead of supporting future generations of women, gatekeepers withhold the truth from their young charges both in what they propagate through their teaching and "in a conspiracy of silence" (1988b, 178) as well.

Herrera-Sobek's critique can also be applied to the experience of Cleófilas in Cisneros's "Woman Hollering Creek" in the eponymous text. Like Roberta Fernández's young narrator in "Andrea," Cleófilas has elder females surrounding her. But instead of mothering this isolated young Mexican newlywed, these Chicanas seem detached and self-absorbed. After her marriage to Juan Pedro, after moving to the United States, Cleófilas is surrounded on all sides allegorically by loneliness and sorrows in the form of these repressed elderly Chicanas. On one side of her house there lives a widow, appropriately named Soledad [alone]. On the other, lives another widow, also appropriately named Dolores [sorrows] who divides her time between her garden, the memory of two sons killed in the war, and a husband who had died shortly after them from grief. Each Sunday Dolores picks flowers from her garden and brings them to the Seguin Cemetery.

Readers will observe Chicana writers weaving this thread through all their texts: gatekeepers treating younger women either with neglect when they should care, or with attention aimed at keeping their female charges in line, according to patriarchal rules and regulations. This is not to claim that Chicana writers do not also depict beloved and respected gatekeepers who genuinely return the love and respect of the youthful protagonists. Nevertheless, even they almost always serve as conscientious perpetuators of the culture's training. They do this in order to do the right thing, according to how their gatekeepers indoctrinated them when they themselves were young into the values they have internalized and now embody. They do this through familism: inequitable gendered power relations perpetuated in the home. Or else, as in Cisneros's "One Holy Night," older women are conscious collaborators inimical to the protagonists, spying on them on behalf of the culture. They have entirely internalized the nonsense fed to them, in the peculiar colonized position of objectifying their own subjectivity and that of their own group's.

Throughout history women have played "the role of collaborator as often as that of victim" (Allen 1996, 171). This is why Chayo, the narrator of another wonderful Cisneros cuento, in *Woman Hollering Creek*–"Little Miracles, Kept Promises"–does not want to replicate the behavior and lifestyles of her foremothers. Cisneros has made the same revelatory journey as Chayo's. Like Cisneros, Chayo does not wish to live in the straitjacket that her family and culture wish to impose on her. On the other hand, she still does not wish to betray her ancestors, to shed her cultural heritage. Cisneros would prefer "fusion" (Ruíz 1993, 122), as would many other Chicana writers.

Interestingly, Chayo remains single. She might very well be in the same position as the letter writer from San Antonio quoted in "Little Miracles" who can't find a decent man in all of San Antonio (where Cisneros lives). It could also signify that Chayo is simply not interested in marriage, as in the case of Felice of "Woman Hollering Creek" and the narrator of "Never Marry a Mexican."

All her female relatives pressure Chayo, many against one. Whenever she attempts to work in her room, they demand that she join them instead. Critiquing the masculinist discourse in this regard, Chayo wonders whether only boys are considered as rational, whereas girls are considered as daydreaming when studying or working; whether boys are ever forced to leave their projects when visitors come in order to "smile and be nice and quedar bien [be good]?" (126).

Girls are so harassed with name calling and other invalidating discourse, with so many repeated dire prophecies of failure and doom that their thought processes inevitably get clogged with psychic pollution, eternal defensiveness, guilt, and a strong sense of inferiority. These are the by-products of the hourly, the daily, the lifelong litany they experience: the cacophony of gatekeeper voices and masculinist propaganda in all the media and institutions of the culture. This goes on mostly in the home, where parents are far more concerned over the possibility of their female offspring rebelling against rules and therefore impose far more constraints on daughters' "individuation" (Haaken 1996, 1072) than they impose on their male offspring.

When Chayo is at home she is forced at every turn to hear her family's accusations and invalidations not only reverberating in her ears but in her heart and mind as well. They complain about and deplore the time she spends alone by herself. They are apprehensive about what she does alone in her room, how it might appear to the community, as if it were something inappropriate. Over and over they demand of their "Chayito" when she will be getting married. They compare her derogatorily with a younger cousin who is already married and they predict that Chayo will "change" her independent attitude and career ambitions just as soon as she meets "Mr. Right" (126). Because only men are valued for the same attitude toward her career and the same interests as Chayo's, but she is considered a bad girl.

Chayo's gatekeepers use counterpoint in two voices to harass her–her mother's and that of another relative's or family friend. The mother's voice, a condescending one, makes a transparent pretense of support. The other voice openly invalidates Chayo as an individual. Both women directly and indirectly attempt to brainwash or propagandize Chayo through creating and reinforcing a sense of guilt into the young woman for not accepting the culture's expectations, their parameters for women. They determine what women should be doing when they define Chayo's artistic productions as "little pictures" and her essence as an individual in the diminutive ("Chayito"). They inflict painful insults on Chayo in order to trivialize what this young woman is really making–art: "Chayo, tell everybody what it is you're studying again. . . . She likes / Making her *little* pictures. She's gonna be a painter. / A painter! Tell her I got five rooms that need painting. / When you become a mother" [emphasis mine] (126).

Her family members are the human beings she loves the most. Because of this, Chayo is most vulnerable to their opinion. Intent on enforcing the culture's ideologies about women, they give Chayo a "double whammy" emotionally, as is done to many women globally. The culture valorizes "an idealized form of motherhood," and on the other hand, it demonizes married women who work outside the home (Segura 1995b, 177). Her family uses this ideology to continually harass her, without ever questioning whether Chayo fits into either one of these molds. It is beyond their acculturation to imagine all the other lifestyle possibilities that she herself might choose–for example, as a lesbian with or without children, and without ostracism or bringing shame down upon herself.

Anzaldúa also bears witness to this treatment of girls to prevent them from turning out differently from what the culture decrees is appropriate for women. She tells her readers that early on she had "a strong sense" of self and that, like Chayo, she had a "stubborn will" that made it possible for her to make life decisions for herself regardless of how inappropriate others found them. Again, like Chayo's, her situation demanded all the belief in herself and strength that she could muster because she endured daily harassment from all those around her. There was nothing in her culture that accepted what she did with her life. So far as it was concerned, "*Habia agarrado malos pasos*. [I had taken up bad ways]. Something was 'wrong' with me. Estabá más allá de la tradición. [I was way outside of traditional boundaries]" (1987, 16).

In her poem "*Cihuatlyotl*, Woman Alone," Anzaldúa, perhaps more powerfully than any other contemporary Chicana writer, testifies to this straitjacketing experience of little girls by their cultural gatekeepers. What should be emphasized at this point, however, is that this experience is universal to all females globally, not restricted only to Chicanas. Anzaldúa describes herself as having had to fight off her own "*Raza*" [people] and her own "father mother church." They all rage at her need for independence, for self-expression of her own needs, desires, and goals, for decision making for herself in order to pursue her own chosen vocation. To achieve acceptance and approval on her culture's terms, Anzaldúa would be forced to conform to her *raza's* demands. To avoid this fate, she determined, instead, "to let your values roll off my body." She exults now that her seemingly endless struggle has at last come to an end– within herself. No longer does she feel the need to strike out in self-defense. There is now nothing further that can be torn away from or added to her self-identity in her society's effort to change her. She now shapes and creates herself. She is "the final work" (1987, 173).

To get to this stage, Cisneros's Chayo, like Anzaldúa, has suffered much, but unlike Anzaldúa she is still suffering. In her isolation she turns to the Virgin of Guadalupe to help her after first revis(ion)ing the saint so that she can relate to her. She confides in the Virgin that she shouldn't imagine Chayo did not get lumps from all sides, how difficult her life had been without her assistance. Chayo then specifies to the Virgin the hurtful discursive codes of control that the collusive female gatekeepers hurl at her, like curses, in their vain efforts to imprison her within the psychologically prescribed constraints that her uncut, braided hair represents. For daring to go on to higher education, she is insulted with terrible names by a polyphonic gatekeeper chorus of invalidation, especially and most hurtfully, that of Chayo's own mother. " 'Heretic. Atheist. Malinchista. Hocicona [Big mouth]. Miss High-and-Mighty. Miss Thinks She's-Too-Good-for-Us. Acting like a bolilla, a white girl. Malinche' "(128). Somehow Chayo still has sufficient spirit to attempt to speak up, even though every time she does, she is vigorously excoriated and suppressed as though she were somehow the wrong one, not them.

Anzaldúa's comment on "hocicona" and its variants is worth including here, namely that in Chicano culture, "*hocicona, repelona, chismosa*, having a big mouth, questioning, carrying tales" are all code words used to mark a "mal criada [evil girl child]." When used on females they are "derogatory" (1987, 55). In fact, she has never heard them applied to men.

This comment provides a devastating rejoinder to some Chicana critics' defense of Chicanos' mistreatment of Chicanas on the grounds that Anglo men have humiliated Chicano men, deprived them of their machismo. How is it that they don't request Chicanos to be more understanding? How is it that they don't request Chicanos to unite with Chicanas who are verbally abused, if not worse? How is it that they don't request Chicanos to curb the abuse that is heaped on Chicanas every hour of every day in their own homes by their own family members? And how is it that when Chicanas go out into the Anglo world, they have to experience the same treatment? How is it that Chicanos demand that Chicanas make up to them for their being oppressed by Anglos, soothe them, and put up with whatever violent responses Chicanos have as a result, and not the other way around? Why is it Chicanas must always pay doubly to Chicanos and Anglos for Anglo oppression, whereas Chicanos are victimized once by Anglos, but can then feel free to relieve and release themselves of this humiliation by venting it back onto their Chicanas?

The culture also uses certain brainwashed female gatekeepers such as Consuelo in Roberta Fernández's "Andrea." Yet like many Chicana writers, Fernández does not choose to focus on those who run the culture, on men, but rather on gatekeepers, the Consuelos. These women conduct themselves as if they were acting from a sacred calling to impose the culture's construct of inequitable gendered power relations on themselves and all other women. As Anzaldúa points out, our culture, created by men who are in power, shapes our belief systems. Prevailing "paradigms" go unquestioned, unchallenged and are perpetuated down the generations by the offices of the gatekeepers, collusive women who play an integral part in this ongoing process. Men create the rules and regulations, but it is gatekeeper women who "transmit them" (Anzaldúa 1987, 16).

Fernández gets around to Consuelo's voice very late in the story "Andrea." It is only at this point that she herself can enunciate and testify to her position and thereby give it the strongest possible validity. It is only at this point that readers become fully aware that the author is addressing the issue of a gatekeeper's intransigent adherence to her culture's traditional gendered role requirements for women. Fernández does this only through Consuelo's voice. That voice speaks only and always, not for female possibility, but for female constraint. Consuelo's reasoning is traditional also. She accuses her sister Andrea of selfishness, of self-centeredness and of violating cultural demands and expectations, as well as of violating religious codes of ethical conduct for women.

Consuelo perceives herself as altruistic and her sister as selfish. Although the family became poverty stricken after the death of the girls' father, Andrea failed to comprehend their predicament because she always had her own personal wishes gratified, even at the expense of others. After moving in with Consuelo and her husband Tomás in San Antonio, Andrea, in Consuelo's opinion, never made any contributions to the family expenses. Preoccupied with the pursuit of her own career, she followed her own agenda: getting voice lessons, buying beautiful clothing, enjoying all the pleasures of youth. Consuelo claims to have learned during this period of time to have no expectations about her sister in terms of help and admits to having been very resentful of this discovery. That she still evidently resents Andrea's conduct in the present reveals that Consuelo is convinced that Andrea violated the rules she believes in.

Consuelo harbors an even greater grudge against Andrea. She lacks a sense of filial duty. She did not give their mother her due. Because of Andrea's absorption in her career, "Mama" would not hear from her for months. In Consuelo's opinion, Andrea is so self-absorbed that she never even showed any concern about or interest in her mother's or sister's lives. Consuelo gives as an example that when she was widowed, Andrea did manage to take off from work to go to Tomás's funeral. But then she refused to stay with Consuelo any longer, despite that difficult period for Consuelo, on the grounds that she had unavoidable professional engagements in New York. Consuelo felt betrayed that Andrea had repaid her with coldness and lack of consideration after she had done so much for her.

What also hurt Consuelo was Andrea's reporting to people that Consuelo did not approve of her because of her career, traipsing freely all around the country with a troupe, acting and dancing in theaters. Consuelo claims, however, that she lost respect for her sister because of her egomania. Consuelo has already advised the young narrator not to enter the dance profession because it leads nowhere, so that her protestation that she did not disapprove of the same profession for her sister does not ring true. Tellingly, she has no regard for the fact that Andrea scrupulously keeps her professional commitments. She insists only that Andrea commit herself to family loyalties and duties as her priority, thereby projecting her own values onto Andrea.

When Andrea claims that the insignificant amount of letters she did manage to send to the family should serve as proof that she had communicated with them, Consuelo violently tears the letters–precious, irreplaceable documentation of a unique and wonderful career–into small fragments. In retaliation Andrea tears the letters into even smaller pieces and flushes them down the toilet. Years later, when Consuelo comes upon an album collection of photographs of Andrea's career, she tears them up as well. The photographs are the only surviving evidence of Andrea's success. Like the letters, Consuelo shreds the photographs into small pieces. Only this time she puts the pieces into a bag, goes down to the river, and throws them in. Clearly her outrage about her sister's career, as well as her envious hatred, takes the form of metaphorically obliterating both her sister and her career.

By these two extreme and destructive acts, Consuelo successfully obliterates all evidence of her sister's public successes, of an alternative history that could expand Chicano culture's definitions as to what constitutes women's success. Consuelo also obliterates proofs of Andrea's having freed herself from their culture's constraints against women: that she had lived and not died, as the culture decreed is the appropriately inevitable plot sequence for women who disobey its rules. Andrea, instead, had gone on to have it all–career, husband, home, and family. The evidence that if Andrea had it all, then other women could as well, goes beyond the culture's prescribed parameters for appropriate female conduct. The letters and the album full of photographs do not justify Conseulo's circumscribed and stultifying life, and that is why she destroys all evidence of their existence.

There is another proof of Consuelo's active participation in perpetuating the suppression of women outside of the culture's parameters of what constitutes female success. Her eloquent claim that such ambitions lead nowhere discourages her cousin, the anonymous young narrator, from pursuing a career in dance when she was a young girl. By this means–negative masculinist discourse–the young narrator is diverted for many years from practising what had been her chosen pursuit. By structuring the young narrator's eventual antagonism to female repression into the form of a story that exposes it, Fernández is thereby rejecting it. She does so paradoxically, also through the means of negative masculinist discourse.

Code words signal to women what their limits as women are and what is expected of them. Most women are manipulated by these words simply because they accept and trust without question what they are told by authority figures. Women who accept their cultures' words/codes/discourse–the ideology of proper womanhood–are considered acceptable and appropriate participants in patriarchal society. Thus it is that when the young narrator finishes her first dance recital successfully, tears streamed down Consuelo's face. The narrator wonders what those tears really mean, what internal emotions they project. As a result of not knowing for sure whether she has Consuelo's approval, the narrator then begins to feel tired and confused, although after such a success she should be delighted and excited. She trusts Consuelo's judgment, her negative attitude toward dancing, for example, and abides by her advice and judgment in most matters for a long time. Dancing is literally the girl's choice of career and metaphorically the symbol of freedom, of free choice for women in their lives. At this point in her young life, she trusts her cousin Consuelo's guidance and advice and that of other authority figures, "the nuns, my school counselor and my mother." This trust is the source of her premature and self-destructive decision by her junior year in high school to pack away her dancing shoes, to concentrate instead on her schoolwork, to be more "practical" (124).

Ever philosophical, Andrea reasons that Consuelo's finding and destroying the album that recorded the progress of her career was necessitous. It thereby served the purpose for which it might have existed in the first place–to be destroyed by Consuelo. Destroying the album enabled Consuelo to express her resentment of Andrea's lifestyle fully and freely. By doing so she negated the possibility of public success for a woman who dares to break the traditional rules for her gender. She also evaded the possibility that she, not Andrea, might have been wrong all these years. Consuelo's resentment of her sister on the basis of her convictions about the definitions for right and wrong conduct for women, imposed on women by the culture and by gatekeepers such as herself, may very well have been unjust. She refuses to even look into this possibility. If she ever would, her worldview might be torn to shreds, like Andrea's letters and Andrea's photographs.

Consuelo refuses to bear the thought of her sister's fifteen years in the spotlight. It would make all that she believes in and lives by erroneous. It would make her life worthless. She refuses to face this possibility, to come to grips with the heresy that pursuing one's desires freely might lead everywhere for a woman. Staking one's life entirely on living out the ethics of care might lead nowhere. In tearing up her sister's letters to the family, as well as the album memorializing Andrea's successful career, Consuelo is obliterating the evidence that a woman can follow her ambitions and be simultaneously loving, caring, and decent. This is all evidence that would destroy the culture's decree that ambitious women are unnatural women who invariably end badly. As such, they are never supported, applauded, or put forward in any way as role models for younger generations of Chicanas. Instead ambitious women are condemned, punished, and ostracized, declassed or unclassified. They are ignored by all around them, including the media, when they pursue their own self-fulfillment. They are "imprisoned in a borderland not limited to geographic space . . . that resides in a space not acknowledged by hegemonic culture" (Saldivar-Hull 1991, 211).

Using a perfect symbol for the rigid, closed-off Consuelo, Fernández depicts her as ending up unable to hear anything. She becomes completely deaf, but now able to indulge herself fully in reliving the past. Refusing to hear anything other than what she wants to hear, Consuelo consequently has lost her hearing. This disability ensues from her refusal to accept any other value systems than what she inherited by tradition and from her obstinately continuing into a future closed off forever to the possibility that the traditional cultural model for women is not universal law, but literally man-made law. Her Mexican and Chicano tradition is a closed system whose gendered class constructions in the form of the subordination of women to men within family confines do not satisfy or serve women's full needs and desires as fully defined human beings.

Readers will observe that familism (valorized by traditionalists as "family values") is condemned and opposed by the vast majority of Chicana writers and critics as sites of economic and political exploitation for women. At best, Chicana writers and critics are ambivalent toward the practice of familism. Some authors, like the courageous Roberta Fernández, even indict "male-identified women" like Consuelo, who, by accepting and internalizing patriarchy, deny their connection with other women and instead recognize only male domination (Pérez 1993, 60). Nevertheless, despite Chicana writers' struggle against familism, all studies have so far shown that it prevails "even among Hispanics who have become highly acculturated into the larger American society" (Knouse et al. 1995, 2).

Chapter 3

Discriminatory Gender Success Models

In Cisneros's "Bien Pretty Lupe" in *Woman Hollering Creek*, Lupe takes a job as an art director at a community cultural center in San Antonio. She and her lover have broken up because he has gone off with another woman–a blond, white professional woman employed by Merrill Lynch. Eddie luxuriates in Chicano culture's prerogatives for males, while cynically making use of Anglo opportunities for men of color to which Lupe, a Chicana, does not have access. As Segura informs us, the unjust "interplay" between gender, race, ethnicity, and class creates a situation where Chicanas receive less income and status than either Chicanos or other workers. Thus Chicanas and other women of color suffer from "double jeopardy" after they enter the workforce and from lack of mobility thereafter.

As I have pointed out elsewhere, what Segura views as "double jeopardy" for Chicanas because they simultaneously belong to "two historically disadvantaged groups (women and racial-ethnic minorities)" is too simplistic a conceptualization. Chicanas and other ethnic and women of color actually experience triple "jeopardy": from Anglo men and women and from their own men to the point where they are "outclassed."

Like most contemporary feminists, Segura sees class as intersecting with gender, race, and ethnicity, whereas I see these three elements as markers that invest certain dominant individuals in a culture with class status and divest others of such status. As Segura herself concludes, Chicanas are employed in far lesser numbers than Chicanos who, on the other hand, have better employment rates than other groups. She sees these numbers as reflecting inequitable gender, ethnic, race, and class power relations, although educational levels of attainment do impact on possibilities of upward mobility. In addition, the burden of home and family responsibilites also impact on Chicanas. Both constraints on Chicanas reinforce and perpetuate the system of masculine privileges, as well as the impression that Chicanas are not committed as much as Chicanos to work (outside the home, of course) (1995b, 176–177, 178–179, 181).

Cisneros exposes through her writing precisely what Segura has maintained: that options for Lupe and other Chicanas, even though they are as well educated as their men, are very much more limited for them than they are for their men and for other women. In fact, inequitable gendered power relations do not so much intersect with class as create class inequities by denigrating women and demoting them to lower economic class ranking–as in this case, Chicanas–solely on the basis of their gender, race, and ethnicity.

Lupe has supported her lover, paid both their college loans, and the rent on their tiny apartment by working as a waitress. In good times he had found the apartment to his liking, but when he met someone who could give him more, Eddie complained about the conditions of his life with Lupe. She scorns Eddie's hypocrisy in endlessly mouthing politically correct discourse about human rights' violations in Central and South America and South Africa, while he has not the slightest interest in blacks and children in the ghettoes in the United States, or Lupe herself (as a Chicana). Furious and grieving that Eddie has turned out to be an opportunist, riding on the backs of all those who fought in good faith for improvements for people of color, she also condemns him for not even having the "decency" to leave her for another "woman of color" (142).

Christine Sierra's study of Chicanas in academia found that Chicanas and mainstream Anglo academic males were "significantly different." Influenced by feminism, Chicanas now challenge the separation of what has traditionally been considered to be private, "community-based commitments and personal responsibilities" from the public or "professional" world. Such a division effectively declasses women by placing them outside of society's class ranking parameters. For these reasons Chicanas call for transformation of their "communities" and their workplace in order to change "the basis of power and influence" (1986, 7) in Chicano culture.

According to Segura, traditional patriarchal human capital theory divides the working class by occupations "stratified by race and gender criteria." This model removes the focus from human beings, especially women, who suffer inordinately from poverty due to lower class stratification. She would focus, instead, on "societal mechanisms" that cause Chicanas to be outclassed. She blames the patriarchy for hitherto having prevented "an organized, coherent challenge to [its] "prevailing social order," perpetuating itself through a "reserve army of labor" (1986, 60) of women that it has forced into existence.

Segura's brilliant observations here relate to one of the major themes of Chicana literature: how "a reserve" population of the female underclass is ensured at home as it is at work. Women are *man*ipulated so that they are tracked by the culture into a "sexual division of labor" (Lopez-Garza 1986, 72). They are consistently trained and deployed to do work which is basically conceptualized as a continuation of the work they do at home. This is the case, Marta C. Lopez-Garza tells us, because men take over control and positions of high class ranking, whereas women are allocated the most menial positions (Lopez-Garza 1986, 69).

This is also accompanied by a matching discourse that inscribes into women the desired hierarchical patriarchal perpetuation of certain knowledge formations. Lopez-Garza also reflects on the claims advanced from all sides that science and technology are magical panaceas for so many ills, including poverty. She argues that no matter how advanced the technology, inequitable gendered power relations must also be taken into account, particularly in regard to improving negative conditions relevant to women's work. Since women represent more than 50 percent of the population, there can be little hope for societal improvement, otherwise (1986, 73).

Without taking into account what Lopez-Garza calls "sex-specific inequities in power" and what I call inequitable gendered power relations, she believes that it is impossible for political economists to explore and theorize about "the transnational labor process" and the working class as "the international division of labor." A view of the working class as a "labor power" occludes class and gender divisions. If the working class were viewed as a group politically and socially, differences in political and social power based on class and gender divisions across cultures and across nations would be exposed in the so-called "international working class" (1986, 89).

Ample proof that inequity exists within their own group for Chicanas has been found in relation to "the occupational distribution" (Segura 1995a, 130) of Chicanos and Chicanas in comparison with that of white men and women. Not surprisingly, Chicanas earn less than Chicanos. That the statistics also reveal that white women's incomes remain lower than white men's exposes gender as classed and that it operates entirely in favor of men against women.

Although Lopez-Garza views this "sexual division within labor" as a topic needing research, I doubt if she intended the research to include literary works. Nevertheless my project extends her perspective to analyze the works of Chicana writers. I have found that Chicana authors depict how their characters' lives in terms of their work experiences are economically affected by a world in which wherever they turn and whatever they do, "women are defined in terms of men" (Broyles 1986, 185).

As Blea points out, Anglo discrimination according to class oppresses Chicanos in the lower rungs of the socioeconomic ladders, but she fails to include Chicanas as a class in her victimization model (1991, 139). Further, when she argues that because in order to enhance their profit margins it is necessary for the upper classes to have lower classes to exploit to those ends, the same could be argued as true for all women in all gendered economic and social classes, not only poor women. In all classes women are used to expand profit margins for all men in social, political, economic, educational, and especially religious and family institutions, and both physically and emotionally as well.

Cisneros's "Bien Pretty Lupe" illustrates this in terms of Eddie's maximization of profit for himself in his act of leaving a Chicana who has done everything for him. Instead he chooses a white woman whom he believes can do much more. Eddie is depicted as driven only by a ceaseless, ultimately successful drive for upward mobility at the expense of Chicanas. What Janice

Dewey discovered in Estela Portillo Trambley's play *Doña Josefa* about a
lesbian benefactress to her community who commits suicide, can well be true
here in terms of outclassing women. This is accomplished through patriarchal
gendered success models: "Overshadowed by dominant, partial, and repressive
cultural values, all women, women of color, lesbians, *are displaced and
marginalized*, and Portillo knows this both personally and politically" (1989,
46).[1]

Chicana works are organized for the most part by what they are attempting
to expose in terms of class relations of power in two cultures, primarily in terms
of gender and race. Pierre Maranda defines as "semantic charters" or "signifying
systems" those "culture specific networks that we internalize as we undergo the
process of socialization" (cited in Alarcón 1989, 106). Most women accept them
without question because they are exposed to them as terms in relationships,
church dogma, and sex role typing. Bernice Zamora wittily illustrates this
problem in her poem "Pueblo 1950." She remembers that when she was twelve
years old she received her first kiss. Her mother said "shame on you," her
teacher said "shame on you," she herself then said "shame on you" (1993, 315),
but not a soul ever said anything at all negative to the boy who had kissed her.

One of the themes most common to Chicanas is the refusal to be objectified
according to gender roles and relationships, as well as to be the victims of racial
and economic exploitation (Yarbro-Bejarano 1988, 140), although racism may
rub off on the objects of racism themselves, in this case, Chicanas. In "Saints,"
for example, Denise Chavéz's young narrator Soveida exposes this phenomenon:

Saints are also culturally rooted, like San Martin de Porres. He is the first black man I
ever knew about. He is very handsome and always seems happy. He is a saint for all
displaced people; himself an outcast by color. He is somehow very dear to all Mexicanos.
He once worked with lepers and the poor. He is so nice! We embrace him like a brother
and admire his thick curly hair, not unlike our own. He is a saint for all Latinos, a get-
ahead saint, who is loved and accepted by all the *viejitas* who would never allow their
daughters (¡*Ni los mande Dios!*) to marry Black. (1992, 40)

In Fernández's "Andrea," Consuelo's prickly response to her white female
employers when she worked as a thirteen-year-old maid, reveals that she already
perceives them as exploiting her. They are racially and socially condescending in
their assumed genetic and class superiority, as troped in their giving her
hand-me-down clothing. But Fernández shows the other side of the coin to
racism, an alternative response to these same white employers. Consuelo's
younger, more mellow sister Andrea receives a great return on her investment of
trust when those employers reveal another aspect of their ethnocentrism and
racism–condescending patronage, or, in this case, "matronage." They lavish
every kind of material and educational benefit on the innocent, vulnerable,
trusting child–in order to improve Andrea's status socially and further her talent.
A problematic in this story, then, is how Fernández intended the reader to
interpret the polarity here between Consuelo and Andrea's responses toward the
white female employers. Is Fernández positive, like Andrea, or negative, like

Consuelo, or ambivalent toward Andrea's ambivalent employers who are insensitive and exploiting, but also generous white benefactresses?

Herrera-Sobek and Viramontes make the claim that in this story Fernández has broken previous stereotypes of Chicanas. The story is also of significance because it shows the clash between traditional cultural constraints on women (as embodied in the character of a female gatekeeper of those values). It also delineates the character of a female who simply goes out and does it all by fulfilling her ambition to dance in the traditional Spanish theater. Andrea succeeds, but within the traditional choices open to her for self-expression. She then gives it all up after marriage. Her dancing career provides the axle upon which the wheel of the story turns. It provides the center from which radiate the diverse lives of her sister Consuelo, the narrator's mother, other female family members, and the narrator herself. This structure permits the young narrator to meditate at great length about the consequences of Andrea's life for everyone related to her. They are self-reflexivity and self-understanding about her life as well as theirs. Faced at the end with choosing between the two alternatives, the young, ultimately feminist narrator finally decides to go one better: to do it all, always.

Again, Herrera-Sobek and Viramontes consider this story unique because the author writes about Chicanas who live different lives from those Chicanas previously portrayed in Chicana literature. They make this claim on the grounds that Fernández's characters are not "*campesinas* (peasant women) or the urban poor but lower middle-class Chicanas leading dignified productive lives" (1988, 33–34). By creating such characters, Fernández provides an alternate view of Chicana lives. In "Andrea," we read about women who work hard. This is not unusual. But these women are also educated, and have hopes for their future and for future generations of Chicanas.

Herrera-Sobek and Viramontes's observation is only partially true. The young narrator does eventually conform to the description of the Chicanas above, so pleasing to Herrera-Sobek and Viramontes that they conveniently omit the truth, as Fernández describes it. For although they are hardworking, neither Andrea the dancer nor Conseulo the gatekeeper is well educated. Certainly Consuelo does not lead a productive life, nor does she entertain future hopes either for herself or others. This quality is symbolized in her frustrated, embittered personality and her deafness in later years. When they plan to take a trip back to their homeland, Consuelo becomes a fifth wheel in her brother-in-law's Italian family group.

Andrea and Conseulo, and their cousin, the narrator, allegorically represent differing worldviews about life. Consuelo, represents a problem for women that "outclasses" them. Andrea represents a solution that situates women as respected members of and within their culture in their own right. Their cousin's perspective is limited until the end of the story. The reader's perspective is expanded through the device of the photograph album, consisting of family memorabilia and featuring material connected with Andrea's performances, her roles, places where she and her troupe had performed, dates, names of the theaters, and program information. Another purpose of the album is to create a meaningful repository of family events in an attempt to link them with the family's history going back to San Luis Potosí in Mexico just prior to the revolution. So the narrator claims, but she is unreliable. And history is not what Fernández is altogether about, although she is acclaimed as a historian of Spanish traveling theater in the Americas. In "Andrea" she constructs a feminist revision of Mexican and Chicano history in terms of women, including women's experiences and perspectives within that history.

For the women in the family, the album also represents Andrea's acting-out of the Cinderella myth. Women globally identify with the king's neglected daughter (the Chicana oppressed by Anglo and Chicano rulers), abused by her stepmother and stepsisters (Anglo women), and languishing in the cinders as a kitchen slavey (consigned to thankless homemaking jobs). In every culture globally, because women in all cultures experience inequitable gendered power relations, this myth resonates powerfully for heterosexual women. They dream that after a seemingly endless period of waiting, Prince Charming will arrive and carry them away to conjugal happiness forever afterward. This myth is more real for women, including the women of Andrea's family, than even Andrea's glamorous life.

The narrator's purpose, then, is to explore the possibility for women of living a life whose trajectory resembles that of the Cinderella story as a solution to the private life of routine drudgery. The narrator therefore sets up the Cinderella possibility in the person of the glamorous and successful dancer and later model wife and mother, Andrea, as opposed to her drudging sister Consuelo. The latter always conceives of any female who does not sacrifice her own personal needs to those of her family's as the embodiment of evil (Ruíz 1993, 111). Both types of Chicanas battle for supremacy in the narrator's mind– Consuelo "defining, creating, and enforcing discursive regimes of disciplinary truth" (Luke 1995, 59). As for the narrator, the third type of Chicana, she represents the next generation, the feminist generation to which Fernández belongs.

As with the Cinderella story, this conflict between obedience to and perpetuation of the traditional, as opposed to striking out for oneself, not only occurs in the Chicana narrator's mind. It is a binary or dialectic in most women's minds, given the nature of the global culture into which we are born. In Chicano culture, however, the questions arise in a specific form for the narrator: Can a Chicana live simultaneously in two cultures? Can a Chicana Cinderella, for her advantage, for her fulfillment, blend an Anglo optimism that yet discriminates against Chicanas and allows them limited access to resources, with Mexican "macho" culture which limits their upward mobility even more, decreeing that "woman's place is in the home"? (Ruíz 1993, 110).

Through the device of the album, Fernández subtly depicts the major qualities of the two opposing sisters, Andrea and Consuelo. These sisters are nieces to the narrator's mother who made the album. The story details on its surface the sisters' nearly lifelong, irreconcilable differences in perspective and lifestyle. On one level, therefore, this story is a realistic tale of the differing lives and attitudes of two sisters who represent the past and the present (Dernersesian 1993, 45). It is also the story of their cousin, the narrator, who is situated in the middle, torn between the two, until she chooses the direction in which she will ·go. On another level the story is an allegory. Consuelo represents duty to tradition, obligation, and familial and customary ties, as opposed to Andrea's dream of individual female Cinderella-like success through romantic ambition. The differences between the sisters can be summed up as two opposing positions that fit into the paradigm of conflicting prefeminist perspectives, with the unnamed, ultimately feminist narrator torn between them for a long time. Sympathetic and inclusive of both perspectives, she eventually goes beyond both, to feminism.

Andrea is at first described by the narrator in fairy-tale terms, as an "exotic" and "bewitching" relative who enchants her because she had danced on stage "in the limelight of make-believe and far-away" (112) and was able to do so because she was self-confident. Andrea was a golden child, because from her very first appearance on earth she was the favorite child, the apple of her mother's eye. From a need to "root for the underdog" the narrator is more drawn to Andrea's dour sister Consuelo, significantly ten years older than Andrea. The narrator begins by preferring Consuelo's heaviness of expression in pictures on the other side of the album from those of Andrea whose face is smiling and dimpled.

From the beginning, then, the narrator sets up a polarity of opposition between the two female perspectives. Although sisters, the traditionalist elder had been unwillingly uprooted from San Luis Potosí, from her beloved ancestral home in Mexico where she had lived with her grandparents and cousins. At the age of thirteen, the contrast between Consuelo and Andrea is already marked. Consuelo had to do housework at the Army post at Fort McIntosh for a white woman, a poet of sorts from Connecticut, whereas Andrea had become this woman's protegée. Together with another army wife, a piano teacher, the two older women had provided Andrea with a multiple fairy godmother, just as happens to Cinderella. From the beginning, then, Andrea lives the dream–acts it out–whereas Consuelo is forever the kitchen drudge and nothing more.

Ignoring Consuelo, these fairy godmothers had taken it upon themselves to nurture Andrea's talents by paying for her training and clothing. In contrast Consuelo held herself aloof from these women and inherited their cast-offs. She felt contempt for the women because in her opinion they treat Andrea like a doll.

The narrator's mother, their aunt, serves as chorus. She muses aloud to her daughter that the source for Consuelo's strong objection to Andrea's career was her distrust of Anglo colonizers and their motives. Consuelo, she points out admiringly, always had a strong sense of self and held herself aloof from her employers. Just as admiringly, she adds that on the other hand, the employers and Andrea engaged in a mutual admiration society. In her opinion, the fairy godmothers did all they could for Andrea. Consuelo's childhood had been dark and difficult, whereas Andrea's had been "magical" (117).

The narrator objectifies Andrea primarily in the role of a performer as she gazes at the pictures in the album, "hands crossed at the back of her neck . . . little heart-shaped mouth . . . the dark sequined dress and its long *cola* [train] spread out on the floor" (109). Andrea's illustrious career lasted fifteen years, climaxing in her performing in *Don Juan Tenuo* in the Teatro Hispano in New York (109). Fernández is here threading historical actuality into the narrative by creating the character Andrea as a performer in a Chicano traveling theater. Such theater goes back to sixteenth-century "nativity plays."

The narrator's Tía Griselda, together with her mother, serves as another member of the realistic, down-to-earth pragmatic chorus. She gives readers the first clue that there is another dimension to Andrea besides that of a performer. In fact Griselda hesitates to describe Andrea as only a performer because in real life the latter was never artificial. She reinforces this distinction between Andrea's own persona as opposed to her stage presence, her ability to assume when performing the traditionally prescribed movements and steps. The narrator's mother tells her daughter that Andrea is another person at this point in time from the performing Andrea. She does this to clarify for the narrator the distinction between Andrea's stage persona for fifteen years long ago and her new persona for the past fifteen years, once she married and left the stage forever.

For her stay-at-home aunts, the wondrous pictures they received in Andrea's packages served as pleasant distractions from household routine. They loved to imagine romantic adventures for their niece based on the sparkling expression of her face. According to Andrea, her aunts' fantasies about her are in complete contrast to the reality of her life. Not surprisingly, however, the narrator's mother confides to her that the stories they had made up about her excited their fantasies and pleased them far more than those their niece would tell them. Andrea's new persona is captured in a snapshot of her putting the finishing touches to a large snowman in St. Louis, where she had moved with her husband and two children after she retired from dancing.

So what was Andrea really like? What are the qualities necessary for a woman who would get it all, for a woman who would live with it all as every-day reality to her, all the while her family lived on a lesser level in their safe realities? Interestingly Andrea combines the qualities that the narrator is imposing on herself with those that she is being trained to slough off. She is unassuming and pragmatic, although at the same time she exudes charm and talent. She did whatever she wanted to do, fully expressing whatever talents she possessed. She traveled with the successful Spanish traveling troupes, dancing with them. Once she married, however, she left this life behind and never thought more about it. So far as she was concerned, she had entered another stage in life, and the previous one had ended. She lived only in the present. "[L]e dijo adiós al teatro para siempre" [She bid farewell to the theater forever] (112).

She is unlike Consuelo who would obliterate Andrea's creative side if she could and prevent her sister's dancing in order to forward only the patriarchy's limited construction of woman as entirely house-bound and husband-bound. On the other hand, Andrea sees the chasm between them simply as an opportunity which makes possible "the intermingling of sameness" (Consuelo representing the "sameness" of marriage and motherhood) and "difference" (Andrea representing the "difference" of her dancing career out in the world) (Gwin 1996, 889).

At face value, Andrea's solution to rapprochement with her sister seems eminently practical and reveals a tolerant, easygoing nature. From a feminist perspective, her solution is sequential. Her career–performing and dancing–comes before marriage and motherhood. She never considers simultaneous possibilities. In contrast, her cousin, the narrator, speaks from a younger, feminist perspective. Her earliest dream, significantly enough, is to spend her life dancing. She vows that if she had been Andrea she would never have stopped dancing, never have ended her career. Her youthful bravado is highly ironic at that point in her life, because for a long time the narrator gives up her ambitions for supposedly practical reasons. On the other hand, Andrea freely chose her retirement after fulfilling all her dreams.

The narrator's mother claims that Andrea had reasoned it out once with her, concluding that fifteen years on stage had given her happiness. After that time, she had begun to desire the greater stability of family life in a fixed home, that basically she could not continue living a life in which she served "two masters" (112). Obviously she conceptualized her public career as her first master and her private home life as her second master, sequentially, rather than simultaneously. Here the narrator's mother who is both Andrea's and Consuelo's aunt, represents the community of women surrounding and circumscribing the young narrator when she maintains that a career and marriage for women are "two masters." She conceptualizes them, not as intersecting possibilities, but as a rigid binary, as does Andrea herself, the glamorous and successful career woman.

Marriage and motherhood have always represented a point of no return away from public life for women in careers. Even today, many Chicana feminists, as well as women around the world, find the apparent paradox of combining a career with marriage and motherhood impossible to resolve. Somehow, however, it never seems to pose a problem or even seem paradoxical for their menfolk, because it doesn't have to be either a problem or a paradox for them. They are comfortable with career as their first priority and raising a family as a second priority, whereas women are defensive about pursuing careers due to the way both genders are acculturated in terms of their working lives.

The culture's inequitable gendered power relations in terms of gender success role models are so constructed that the pursuit of a career out in the world is extraneous to the definition of women's roles and an easy option to eliminate at the slightest difficulty. Marriage and motherhood alone are considered vital work for full career status as a woman. Indeed the Cinderella story does not contain the role of career woman in its plot line. The only job that Cinderella performs before she crashes the prince's ball is that of a kitchen maid, a job done by all women everywhere as a matter of course, unless they are of the very highest class. Then they hire some Other woman to do it as substitutes for *them*, never for their men.

For a long time, the narrator prefers the soulful, sensitive, cautious, conventional Consuelo to the artifice of Andrea. Yet at the same time, she disagrees with Andrea's decision to give up worldly success for marriage and domestic life. According to general consensus, Consuelo had disapproved of her sister's career decision and mystifies her family by never referring to those fifteen years. The narrator then discovers other perspectives, other realities: the depth and complexity of her perspective increasing as the narrator matures. Finally, on actually meeting the two sisters, the narrator discovers that the polarities, the differences in their preferences remain. Andrea contends astutely that the major differences between her sister and herself were accrued during Consuelo's childhood when Andrea had not yet been born. Andrea was born in the United States, Consuelo in Mexico, and Fernández is thereby indicating that this distinction makes all the difference in how they were socialized.

When Andrea finally meets the narrator for the first time, Andrea embraces and kisses her. The narrator, feeling uncomfortable, rejects her. On the other hand, she feels comfortable with Consuelo, especially with her gloomy facial expression. Because she secretly observes her with distrust and scarcely concealed disapproval, Andrea's presence continues to make the narrator uncomfortable. Meanwhile, Andrea, basking in being the center of an admiring group of family and friends, chatters away. Charming and spontaneous, she lifts the spirits of everyone around her, except for the narrator and Consuelo.

Why does the narrator here in the beginning identify more with Consuelo, the sad, the sombre, the burdened woman, the failure? Consuelo is practical (as is Andrea) and traditional (as is Andrea). The only difference between them is that Andrea's practicality includes leaving home and family to dance on the stage. Consuelo, however, advises the young, ambitious narrator that dancing is something she can do as long as she is a child, but that when she gets older she should not keep up with it. Indeed Andrea herself does not continue dancing once she reaches a certain age. It is untrue however that dancing for Andrea did not "lead" her "anywhere" as Consuelo maintains to the narrator.

Consuelo's gatekeeping of this unexamined belief system is here imposed upon and indoctrinated into the credulous young narrator, even though in reality Andrea has called it into question by having led a fulfilled life. She danced as long as she could, most probably according to her biological clock, then married, and raised children. Furthermore she is still living, apparently happily, with her husband Tony. The latter is as extroverted as Andrea, and according to her, the couple have a good time together. Andrea is not an isolated housewife either, but also enjoys friendships and many social activities in St. Louis.

In contrast, Consuelo has married, been widowed, and is childless. Her attempt to return to St. Louis Potosí, her birthplace, lasted only a year because it was no longer the same as it had been. She attaches herself to and identifies with Andrea's traditional Italian in-laws and plans a visit to Italy with her brother-in-law's sister that never comes to pass. Significantly, again in contrast, Andrea and her husband Tony did go there on their own, but obviously they did not take Consuelo along with them.

Consuelo is safe and conventional, a stickler for going by the rules, "[a]lways . . . so strict about how we should conduct ourselves as a family" (116). In this regard, it turns out that Consuelo's chief source of rage against Andrea is not so much that Andrea had enjoyed her dancing career–has had it all, in fact–but that Andrea shatters time-honored customs, traditions, and family obligations in doing so, by finding self-fulfillment.

Consuelo embodies a traditional woman who has totally internalized her culture's model for what constitutes success in a woman and acts on that suspect model without ever questioning it. Gonzales-Berry might well be cautioning readers against women's declassification, or being "outclassed," when she urges women to destroy masculinist discourses because they have inscribed "so much self-hate" (1995, 123) into women, and I might add, so much *amour propre* into men.

Through Andrea the narrator finds out how difficult Consuelo's life had been, how very opposite the sisters are. Andrea can hardly believe how different she is from her sister, to the point where it mystifies her (116). Andrea has always lived spontaneously, in the moment. In contrast, Consuelo has always brooded about the past, her once strong ties to family and ancestors, to all she had left behind in San Luis Potosí, in Mexico. As a child she had felt uprooted, and still feels "transplanted" (116), whereas Andrea lives only for the moment.

Consuelo's nostalgia for the past is more typical of Chicanas than Andrea's spontaneity, according to Rebolledo and Rivero. But they use the past for feminist purposes. Marginalizing contemporary life, they focus on the past glories of their culture, lauding its communitarianism, rather than individuality. They do this as a means to question and critique the worship of individualism, of capitalistic materialist consumerism of their current oppressors, the colonizers, and the dominant Anglo culture (1993, 18).

This difference between the two women not only is the difference between two sisters. It is a historical and generational one between the immigrant Mexican American generation and the next generation of Chicanas. It is also a difference of approach to the questions of how females should live life–the differences between the traditional, prefeminist, and feminist women. Traditional, prefeminst women attempt to continue the past into the present. They cling to the past, as Consuelo's resentment of the present reveals. Feminists take the past into account, critique it, but bring it forward into the present. Although they stress the present–living fully in the present without gender role constraints, they are continually embattled, continually struggling with the need to be self-reflexive and to question the shibboleths around them that perpetuate inequitable gendered power relations.

It is Fernández's opinion, therefore, that the difference between the sisters lies in their different experiences and their different responses to different external events and histories. Their responses to situations differ because their consciousness encountered different situations. Their subject identity is contingent on external forces, the complex of situations around them. Such a postmodern attitude does not account for the possibility of internal, individual agency. Note the self-reflexivity lacking in Consuelo when she piously replicates the belief system she has learned and believes in without question: dancing, that is, freedom, gets women nowhere.

Andrea, on the other hand, is flexible and advises her cousin to adapt to her environment, but the adaptation must be rapid, instantaneous. Change is constant, even though "essences remain the same." Andrea uses herself as example. Although she has experienced many "dramatic changes" during her lifetime, she has still "remained the same person" (118).

Both sisters are alike in remaining fixed in their basic personalities, belief systems, values, and training. Although Andrea may remain fixed inside, she adapts and modifies outwardly so as always to get what she wants from the system. Consuelo remains dogmatically, righteously fixed in her value system. She seeks to retain control over external situations according to her notions of how things should be. She does not yield in her opposition or forgive when her notions of reality and truth are violated. Her reality, her truth, is the only truth. This is why Andrea, the fluid, spontaneous character is always laughing, while Consuelo, doggedly fixed on tradition, is dour and full of rage and resentment.

Consuelo acts according to her training for a respectable Mexican woman. Her personal needs are sacrificed, never taken into account in relation to doing what is right, whereas Andrea incorporates and integrates personal desire with customary public rules and regulations for women in such a way as to please others as well as herself. She thereby stretches parameters without violating them.

As for the narrator, she does not fully realize how unique Andrea is until she has matured to young womanhood. The illumination finlly dawns in her when she discovers that none of her classmates has any successful female relative in their families that they could boast about, or even such a relative in the past. In the latter respect, they view the narrator's photograph album as a fitting reflection of Andrea's unique career that they admire as courageous, even daring, and rare for her time (124). Further she discovers that Andrea had never made a fuss about her success. She just went and did it, without the price that the culture, the media, the gatekeepers–all circumscribing women–insist to women that they will have to pay if they transgress traditional bounds.

But there is a price for transgression. The conventional woman, the cultural gatekeeper, responds with corrosive jealousy and enmity, as embodied in Consuelo. This poisons Andrea's life on a literal level. On an allegorical level, it can be interpreted to mean that enterprising women are bombarded with naysayers and gatekeepers from all sides, including their own sisters. Consuelo would rather be right about her values than relent and be more tolerant, even accept difference. She would rather turn "back in the end to her familiar life, confronting, instead a *different* form of death: a life of habit that is no longer life" [emphasis mine] (Piper 1995, 168–169).

The author structures the narrative in a circular manner, unpacking levels until she gets directly to the heart of the matter. First she gives clues as through the eyes of the idealistic young narrator. Her mother, Andrea's aunt, dotes on everything Andrea does. In fact, she is the one who makes the album. Instead of ending the story at this point, Fernández sets up an acceptance of paradox and difference. According to Andrea, it is only after the album's destruction that real conversation between the sisters takes place. Once the letters and the photographs that represented the part of Andrea's life which so enraged Consuelo are destroyed, the sisters then become closer, as they might have started out and then continued throughout their lifetimes.

But this is not really the case. Andrea, in maintaining that she totally accepts Consuelo, is once again adapting to a seemingly impenetrable barrier. Most crucially readers discover that Andrea has, in fact, always secretly admired her sister for being her opposite, for being a woman who had never once in her life deviated from rigidly upholding the traditional values she inherited. Andrea sums up her approach in response to such a hidebound, tradition-perpetuating sister. She shrugs her off by advising the young narrator that people should avoid unpleasant situations that do not affect them or have any bearing on their lives (126). The narrator, however, remains traumatized by Consuelo's willful destruction of the letters and the photograph album, her erasure from the public record of the life and professional accomplishments of one of the successful women of the previous generation.

This erasure leads the young narrator to a dramatic revision of her own life's hitherto safe course–to reconstruct her own blue album which she had begun for herself while she was dancing and had discontinued on the advice of Consuelo and her other relatives. Blue is the color of hope and fidelity to a dream. The young narrator offers assistance to a classmate who is working on an exhibit about women in dance. The narrator can no longer help out with the old album of Andrea's photographs, but she can help by returning to the dance, to pursue dance as her career, however she can do so. This statement echoes Andrea's advice to her young cousin, the narrator herself, to dance (through life), to perform any way one can through adaptation, through ingenuity. Although Andrea uses the trope of the dance, she is talking about her personal solutions to the culture's constraints on women. Her philosophy is to do life, however and in any way one does it. Not through outward rebellion, but to work within the environment one finds oneself in, to make do as best as one can: "You must adapt to the situation on the spot" (118).

Heeding Andrea's advice, then–no longer passive, no longer brainwashed into putting up with her culture's artificial constraints against her ambitions because of restrictive and false success models for women–the young narrator finally realizes what she has to do. For the first time in her life she will not permit anyone to prevent her from doing so. She hears a clear-toned voice in her head–doubtless Andrea's–telling her that "de una espina salta una flor" [from a spine blooms a flower].

Once again, as in her childhood, the young narrator "hears the Spanish melodies that had filled her head in her childhood and shadowy figures in lacy white headdresses beckon her to join them" (126). She will perpetuate the tradition of the long line of invalidated and eradicated women who have always fulfilled their ambitions despite their culture's denial of their existence. The young narrator will return to dancing–if not literally to the dance, then to making the moves she wants to make to develop herself through her life. She will do whatever it is that perpetuates and continues the pursuit of a woman's full and successfully lived life on her own terms.

There are male ancestors–fathers and grandfathers–all dead. There are husbands, also all dead or far away, off the stage. There is only one male living, a very minor character, Tío Menos (significantly, Little Uncle) whose function seems to be to organize Welcome Homes when Andrea gets off the train on a visit home and to provide her adoring relatives and friends with "noisemakers." Fernández does not confront, does not preach, but no male plays any significant part in this story. They do not have to be present. Men comprise the gender that runs the system and that the system values, and men have created the oppressive constraints on women. For as Inge T. Boer puts it, "The ultimate transparency of power is established by absence" (1996, 49).

Is Fernández taking it for granted, without explanation of any kind, that readers will be familiar with the Mexican value system to which Consuelo so rigidly clings? Will future readers be aware of the enormous reach and power, the global nature of the cultural constructions for gendered power relations that declass women, that limit options for women's success, and that have been so inimical to their self-fulfillment? Where writer/critics such as Cherríe Moraga and Gloria Anzaldúa allocate much space to delineating this problem, Fernández focuses on exposing differences in terms of solutions through the creation of three different and differing women. Consuelo is the hidebound traditional woman who believes wholeheartedly in what she was taught and will allow no woman in her reach to deviate from that truth on penalty of figurative death, such as erasure from history. Andrea is the woman who lives with this historic constraint all her life, whatever she does or doesn't do, no matter where she turns, whatever her other successes in life. She permits this constraint to influence her, because she valorizes compromises. She bends and modifies and twists to get along with and to appease her traditional sister(s) while always adhering to her own desires.

Finally the feminist in the guise of the young narrator continues where Andrea has left off. The deafness of the traditional woman goes both ways. Not only can she not hear, she herself also no longer communicates, nor does she reach out to do so to succeeding generations of women. Because of this failure, the young narrator and the new generation she represents are no longer frustrated and constrained by wrong (headed) advice from all sides. Feminists can hear and follow other voices, other songs, other dances. Although the traditional woman cannot hear what they have to say, feminists, without the rancor and ill feeling the traditional woman displays, do still hear her and do understand and sympathize with her position.

However, they may not choose to listen to the traditional woman. They go their own way, a different way from hers, although the feminists live with her side by side. Every day of her life Andrea has to deal with her traditional sister's *invidia*, her commitment to the failure of feminism and the triumph of tradition. The feminist, free of her traditional "cousin" and removed from her, still identifies with her, still loves what she embodies–tradition and a stable value system. But whereas Andrea adapts to and compromises with tradition, the feminist narrator ultimately comes to know and to understand "what she has to do and . . . will not allow anyone to dissuade me from it without compromise" (126). Andrea, unlike Consuelo, does not adapt "to a world of oppressive social relations." She does not attempt to change what she finds; rather she wants to make the best use of it. Only the feminist young narrator at the end will repudiate Consuelo's rigid acceptance of the world as she finds it and Andrea's adaptation to that world and all its given conditions as a priority while waiting quietly and patiently to fulfill her needs when she can. The young narrator will move forward, instead, to a transformation of "the very conditions that promote such conditions" (McLaren 1996, 181).

Unlike Andrea who is guided by Consuelo in her childhood, the young narrator will follow her desires. The narrator is nameless because she represents an entire generation. She will dance her own dance the rest of her life. Unlike Andrea who gives up dancing after fifteen years in order to marry, the young narrator will dance without simultaneously compromising. Nor will the young narrator follow Consuelo (tradition), using Consuelo as referent, because the narrator will not follow two masters simultaneously–her desires and the culture's decree that women cannot have a career and marriage. She will fill in "the discrepancies [that her cousins both represent] between women's desires to act and define themselves and the world's reception and suppression of those desires" (Gonzales-Berry 1995, 123).

It is Consuelo who is noticeably quiet and Andrea who talks too much in the narrator's early opinion. Consuelo, obedient to the very labels her culture uses to restrict and limit women's activity, socially as well as intellectually, ends by becoming totally deaf.

Rebolledo's conclusion is that Fernández is not denying the validity of the two sisters' lives, of how they chose to live life as Mexican women and first generation Chicanas. She created them to embody the complex situations of the lives of women from these cultures. However, in addition, she adds another perspectival dimension through the young narrator that is unique to her. She achieves this through a circular structure that repeats and overlaps itself by means of a variety of voices. Thus Fernández offers a paradoxical diversity of windows onto varying truths, all through the use of Spanish, Mexican, and Chicana cultural contexts. These are the historical references to the touring troupes and theaters in which Andrea dances, the places these troupes toured which supported their work, the dances and plays they performed, and their costumes (1988, 137).

Also through her frequent use of Spanish proverbs, Fernández condenses each thematic incident in such a way as to stretch the boundaries of their discursive meaning to signify and justify women's choices in different situations, as in a myth or an allegory. Additionally Fernández uses a chorus and traditional adages to point the meaning and the moral of the characters' perspective on a situation as in a traditional morality tale or homily.

The narrator, who has the last word, perpetuates the Spanish saying, perhaps punning covertly on its meaning for all women in the future: "De una espina salta una flora." Figuratively speaking, from the (rule of the) phallus will emerge a womb. We may find that we obey a traditional masculinist value system to benefit and replicate the experience of male rulers and their discourse, but we can adapt these adages, as Fernández is suggesting, for our own needs. Thus it is that for us in living our lives "de una espina salta una flora." The Tao has a similar concept of life, namely, that water lilies are rooted in garbage, to signify that the enlightened human being is rooted in the material circumstances of life from which (s)he rises.

So it is that the nameless young narrator of Fernández's "Andrea" comes to a point of illumination. She makes a conscious reevaluation of her prior perspectives and choices, of how and why she came by them. She then consciously chooses to assist in actual physical activities in relation to her project of dancing in any way she can. Not only verbally, but in practice, as well.

In Cisneros's story "'Mericans" in *Woman Hollering Creek*, the children play in front of a church, awaiting their grandmother's emergence from her prayers out into the light of day. As they do so, they reveal a mysterious anomaly. These children, male and female, as they interact with one another, have already internalized without question sexist cultural messages in terms of inequitable gendered power relations. They have already learned the constraining limits within which we "'perform' gender" (Walters 1996, 856).

The narrator is told repeatedly by her brothers that they cannot play with a girl. They use the term "girl" as an insult, for example, that she throws a ball the way a girl does. The narrator's response is to attempt to stop from crying, because only girls cry. Through this narrator, whose name we discover later on is Michele, Cisneros seems to be advocating role reversal as feminist. Or as Alarcón puts it about internalizing such a perspective: It is "a male ideologized humanism devoid of female consciousness" (1981, 188). Michele displays this same kind of colonized attitude, created by her having already internalized and maintained "relations of power and discipline." "Gendered spaces . . . whether they be the Mongolian *ger* or academic secretarial offices in the United States, contribute to the maintenance of prevailing status differences" (Gwin 1996, 872). Such moves on the part of young females like Michele are due to attempts to "find their place in male language, law, grammar, syntax." As a result, they grow "completely divorced from themselves without knowing it" (Gwin, 1996, 872).

On the other hand, all the children in Michele's group, both male and female, are somehow already alert to American exploitation of Mexicans. They are quite sophisticated in their critique of institutionalized racism in terms of racist power relations. An American tourist from "that barbaric country with its barbarian ways" (18) gives Michele's brother Junior a handful of chiclets in exchange for her taking a photo of him. In the American tourist's imagination, this snapshot is already a memento of an exotic, alien culture, until Michele and another brother come up to the tourist. Junior addresses his siblings in every-day American lingo, causing the tourist to be struck with disbelief that the little dark "foreign" boy is able to speak English.

Readers might question at this point why it is that Junior is so aware of racism, of racist inequitable power relations, but does not show the same awareness of and sophistication toward sexism and gendered inequitable power relations. In fact he internalizes and perpetuates sexism to aggrandize himself. Readers might also question at this point why his sister Michele, the narrator, already suffers from lower status because she is a girl and why she also internalizes and perpetuates this sexism. Her brother's name "Junior" indicates that any junior male is already indoctrinated into and is capable of perpetuating the Chicano concept of masculinity.

Michele replicates the masculinist notion of male superiority to females by accepting Junior's qualities as preferable to whatever qualities are identified as female. For example, Michele buys into them by refusing to cry because only girls cry. In this way Michele thereby devalues what are deemed by her culture "female attributes" in a tearful "reappropriation of the attributes of the other"–to pun on Naomi Schor's apostrophizing of Luce Irigary's perspective on this problem (1989, 48). What is constructed is not masculine (in this instance, crying). Instead Michele perpetuates the valorization of what is constructed *as* masculine (attempting not to cry). One wonders why Michele did not question what was inherently female in crying, as both sexes have tear ducts.

So what is inherently unmasculine about crying? Are we "just fighting for access to 'what the boys have'"? (Walters citing Whisman 1996, 860). If Michele continues in her path of "identification with the aggressor" (Haaken 1996, 1087), she might very well end up like most women, developing problems in relation to low self-image and low self-esteem because of that identification. For although Junior and Michele are only young children, nevertheless they already know what is racist, what is discriminatory, yet they are simultaneously, inexplicably unaware of the nature of sexism and what is sexist.

In Patricia Preciado Martín's "La Virgen de la Soledad" [The Virgin of Loneliness] in *El Milagro and Other Stories*, the author sustains a painfully ironic tone and discourse in this cuento that makes it unforgettable. The Sierra Encantada Guest Ranch outside of Tucson was originally owned by Don Estéban Romero, "fabled" for having been a pioneer in the area, for his good blood and looks, his prize-winning livestock, his excellence as a business man, "and his way with women and horses" (74). Nowadays what the guests at the five-star ranch find most interesting and moving about the place is its romantic history, especially in relation to Don Estéban Romero's first wife, Dolores Cárdenas de Romero (1865–1885). Her gravesite attracts the most attention, as evidenced by the various floral tributes placed there. The crucial language here in terms of exposing the "outclassed" life of a Mexican woman, even of this obviously high born woman, lies in the presumably callous expression Martín uses about the Don, that he has a "way with women and horses." The Don situates female human beings as property on the same level as animals. Since ancient times, as in Greece, such a status for women, or lack of status, was legal. It also served as a signifier of classlessness, since animals have no legal class status.

Dolores, "the child bride" of Don Estéban, "died without producing him an heir" (77). That is all that mattered to him and apparently everyone else in her culture. By using Dolores's diary as a device, the author exposes the cause of her death: Soledad or Loneliness. She is a beautiful, sensitive young woman, totally dependent upon the husband who neglects her, has no use for her, and acts as if she did not exist, as do his ranch hands. After she has cooked their meals, Dolores stands at the kitchen door while her husband and his vaqueros gather around the table "in silence." The only time they talk is "to tally the day's losses or to plan the next day's foray." She watches them carefully, closely, "obedient, waiting for a word or a gesture to banish my loneliness. Nothing." At night when her husband ends his meals, he "listlessly" pushes his food away from him to indicate he has finished. Then still silent, still ignoring his wife's existence, he goes "into the sala to read or brood by the light of the kerosene lamp" (79).

Here the author reminds us of the basic patriarchal organization and structure of human culture as we have known it for thousands of years. In relation to one family, Martín is troping the way of the world, or what I sometimes call "Men's Studies," meaning that every aspect of life is viewed from that perspective, the study of men and men's activities. Likewise, Dolores (whose name means "sorrows") experiences her world the way the larger world is run. The world is of, for, and about men and their doings and interests in every way. They relate to each other in all the areas of life that they alone have determined are significant and relegate and isolate women to the kitchen and to the bedroom. Thus as in the world outside where women are liminal, except for a few select, constraining purposes, Don Estéban has nothing to talk about with his wife and neglects her. He is only with her in their bed. She waits there for him, "my hands folded in prayer on my empty womb. When I awake to the first rays of the sun, he is gone" (79).

Dolores is brainwashed, having totally internalized her culture's concept of woman. She experiences this concept as unbearable pressure because she wants to succeed, to have a place in her world. Without being able to produce a son and heir for her husband, she is nothing, nobody, and obligingly proceeds to become that by dying. Because his wife is not conceiving, her husband no longer even wishes to lie with her at night: "'Let me take you in the buckboard to town. This is no place for a woman,' he says" (80).

Literally and figuratively, then, Dolores has no place any longer in which to live, for there is no place for a woman other than as a wife and mother in her husband's home, in the man's place. She refuses to go to town, however, despite her terrible isolation because she does "not want to suffer the inquiring glances and raised eyebrows of the clucking women. . . . 'Todavía no?' [Still, nothing?] They pat my abdomen maternally" (80). Unfortunately, according to Martín and to other contemporary Chicana writers, gatekeeper women who collude knowingly or otherwise act as accomplices with the oppressive patriarchy.

These gatekeepers advise Dolores that the solution to her problems is "'to make a manda'" to the Virgin, that she "' is the answer. La Virgen embarazada [pregnant Virgin] will come to your aid and answer your prayers'" (80). Obediently, Dolores prays to "La Virgen embarazada." She kneels every day "[o]n the sharp stones of the arroyo until my knees bleed" (80). Despite all of Dolores's "litanies and lamentations" (77), this manifestation of the Virgin was not the one to which Dolores and her life and death were dedicated, but that of La Virgen de la Soledad:

By far the most popular destination of the tourist pilgrims is the aforementioned shrine of La Virgen de la Soledad, which the grieving and shocked Don Esteban built in memory of his beautiful tormented wife. . . . La Virgen de la Soledad, laden with the secret entreaties of so many, gazes serenely down at the sun-baked tourists and the ever-flickering candles that they light in the hopeful notion that their dreams and prayers will be fulfilled by the intercession of the soul of Dolores Cárdenas de Romero, who wasted away of tristeza y melancolía [sadnesss and melancholy] in the year of the Great Drought–of the desert and of her womb. (78–79)

Martín's understated sarcasm which she deploys to mask her outrage and fury at the drought in which women live, should also be noted as a major characteristic of her work, as well as of the majority of contemporary Chicana writers discussed in this text. Cisneros's cuento "Los Boxers," in *Woman Hollering Creek and Other Stories*, without using one angry word, nevertheless conveys this same outrage. Seemingly a light, brief monologue orated by a widower in a laundromat, almost like a one-act play, an elderly Chicano boasts about his newfound skill in washing clothes since his wife's death. At the same time, he exposes his deceased wife's unappreciated labors in the home while she was alive. This cuento is actually written to make the point that on occasion men too suffer from inequitable gendered power relations as a form of accidental byproduct of this evil that they direct at women.

Additionally, "inherent in the system of patriarchy" is the "differentiation of old age," which this cuento exposes:

Historically, women have been consigned to the domain of the private, the domestic, the home, where they are held responsible for rearing children, nurturing them literally and emotionally, as well as being available emotionally to other members of the family, and friends. They are also held responsible for the family's social life, and for keeping track of all religious ceremonies and holidays. Suddenly, a man who has always led his life outside the home, in the workplace [*sic*] and out in the community "providing for the family's economic susbsistence" loses his wife. (Facio 1996, 38)

Cisneros, in taking the materialist feminist perspective that women's unpaid labor in the home makes it possible to perpetuate the work force, chooses an especially difficult and tragic time for the male in question to discover this problem. In "Los Boxers," Cisneros exposes a traditional working-class male's gender perspective in the process of being radically transformed for the first time in his life. Through this means he finally achieves enlightenment as to how many hitherto unnoticed ways his wife's unremunerated labor has made his working and private life possible and seemingly effortless.[2]

The widower is talking to a young woman who is accompanied by a little girl. He shares with her all the expertise he has acquired washing clothes in the laundromat. Many readers would find his suggestions worthwhile, for example, to use ice cubes on spots, or to classify and separate the wash by weight. In addition, clothes should not be left in the dryer. They should be removed as soon as the machine stops spinning. If not, he explains, the clothes will have to be redone, as I myself know full well from many personal disasters.

The kicker comes at the end. We discover that the widower has achieved all this expertise only recently. While his wife was alive, he did not appreciate his wife's expertise because by virtue of his masculine divine right he had never done a thing for himself, or ever so much as imagined that some day he would have to do so. But now he appreciates having hands-on experience in taking care of himself. In retrospect he appreciates the luxury of having had the services of a wife who had so completely internalized the culture's decrees for women and who had probably died like an old burro from overwork. He pays tribute to her cleanliness, her neatness, and high standards. Even though their home was old, it still appeared new because all the "towels, sheets, embroidered pillowcases, and them little table runners like doilies, them you put on chairs for your head, those, she had them white and stifflike the collar of a nun." Everything was starched and ironed, even socks, T-shirts and "los boxers" [boxer shorts] (132).

Now that he has lost his wife, he realizes what he has lost, and that perhaps he and the culture had worked her into her grave due to her unremitting labors to conform to the image of a perfect wife. Perhaps he should have shared the duties that he and the culture delegated only to her in their home. As I copy these words, I see in my mind's eyes my own beautiful, but arthritic mother standing at the board, ironing with hands like claws, the same items listed above, as well as stacks of handkerchiefs for my father, while her friends and I mock her for doing so, all to no avail.

Gloria Anzaldúa's eerie story "Ghost Trap" is either coincidentally or purposely written as a companion piece to "Los Boxers." While describing the widower as helpless without his woman, Cisneros, at the same time manages to reveal all that his wife had done to serve his needs, to make his life comfortable and as aesthetically pleasing as possible. In contrast, after two weeks of widowhood Anzaldúa's protagonist, an elderly woman, finds that her husband's ghost has returned to her: "[H]e would follow her around the house and to the backyard" (1992, 40). Her response is to miss "her solitude" and to feel "stifled." Then he begins to demand "clean clothes," which creates the terrifying possibility for her of the strongest community "censure" she could imagine herself subjected to as a Chicano widow if she ever dared to replace her husband "with another man." Her husband demands his dinner (although as a ghost he cannot eat, of course) and beer (although he cannot drink). He angrily criticizes the brand she buys for him. Again the necessity to go to the store to shop for the ghost's beer exposes her to the fear of suffering community ostracism, this time on the grounds that people would think that "her grief had driven her to drink" (1992, 41). Finally:

Tending to his ghost seemed to take all her time. She began to resent all the washing and cooking and trimming of his hair and toenails when he was alive. Just when she thought herself free, the pisser was back and more trouble now that he was dead. Her only consolation was that she didn't have to wash his smelly socks and dirty underwear. But her two-week-old *vida* [life] was no longer her own and she wanted it back. How could she stop her *marido muerto* [dead husband] from returning? (1992, 41)

Her solution is to construct a ghost trap, which is a miniature of their house put together "with Popsicle sticks and glue" (1992, 41). She places the trap in a safe spot between her husband's grave in the cemetery and her home. However, fearing that his ghost would be able to emerge should the ghost trap be endangered or destroyed, she brings it back home and puts it under her bed. That night, her husband's ghost returns and demands sex from her, which she refuses. "Next morning she woke with deep grooves down the corners of her mouth and bruises on her mouth, breasts, arms, and inner thighs. She peered under the bed and saw that the door of the casita was open. She walked from room to room looking for *el pinche desgraciado* [the mean, selfish bastard] and muttering to hersef, How am I going to get rid of that fucker?" (1992, 42). She then decides to take the ghost on literally, not only with words:

That night she plugged in the vacuum cleaner and put it by her bed. She tugged on two of her sturdiest corsets. Several pairs of pants and three shirts, turned off the lights, got into bed and waited. She jumped out of bed, fetched her heavy iron skillet and hid it under the bedcovers just in case he'd taken on more substance than the vacuum could handle. Come on cabrón, vente chingón [goat, come on you fucker], she said under her breath. (1992, 42)

Whereas Cisneros's widower in "Los Boxers" lives on, each day increasingly aware of all it had meant for his wife to keep their home, to care and feed for him, to make life pleasant and graceful for him, Anzaldúa's nameless widow learns otherwise. She had begun by grieving. Each day that passes brings her a greater awareness that she has devoted an entire lifetime of service to a crude, brutal, and ungrateful husband. Widowhood literally raises her consciousness to the point where she begins first to appreciate and then to treasure her freedom, her peace, her newfound ability to do as she likes, to be self-motivated, to live for herself according to her own needs. Her husband's ghost reminds her of all the ways in which she had been held captive and had lost her freedom as an individual in the institutions of matrimony and familism.

Both Anzaldúa's and Cisneros's cuentos expose the downside of gendered familism, when too much service and nurturing is demanded of women and too little of men. These cuentos almost seem to have been written as if to illustrate Facio's conclusions after researching in a senior center about "the ideological premises and underlying implications of familism, namely, the value of male authority over females" (1996, 13). Although "family values" are not specific only to Chicano families, nevertheless, Facio found that they comprise the primary "component or dynamic" for Chicano families which continues to make its demands on Chicanas, even after widowhood, as we have seen in "The Ghost Trap."

Familism, Facio concludes, basically defines Chicanas only as "wives, mothers, and grandmothers," and all training hinges on those roles only. The truth is that not all older Chicanas are involved in family situations, are no longer wives and mothers, and never were directly living lives related to the roles assigned them in what the culture decrees is "a traditional family structure." Facio therefore suggests tactfully to Chicano culture that it stop "'lumping' married and unmarried women together as if all women were alike" (1996, 13).

Older Chicanas should be analyzed, not as they have hitherto been, as individual entities adapting to the aging process, or in relation "to technology," but rather "from a political perspective." Then the major emphasis would be on how we could "optimize the aging process." What familism really means would be exposed. Inequitable systems of "social power and inequality" situate the Chicana family within "the system of production." The "economic exploitation of Chicanos" is reinforced by the traditional "role of the elder in the family." The Chicano family is used to mediate "capitalism and aging" because the way in which women are kept in the home to provide and sustain workers makes it economically feasible to maintain and perpetuate a capitalist racist, sexist system. For these reasons, "capitalists as a class and men as a class are seen to benefit from the social relations of patriarchy and capitalism" (Facio 1996, 14). I have already debated the critics' habit of linking inequality in gendered power relations only with patriarchy and capitalism as if they were two different entities on the same level. It is my conviction that capitalism is only one "ism" out of many and that patriarchy shapes all "isms" that comprise all cultures globally.

Facio believes that feminist theory could shift the Chicano culture's emphasis away from embedding women in the traditional "structure and functions of the family" and from the erroneous assumption that they "benignly benefit the elderly" (1996, 14). Instead the focus should be on how "gender and class dominance transcends the family and continues into old age. . . . Chicana grandmothers would be more than matriarchs; they would also take their place as players in the historical and societal process of gender oppression" (1996, 14–15). They provide the dubious luxury of free childcare and homemaking services to the family's workers. Thus they free generations of workers in their turn to continue uninterrupted in the workforce. Meanwhile employers remain seemingly detached and removed, but greatly benefit by this process by which female family elders are virtually enslaved.

Cisneros's and Anzaldúa's stories call for the widower and the widow, and, by extension, for all of us, to reassess "past traditions in the midst of contemporary realities." Both males and females were and are socialized into uncritically accepting cultural mythologies about "old age: that it would bring harmony, status, respect, and solace." But the reality is that elders are living lives of "poverty, family structural changes, differential life expectancies, longevity." Clearly the authors of both stories are calling for a cultural reassessment and redefinition of old age, primarily in regard "to traditions that reinforce a gender hierarchy" (Facio 1996, 15).

Facio has also noticed an interesting "dialectic" in terms of Chicana "grandmotherhood" that "The Ghost Trap" brilliantly illustrates. The new widow's fears of community ostracism are all based on situations in which she might be viewed and construed as no longer living in conformity to her former "caregiving and nurturing role." Her widowhood in old age has suddenly brought her a newfound independence. This is the first time in her life, in fact, that she has had the time to think about herself at all, her needs, what she wants to do with her day, her life, without the ceaseless burden "of caring for a . . . spouse" (Facio 1996, 92).

Because of the way she has been brainwashed, or to use the more genteel term, "socialized," as Facio does, about women's obligations and duties to service men, Anzaldúa's generic old widow would continue to accept her role forever without self-reflexivity. Her automaticity in continuing in that role for the first days after her husband's death reveals that she began by doing so. However, as a result of her experience with the ghost, she begins to realize that she will from now on conform to the expectations of her role as a widow, as an elder, only when she is treated with respect and "not taken for granted."

The conduct of her husband's ghost, as well as his discourse, makes it evident that he is still/forever lacking in this regard, due to the "traditional context" in which he lived and died and now continues beyond death. The problem is that the old widow achieves community respect only if she fulfills "the cultural expectations of caregiver." Not only that. Even though she is widowed she knows that she must appear to "remain single and refrain from seeking male companionship" in order to retain community respect (Facio 1996, 94). Otherwise she will risk being "judged as a 'bad' woman or *una mujer sin verguenza*." When young, she was expected to remain a virgin until marriage and now, as an older woman, she is expected "to be celibate after marriage" for the rest of her days.

As is obvious from her husband's ghost's selfish sexual demands, they are neither designed to include his wife in the matter, nor to give her any pleasure, just as was the case during his lifetime. Thus the widow's status is one of private self-fulfillment but public "powerlessness" so long as her husband, his ghost, and the community can observe her in her privacy. External wardens create a prison house for her of "cultural expectations, ageism, and patriarchy" (Facio 1996, 94) the moment she sets foot outside her door. They permit her no right to define herself, as she quickly discovers–within only two weeks! Nevertheless she takes it upon herself to shape her own pleasures, her own schedule for her days and nights for the rest of her life, to exorcise her husband's ghost forever. But privately.

Facio calls for more than a private solution, such as the ghost trap affords the anonymous widow. She appeals to the Chicano community to acknowledge "the contributions" older Chicanas make and permit them to "define their sexuality" regardless of traditional outmoded stereotypes that were invalid in the first place. When they do so outside the parameters of the community's oppressive straitjacketing, the community argues that such older women are eroding "tradition." This complaint turns into an artificial culturally constructed constraint, because it serves only "to perpetuate [an] older woman's oppression."

Facio's solution is to call for the Chicano community to reject these demeaning and harsh stereotypical expectations for older women as inherited from the Anglo colonizers. Ultimately the community must "take responsibility for oppressive forces toward women, both in the larger society and within the Chicano community" (1996, 108). Such a solution makes it appear as if she attributes the fault primarily to the Chicano community for straitjacketing older women into artificial and false cultural stereotypes about their sexuality. She implies that older Chicanas' problems stem from Chicanos having internalized the "colonial" power's system of inequitable gendered power relations and gendered success role models for their older women. The "oppressive forces" of inequitable gendered success role models for older women existed first in the external Anglo culture and then influenced Chicano culture. I would expand her observation to argue that such oppression of older women is characteristic of all cultures globally, simultaneously.

This is by no means to deny the influences of external mainstream Anglo culture on the Chicano community, especially the influence of the media in terms of consumerism. Ruíz notes in this regard about Chicana adolescents that they "developed a shining idealism as a type of psychological ballast." Some of them became members of the La Raza movement, pinning their hopes for "upward mobility" on education. Other adolescents dreamed, instead, of an easier way to assimilate, by means of "the application of Max Factor's bleaching cream" (1993, 122).

Blea sees a connection between poverty, immigrant women, and "marketing" that seems to be irrelevant on the surface. However, Chicanas, like any other group, can fall prey to what the media projects to the consumer as an ideal way of life. The media's goal is to promote consumerism so that the consumer will forever keep consuming (1991, 90). She argues that Anglo culture thereby entraps Chicanas and that their traditional value systems emphasize communitarianism, not an insolated, individualistic, consumeristic way of life. If Chicanas unwittingly adopt such a way of living, then they will be alienated from their community, but still not be accepted by the powers that be, the Anglos. Such a double alienation would be impossible if Chicanas became aware of their own qualities as Chicanas and took pride in them, as Ana Castillo does. A Chicana who is dark skinned should not pretend to be "exotic," to be an Asian or

Native American. A Chicana does not have "Asian eyes," nor is she from a reservation. But most of all, Chicanas do not "go artifically blonde." Instead, they should be, as she is, proud of the fact that "[t]he sun . . . gravitates to" her "dark pigmentation" (1995, 89).

The story that best illustrates Castillo's protest against the colonizing of Chicana mentalities and Ruíz's warning against Chicana "faith" in consumerism taken to its extreme, as well as Blea's critique, is Helena María Viramontes's "Miss Clairol." Viramontes plays upon the most powerful, sacrosanct concepts in Chicano construction of women—the mother as major source of nurturing, the mother and child model—as personified by the Virgin Mary. Those Chicanas who fall prey to Anglo American capitalistic consumerism can destroy this precious, hallowed construct, according to Viramontes.

First, of course, such Chicanas have to internalize alien values for beauty based upon ideals impossible to realize because such models are slim, blond, and have fair Caucasian features. Obsessed and preoccupied with false romantic visions which they receive from omnipresent advertisements and commercials, these Chicanas neglect and ignore the true source of love, acceptance, security— their own family members. As Ruíz explains:

The ideations of Americanization were a mixed lot. Religious and secular Americanization programs, the elementary schools, movies, magazines, and radio bombarded the Mexican community with a myriad of models, most of which were idealized, stylized, unrealistic, and unattainable. Even the Spanish-language press promoted acculturation, especially in the realm of consumer culture. Aimed at women, advertisements promised status and affection if the proper bleaching cream, hair coloring, and cosmetics were purchased. "Siga las Estrellas" [Follow the Stars] beckoned one Max Factor advertisement. (1995, 73)

Thus many Chicanas pursue their impossible dreams with brand-name products in stores like K-Mart, where Arlene, the protagonist of "Miss Clairol," shops with her ten-year-old daughter Champ. This bargain store represents a cheap and tawdry concept of sexual attractivness to which Arlene completely succumbs. Viramontes spares readers no illusions, such as the ones she gives Arlene. Her descriptions of Arlene's body parts and what she does with them are meant to repel readers by the gross, unnatural uses to which they are put. Nothing fits. Nothing is right. The reality of Arlene's fleshly being is at odds with the types of women for whom these fashions are created. Her stomach spills over jeans that are so tight she can't bend to reach the boxes of Miss Clairol at the store.

Later on when Arlene is preparing for a date, she bathes with brand names like Jean Naté, lying back in the bath and relaxing as the model does in the drawing on the Calgon box (103). She sprays Aqua Net hairspray over her once soft black hair, now platinum blond; a few weeks ago, red; and before that, auburn, all courtesy of Miss Clairol hair dye. She teases and tames "her ratted hair," folding it back behind her head in "a high lump."

She then forces her heavy arms up through the dress while holding her breath, but she is only concerned with the swishing sound the dress makes when she walks. Arlene then proceeds to make up. She paints her brows, making them two even arches, pencils them thickly and high, paints her eyelids "magenta," then outlines her eyes with "black eyeliner, like a fallen question mark." Arlene does all this with trembling caution, frequently stopping to judge her handiwork, because the Arlene she sees reflected in the mirror should not be the same Arlene "who has worn too many relationships, gotten too little sleep."

After applying "chalky, beige lipstick" to her mouth, Arlene sits down on the toilet seat to pull on her stockings and attach them to her girdle. As she does so, she fantasizes about how her date will release her nylons from her girdle, how she will pull them slowly down her legs, pointing her toes. Arlene applies powder and *Love Cries* perfume to her public and private parts in order to arouse the man, so that when they dance she will feel his hardness "bulge" through his pants, the signal that she will be able to spend the entire night with him (101).

Viramontes calls Arlene "a romantic" despite describing her in the most repulsive terms. Her hips jigger and quake while she dances. Afterwards her dress gets discolored, her hairdo falls apart. Her mascara smears her eyes "from the perspiration of the ritual, dance spinning herself into Miss Clairol." Arlene stops "only when it is time to return to the sewing factory, time to wait out the next date, time to change hair color. Time to remember or to forget" (104–105). Only at such a time can Arlene be said to be able to escape into romantic fantasies about herself as a woman.

What is the reality beneath this superficial and revolting ugliness? What is Arlene avoiding or forgetting, escaping from in Miss Clairol and all she represents? The sewing factory and abuse from men. At one point, while dressing herself, the towel that covers her slides down, exposing that one of her nipples is "blind" from having been burned with a cigarette on "a date to forget" (103).

Arlene is also avoiding the reality of Champ, her daughter, in whom she has no interest as an individual, only as a reflection of herself. Arlene projects her experiences and her values onto her daughter. While Arlene shops, Champ accompanies her and is exposed to her mother's questions as to what color of makeup and hair dye she should buy, as if she were a retainer to royalty whom Arlene expects in her insecure self-centeredness to focus only on herself. She relates to her daughter only as a bystander in her play, or as a maid. Champ, tragically, is on the way toward following in her mother's footsteps. Both mother and daughter speak Spanglish, code switching primarily around the terms of knowing and not knowing. Arlene is always asking Champ in Spanish: "¿Sabes que?" [What do you think?] about her appearance, and the child generally answers that she doesn't know.

In extremely ironic counterpoint to where Viramontes would have Arlene place her love and attention, the author uses popular songs on the radio to underscore her projection of romantic fantasy. She sings along, imagining some ideal, nonexistent lover, promising that she will do anything for his love, for his kiss (103). Meanwhile she does nothing for her daughter, except to fantasize the child as a projection of herself as a young woman when Champ grows up, when she will tell her about making love to a boy.

While her mother is preparing for her date, Champ watches TV, dressed only in one of her older brother Gregorio's impeccable undershirts that he himself launders. It is big enough on her to look like a dress (103). Viramontes may here be intimating that Gregorio, who is prematurely mature, is also neglected, because like Champ, he is capable of household chores which most young boys would not be doing otherwise.

In "Tears on My Pillow," a later story by Viramontes, Gregorio is now nicknamed "Spider," and, again, he is never home (113). Champ, now called Ofelia, worries about her brother. In this story Arlene comes across as a sympathetic, caring mother, although she still coifs her hair in poor taste and is linked with brand names. This time, Champ admires her mother's preparations for her date. And this time Arlene is neither described as repulsive nor deluded, but as spunky. When she creates her beehive, teasing it and pulling it high, Champ "trip[s] out." In her eyes her mother has succeeded in performing a marvelous feat, "doing her hair and blow[ing] bubble gum at the same time without missin' a beat." This time Champ admires how her mother sprays "Aqua Net back and forth, back and forth til her hairdo as shiny and hard as candied apples" (115).

This time Arlene's consumerism is viewed by Viramontes through Ofelia's thoughts. It is not as the result of a foolish belief in and dependence upon Anglo media hype. Instead, it is used as a form of bravado, sassiness, strength, courage, and endurance in the face of racism and sexist oppression that would destroy the spirit of ordinary Chicanas.

This time, Arlene's first request after coming in from work is for Ofelia to "[t]urn off the TV," whereas in "Miss Clairol" she doesn't care about anything else but her upcoming date. Before falling asleep from exhaustion, Arlene then asks after her son, inquiring as to whether he is at home or at school. She still works in the sweatshop, with "pipe guts for ceilings and no windows. All these sewing machines buzzing, buzzing eating up big balls of string about big as my head spinning dizzy and so much dust flying 'round, makes it hard to breathe" (113). The factory is owned by a Jew, who shares the harsh working conditions with his workers, at least briefly, because he is described as in the room "so red he's pink." Nevertheless he does not even allow his workers, all women, to even "go pee cause when you come back, might some other girl be in your place and no more job for you" (114).

Spider is older than Ofelia and should be babysitting for her. Viramontes also insinuated in "Miss Clairol" that Ofelia was becoming alienated from school by describing the child as shrugging her "shoulders when Miss Smith says OFELIA answer my question." In "Tears on My Pillow" the same Miss Smith, an unsympathetic WASP, nags Ofelia to answer her question. This time the child informs the readers that Miss Smith has been calling her "and who cares, I don't know the answer anyways, and the bell rings" (1992, 113).

In her survey, Segura discovered that

Teaching and counseling methods [leave] much to be desired. . . . Yet another major source of discontent among the Chicana respondents was the lack of a culturally relevant curriculum. School curricula tend to be monocultural, reflecting mainly the achievements of Anglo Americans.[3] Sitting daily in classrooms that ignored their culture and history, Chicanas felt alienated from their school settings. These feelings were particularly keen since a majority of the respondents attended schools that had courses in black history and culture. . . . [S]chools should include a more diverse curriculum, and most asserted that if such a curriculum had been integrated into their educational programs, they would have been more motivated to attend classes and achieve. (1993, 208)

The fact is that, as Gloria Bonilla-Santiago found, Hispanic girls in high school did not receive adequate counseling. Exploring the enrollments in vocational schools, she also found that Chicanas face futures with poor incomes and few career opportunities, only vocational ones (1995, 220). School will not bring Cisneros's Patricia in "My Tocaya" in *Woman Hollering Creek and Other Stories*, and others like her, any upward mobility in terms of class status or any upward mobility from class to class. Patricia, who works at her father's small taco place after school and on weekends, runs away briefly out of boredom and isolation, as well as extremely low self-esteem about being Chicana. She attempts to Anglify herself by speaking with an exaggerated English accent and calling herself "Trish."

Segura illustrates Patricia's problem in a study of high school students. After working at fast-food chains before finishing their education, Anglo students invariably succeed in attaining full-time career jobs "in the primary sector." In contrast, minorities and women are tracked into service work like Patricia, or sweat shop labor like Arlene in "Miss Clairol" and "Tears on My Pillow," "since historically they have not had the same job options as white males" (1986, 52).

Certainly in "Miss Clairol" Champ does not spend the time throughout the long afternoon in doing anything related to learning or homework while her mother is dressing. All critics of Chicano/Chicana literature are united in concluding that the acquirement of education is considered crucial. They believe that "social and economic advancement depend[s] on a better education. . . . [that] education [is] a central factor in liberating Chicanos from their status of marginality" (Hernández 1991, 42). Note that Viramontes is indicating that Champ's teacher is Anglo by naming her teacher a "Miss Smith," a "unidimensional" figure "behind a cruel white mask"; "a socially myopic" teacher who distorts the "learning experience" (Hernández 1991, 43, 50); who too loudly emphasizes the foreignness of Champ's Spanish name. By this means, the author is censuring the teacher "for failing the student . . . [and for] the insensitivity of schools toward the educational needs of Chicano children" such as Champ to the point where "teachers' prejudices are . . . the most formidable social barriers facing Chicano students" (Hernández 1991, 41).

Segura writes that "educational success, including high school and college completion, is linked to the class backgrounds of different populations" (1986, 51) and that "[a]mong Chicanos in the public schools, only 23 percent are performing 'satisfactorily' at each grade level" (1995a, 123). In "Miss Clairol," Champ's acculturation is depicted as primarily the result of her mother's example. The lack of sympathetic interest by Miss Smith is a background factor that had it been otherwise might have been sufficient to countervail the dominance of Arlene's values. Blea concurs, maintaining that Chicanas have "their first negative experience with Anglo female teachers and principals." She blames the poor relationship of Anglo educators with Chicanas on Anglo racism, individualism, and competitiveness, in addition to their having "a higher profit orientation than Chicana males and females" (1991, 92). She omits the deep level class elitist attitudes and values of Anglo educators that determine how they relate to students like Champ.

Hernández would define Arlene's flaws of character as in conformity with "[t]he Bakhtinian notion of the disintegrated personality, whose alienation produces an individual existing solely for [herself]" (1991, 96). In "Miss Clairol," Champ watches only variety shows on TV while also trying to phone Gregorio who has not yet come home. Most depressing of all, like a miniature preparing to be like her mother later on, Champ is "busy cutting out Miss Breck models from the stacks of old magazines." She collects, this "array of honey colored haired women . . . in a shoe box with all her other special things" (113).[4]

In the evening before she leaves, Arlene is depicted in "Miss Clairol" as not even providing the child with a meal, or at least making sure that Champ is properly nourished in her absence. Viramontes's rage is evident when she describes the child in the process of efficiently feeding herself, as if she has done it many times. Champ makes herself dinner from "a can of Campbell [sic] soup" from a pot which she finds "in the middle of a stack of dishes" in the sink. Champ has to wash the pot herself before boiling the soup, then has to search "for a spoon." She eats her soup from this pot while watching TV, even while her mother is still home. The can of soup that Champ eats for her supper is as negative a symbol for Chicanas as is Arlene's continual use of blond hair dyes. Campbell's is the typical canned American soup, the antithesis of the traditional association of Mexican food with women's nurturing work designated by traditional Chicano culture as appropriate only for Chicanas in a spiritually and psychically significant way (Blea 1991, 144). In addition, Campbell's employs migrant laborers in their fields, many of them Chicanas, many of them exploited.

Arlene's incapacity to mother is thus exposed on political and social levels, an incapacity Viramontes underlines even more heavily at the end of "Miss Clairol." Although she has sung along soulfully with the music she plays while dressing for her date–songs about loving and kissing, still Arlene leaves without even kissing her daughter good-bye. Showing not the slightest concern for her daughter's well-being, she leaves for her date with the intention of staying out the entire night. Champ is the one who calls out her good-bye to her mother. "It all sounds so right to Arlene who is too busy cranking up the window to hear her daughter" (114–115).

I wonder whether the culprit for unsuspecting Chicanas is indeed the racist consumerism and superficial anti-family values of Anglo American culture.

Perhaps Viramontes intends, instead, to illustrate a grievance: that the traditional strengths associated with familism are destroyed under such conditions. Arlene distracts herself with bogus pictures of beauty and bogus romanticism about men. Viramontes indicates that Arlene should keep a decent home for herself and her children, instead, while maintaining her own pride and well-being as a Chicana. Arlene should take pride in her Chicana appearance and Chicana attitude and not strive to "Americanize" herself at the expense of her racial and ethnic identity.

Although Arlene's degradation is obvious in "Miss Clairol," and although Viramontes agrees in this cuento that "the colonizer's view . . . is true" about Arlene and Chicanas who fall into a similar trap, Blea sees such agreement as a Catch-22. Chicanas fall into the trap only because of the invalidating messages about themselves that endlessly come at them through all the institutions of the Anglo culture. This bombardment causes Chicanas to experience low self-esteem, which, in turn, leaves them open to consumerism and other self-negating activities (1991, 139).

It is at this point that the Anglo colonizers are in trouble, because their ideology gives rise to a liberation movement. Unlike Arlene, many Chicanas have come to the realization that they can only be manipulated by a racist and sexist Anglo culture so long as (like Arlene) they continue to be unaware that they are being manipulated (Blea 1991, 139). True, Arlene and Champ are colonized, and for this reason their values, dreams, hopes, and aspirations are "controlled" by the media and commerials. In "Tears on My Pillow," however, the author is using Arlene and Champ as "a cautionary tale," but has moved away from her earlier perspective. She has now realized the implications of commercialized cultural (de)constructions on Chicanas and is issuing a danger call to her sisters to avoid this temptation.

In this second story, Viramontes reveals more compassion for Arlene than in "Miss Clairol." Readers are here encouraged to identify with Arlene's situation. The author now reveals Arlene as doing the best she can under extremely challenging conditions. In fact, her excess in clothing and hairstyles, her consumerism, are now depicted as components of an indomitable spirit: a courageous, bold, up-in-your face working-class Chicana, determined to live each day as best she can and enjoy her life to the fullest. Further, instead of being a neglectful mother, absolutely insensitive to her daughter, Arlene is now depicted as caring and loving. When her daughter becomes terrified at the sound of La Llorona weeping, which tropes the tragic situation of Arlene and her children struggling in both Anglo and Chicano cultures:

Arlene took me to her bed and I pulled up my feet real close to her. She smelled like cigarettes and warm beer and Noxzema cream. Her chichis [breasts] was soft and cool under her slip, where I put my head. Please, mama make it stop. I asses her to put the TV on real loud, do something, cause La Llorona was crying so crazy, she was breaking windows.
      Sshh, Arlene said, turning off the light, ssshhh. (1992, 111)

Ultimately, the difference between "Miss Clairol" and "Tears on My Pillow" does not reside in the characters, in their situations, or in their perspectives. "Tears on My Pillow" represents Viramontes' move away from a condemnatory masculinist stereotypical discursive model toward focusing on the limited selections for Chicanas. In Arlene's case these take the form of redefining a Chicana's role as "the prostitute mother."[5] She now creates through characterization an externalized La Raza political statement that sharply critiques the influence of Anglo consumerism.

This process is what Yolanda Broyles terms "the dramatic space necessary for the unfolding of a character." Viramontes now has come to view Arlene as beyond her bio/political role, as having achieved a "a new understanding or 'stretch'" (1986, 169) in relation to her character. She achieves this by seeing and feeling deep within and "through the eyes of" another woman, "the other half of humanity" . . . a consciousness of women–in oneself" that didn't exist in the first story (1986, 165). There it appeared almost as if Viramontes is peering at her character from a microscope, instead of writing as if she were an invisible comadre in Arlene's cramped space, as she does in the second story. In "Tears on My Pillow," Viramontes has repudiated any other value system, politics, or class/race perspective externally inscribed from without onto her Chicana character and onto all working class Chicanas.

In describing Chicanas' problems, Adeljisa Sosa Riddell could well be talking of Arlene in "Miss Clairol." In the first story, Viramontes focuses on Chicanas themselves as to blame for their problems, instead of the society outside her frame. This position unfortunately works to keep Chicanas focused on what is lacking in them, as when Arlene is depicted as having internalized Anglo society's consumeristic and romantic attitudes. When they do so, the Anglo oppressors prevent Chicanas from turning their focus of attention in their direction. As in "Miss Clairol," Anglos and their omnipresent controlling institutions can then freely blame Chicanas for a variety of failures. This tactic is geared to keeping Chicanas psychologically enslaved in so many ways: for being bad mothers, "for not keeping their family together" (Segura 1995b, 406) if they leave the home to work, or if they stay at home, if they are childless, or if their families are too large.

NOTES

1. Lillián Leví testifies to this, as well, in terms of contemporary Nicaraguan culture:

The motto of the feminine gender–to belong to others and live for others–begins to be played out as soon as a girl baby is born. By the age of five a girl child from the lowest economic stratum has become a caretaker for her younger siblings. Her body is already bent under loads almost equal to her weight–a pail of water, a baby. She is unlikely to attend school: family income is insufficient and she must help with domestic chores. By ten she will have witnessed many abuses against her mother; she herself will become the object of violent incest at the hands of one or several males in her own family. At eighteen, after an agitated sexual life but no erotic experience, she will become a mother, still without social services, education, job training, or legislation attentive to her urgent problems. (1993, 15)

2. Facio notes in this regard that "widows who were unemployed during their marriages expressed some resentment toward their husband's dominance. They rationalized their past situations by referring to traditional socialization of women. The ideology of women's 'proper place' is that women are moral guardians of the home and therefore should not enter the labor force. Women's family responsibilities should consist of housework, child care, consumption, and emotional nurturance" (1996, 65). She makes the astute perception that not only are the women dissatisfied with not being able to work, but "with the fact that someone else determined her role in the marriage" (1996, 65). The identity of that "someone else" is obvious, as were his objections, on the grounds that it was the male's responsibility to economically provide for the family" (1996, 65).

3. Blea asserts that "most Americans are monolingual, and for the most part, monocultural." At a time when global communications demands "bilingual ability and cultural literacy on many fronts" this monolingualism and monoculturalism has diminished the "power" of the United States, as well as its "status, and prestige in international affairs" (1991, 120).

4. Breck shampoo advertisements were the forerunner of Miss Clairol advertisements. They always featured elegant young white women from upper, socio-economic classes with fair skin, slender necks, and bright, light hair.

Chapter 4

Silencing and Violence

Both Chicano and Anglo cultures, as well as all other known cultures, give men the right to define what the norm is for their behavior, while defining what women want and expect of them as irrelevant or insignificant. Further, wherever and whenever men have the power to make definitions–and this is just about everywhere and in every time–women are nowhere to be found in their discourse (Pérez 1993, 60). The editors of *Cuentos: Stories by Latinas* declare that "[c]lass, race, and education . . . as it combines with sex, are much more critical in silencing the would-be Latina writers than discrimination on sex alone" (1983, viii). I would contend, however, that under patriarchy the Chicana writers I analyze in this text reveal that even women of more privileged class, race, and education are constrained by "the systemic function of silencing" (Kutzinski 1993, 16), whether their cages are gilded, straw, or tin. Or as Alvina Quintana puts it in almost the same terms: "silencing practices . . . are based on patriarchal traditions" (1995, 253).

The primary motive for most Chicana and other Latina writing, as in most women's writing, is the attempt to express themselves within an alien masculinist world of constraining patriarchal institutions whose discourse does not allow for their existence so that their voices are silenced. Cixous provides a solution to the silencing of women, making them invisible. "[B]y writing, from and toward women, and by taking up the challenge of speech, which has been governed by the phallus . . . women will confirm women in a place other than that which is reserved in and by the symbolic, that is, in a place other than silence. Women should break out of the snare of silence" (1983, 283).

Depriving Chicana writers of the "literary authority" they deserve is no different from the deprivation of authority women experience in all the other arenas of power arrogated to themselves by males. Chicana writers struggle to be read with respect and included in the canon as creators, speakers, and writers of a discourse that will be accepted as appropriate to themselves and their group and on their own terms. Their struggle for inclusion into and equality with other authors in the traditional Chicano and Anglo literary canon is no different from their struggle for equality in Chicano and Anglo social, political, economic, educational, and religious discourse (Yarbro-Bejarano 1988, 134).

Elba Rosario Sánchez also speaks eloquently to the lack of a "Woman's Word" in the culture, of having triumphed, despite her acculturation into voiceless classlessness. Although the culture wanted her deprived of her voice, and although she once lived in the depths of silence because of the threat that she would not be considered attractive to men if she spoke out, ultimately her "tongue gave birth" (1995, 63). She then spoke words that challenged the nonsense she had previously accepted. One wonders what the stimulus was that enabled her to break her silence.

In relation to the link for her between her experience of herself as a lesbian and a Chicana, "Silence," Moraga comments, "is like starvation" (1981, 29). Perhaps the most powerful critique of women's enforced silence is Luisa Valenzuela's. She notes astutely that "the mouth was and continues to be the most threatening opening of the feminine body: it can eventually express what shouldn't be expressed, reveal the hidden desire, unleash the menacing differences which upset the core of the phallogocentric, paternalist discourse" (1993, 126).

The fact is that whoever has the power controls the discourse. Pérez, in her critique of Foucault, agrees with him that language is power, but qualifies the perception to note what Foucault did not. Residents of the Third World are not merely passive, reactive recipients of their colonizers' perspective and discourse. They are very much aware that if they learn and use this discourse, they might gain some power over those who do not, or cannot, or will not use this discourse. Nevertheless, Third World people will always experience rigid controls and constraints, even if they do achieve power from those in the other worlds still in power over them (1993, 60).

Neither Foucault nor Pérez notes that the same could be said for women globally. The discourse about men permits them to express as appropriate and positive that which is in reality unjust, oppressive, and conflictual in relation to women. This is the way taught to Junior in Cisneros's story "'Mericans." Although he is very young, he has already internalized sexism. He treats his sister Michele with antagonism and contempt and excludes her from certain activities because she is a female and Other and therefore inferior.

Douglas R. Hofstadter describes the masculine delusion humorously:

In his wanderings, Loocus the Thinker one day comes across an unknown object–a woman. Such a thing he has never seen before, and at first he is wondrous thrilled at her likeness to himself; but then, slightly scared of her as well, he cries to all the men about him, Behold! I can look upon her face, which is something she cannot do–therefore women can never be like me! And thus he proves man's superiority over women, much to his relief, and that of his male companions. Incidentally, the same argument proves that Loocus is superior to all other males, as well–but he doesn't point that out to them. The woman argues back: Yes, you can see my face, which is something I can't do–but I can see your face, which is something you can't do! We're even. However, Loocus somes up with an unexpected counter: I'm sorry, you're deluded if you think you can see my face. What you women do is not the same as what we men do–it is, as I have already pointed out, of an inferior caliber, and does not deserve to be called by the same name. You may call it "womanseeing." Now the fact that you can "womansee" my face is of no import, because the situation is not symmetric. You see? I womansee, replies the woman, and woman walks away. (1980, 477)

In explicating Malthusian theory, Juan Bruce-Novoa indicates the answer to the puzzling question as to why Inés's mother, the bruja in Cisneros's "Zapata's Eyes" in *Woman Hollering Creek and Other Stories*, was slain so brutally. In this story Inés's Indian mother represents women who rebel against the imposed patriarchal concept of family. According to Malthusian "social morality" traditional familism and the structure of Mexican society are believed to be "sacrosanct units." To critique or defy them is to upset "the natural order of things." When this occurs, a domino effect happens, in which, as a result, all the ills of humanity like poverty, crime, and dreaded diseases manifest themselves on earth (1995, 227).

In the case of Inés's mother, her acts as an unruly woman culminated in her extermination by the community of men. From a feminist perspective, however, she was executed because her display of sexual freedom, despite the fact that she was married according to their laws, struck terror in the hearts and minds of the patriarchs of her society. In Mexican culture, the female's public body is heavily swathed, but Inés's mother openly exhibited sexuality through her active interest in and pursuit of men, with the inevitable result that men noticed her womanly attributes. They did this, not with attraction, but with fear and revulsion. Her "aggressive" conduct stretched beyond these men's limits the parameters of the rigidly contained essence of femaleness under patriarchy. Thus her attempts to be proactive sexually, to manipulate her own corporeal essence to pleasure herself, were vain and doomed attempts to act beyond men's control and dominion.

Judging the events in Inés's life and that of her mother's, as well as of the women in her village and other villages throughout the Mexican Revolution, an "archetypal personification of evil" (Haaken 1996, 1083) is embodied in the sleeping Emiliano Zapata, the outlaw underling of Pancho Villa. Inés describes the rapes before the Revolution as committed by the federales who greedily consumed not only food, but also anything else in sight, including other men's property and their women. After the revolution, both armies committed rapes with neither side distinguishable from the other. Inés describes to readers the loud howls the women of a village would emit when they were carried away at night. Invariably, they would return in the morning. Invariably, people would greet them without any apparent consciousness that anything unusual had befallen them overnight.

Inés has no class ranking until she is accorded the very low one of Zapata's mistress. Here is one of the essential traditionally ordained differences between men and women, which can be interpreted as entirely due to inequitable gendered power relations that outclass women. Inés meditates about love, concluding that women are not allowed to have such feelings, even if they wanted to, as illustrated by her mother's fate. What men do is stroke with their eyes whatever women attract them, then lasso, harness, and corral them. Significantly she uses equine imagery that functions on a specific level, as well as on a global one. Zapata in his youth won fame and fortune from buying and selling horses. Culturally also, equine imagery for women is routinely used.

When Zapata met her, he harassed her as she walked in the zocalo [the town square] by riding his horse in her path whichever way she turned, forcing her to dodge one way, then the other, like a calf evading being roped (108). Obviously Cisneros is using the horse and the calf as tropes for inequitable gendered power relations in the patriarchal community. Here we see a combination of sexual violence and power that Pérez astutely observes is the foundation for the permissible violent treatment of women, children, and Other men by white men (1993, 69). However, she perceives this violence as confined to white men only because the term she uses for the Other men who could be the victims of that institutionalized violence is "men of color." Her narrow term therefore exempts Mexican men like Zapata, as well as Chicanos, from inclusion in her paradigm. Evidently Cisneros does not agree with her.

Inés explains, presumably to the sleeping Zapata, but actually to the cruel culture, that although he was handsome, she did not care for handsome men because they imagined they could have any woman they desired. For this reason she acted aloof but proud, not lowering her eyes as the other girls did when men looked at them. This eternal, universal game is played because of the way their relations are structured in the culture. Margarita Fernández Olmos and Lizbeth Paravisini-Gebert make this point as well in terms of my thesis that women are "outclassed" in this culture and in most cultures:

[T]he protagonists' sexual awakenings are neither ahistorical nor apolitical; both occur within specific historical contexts of political violence and upheaval, and great emphasis is placed on the social and class distinctions between the protagonists and their male victimizers. Works like "Zapata's Eyes" couple "eroticism and sensuality" . . . with a critique of sociopolitical structures. (1993, 28–29)

While being ignominiously lassoed by Zapata, Inés is aware that Zapata's men are watching and laughing. Are they laughing in support of their leader in his mock-lassoing charade? Or is there perhaps a hint of something else going on beneath the men's laughter at the sight of a lassoed woman? Might sound equate with meaning here? Is it male bonding and identification with Zapata at the expense of the lassoed Indian girl? Or is it perhaps a hint of a difference of attitude on the part of his men: the possibility of a difference of opinion with Zapata about what he is doing?

After Inés has conducted herself with icy dignity, even while Zapata has prevented her from going on her way, one of Zapata's friends admires the girl's courage enough to joke mockingly at his jefe's expense that she may be small, but she "is bigger than you, Miliano" (108). Nevertheless, despite this cutting and witty put-down of Zapata's methods of fetishized phallic male power as perhaps indicative, instead, of his lack of true manhood, his men make no attempt to interfere in Inés's enforced capture, nor to save her from her fate.

I call attention to this passage because in all the other works I have analyzed so far in this text, men friends are always depicted as gathered around the man in question. They are always laughing conspiratorially against women. This is the only time when a male companion is depicted as mocking another male while he is molesting a woman. They have always been shown as united in their animosity against women, in their bonding camaraderie, and in their unanimity about interpretations of events. They do this so as to cause themselves to be the centered and dominant group, in contrast to the women whom they make small, insignificant, and Other. As Ellen McCracken points out about Esperanza's experience in *The House on Mango Street*, Cisneros's first book, in Cisneros's stories, men treat women with "violence as if it were their innate right" (1989, 67). In "Lassoing Inés," Zapata is probably relating more with his men's opinion than with anything else, except, perhaps, his horses.

When Inés's mother is murdered, her lover participates actively with the other men of the town. This participation reflects "a desire to consolidate partnerships with authoritative males in and through the bodies of females" (Sedgwick 1985, 38). Such a desire is "homosocial" rather than heterosexual. Ines's mother, a bruja, had been taking lovers. On that morning, her last lover colluded with the other men in killing her. She was stabbed in the heart with a greased cane stake, "gang-raped," "a man's sombrero" (111) placed on her head, and a cigar in her mouth. Her corpse was then dumped into her husband's doorway. These signifiers all loudly proclaimed to other women in the village that what happened to this one because she acted like a man will happen to them, as well.

Castañeda explains the perspective which sources such conduct on the part of the men of the community as being ideological in devaluing women, privatizing and reifying them as properties owned by men (1993, 25). Hector A. Torres also uses the term "property," but astutely, in terms of female sexuality in patriarchal discourse where female sexuality is defined as belonging to men and not themselves (1995, 137). Time and again in all their works, Chicanas reject this discourse, perhaps most powerfully here in "Zapata's Eyes" where the bruja who dares to take lovers is brutally slain for acting out her belief that her sexuality is her own to please, as though she were a man.

At the darkest moment in "Zapata's Eyes," readers become aware that Cisneros sees no ultimate hope for change in a system that devalues women to the point where one of them is killed for enjoying men, while it permits men to do as they please. Clearly any and all women are considered outside of class lines when they are exposed as having active sexual desires. Castañeda agrees, when she observes that except in times of war, Anglo culture treats rapes according to both the victims' and the rapists' class rankings (1993, 25).

When women unite with women like the lassoed Inés and her mother in announcing both their sexuality and their right to the free expression of that sexuality; when women unite in refusing to permit grossly unfair gendered relations of power to be perpetuated onto themselves as a group, as a class; when women refuse indoctrination and intimidation couched in masculinist discourse contrary to their best interests and that has nothing to do with their lives, then men will no longer be free to continue their oppression of women (Dernersesian 1993, 52). Men could continue to make up the laws, rules, and customs, the gendered power relations. But when they violate the rights of women, they could be ignored and disobeyed by more than half the population. The male establishment in power makes into legal and religious models whatever they fantasize for appropriate female conduct, including defining highly constrained erotic parameters for all kinds and presumptive classes of women, but never for themselves. Women do not have to accede to their definitions, although many do. These women are what I call in this work and elsewhere "gatekeepers" for patriarchy—women who have internalized and perpetuate inequitable gendered power relations. Beneath the exaggerations designed to frighten off and away all those women who dread disapproval, ostracism, and cultural sanctions lies the truth about what masculinist discourse defines as shameful and heretical about sexuality—that it is so for women only, not for themselves.

Isolated from companionship, Cleófilas in Cisneros's "Woman Hollering Creek" begins to notice a variety of outrages against women once she realizes that her own experience of outrages committed against herself by her own husband parallels theirs. The more abuse she experiences, the more Cleófilas becomes aware of the connection, or as McCracken puts its, "the continuum" (1989, 67–69) between her husband's violent use of his power over her and male violence in a patriarchy. It is this continuum, or as I put it, inequitable gendered power relations that "outclasses" women through violence, as well as by other means. Surrounded, encircled in unanimity and cameraderie by his drinking buddies who share his views, Cleófilas's husband in "Woman Hollering Creek" is further strengthened in his convictions that his conduct and attitude toward his wife are appropriate and normal.

Again, Cisneros composes a doleful litany of what sexism entails—dehumanization. One woman was thrown onto the shoulder of the highway. Another, from a speeding car. One woman a corpse, another in a coma, yet another, bruised from a beating. This litany is followed by another litany, this time as if intoned from deep within Cleófilas's psyche. Cisneros openly indicts all the possible kinds of men whose violence destroys their women: husbands, ex-husbands, lovers, fathers, brothers, uncles, friends, coworkers. It is unchanging, always the same stories in the media of beatings, rapes, and murders of women.

When Cleófilas confronts her husband, his response is no surprise to her. He claims that she is "exaggerating." This word is a masculine discursive coded term applied only to women—like other demeaning terms such as hysterical, nag, gossip, slut in the pantheon of patriarchal discursive mechanisms of inequitable gendered power relations of control and domination over women. This discourse is also deployed globally in all cultures to set a woman to doubting the reality of her experience, as well as her rationality and sanity. Nowhere is this done more brilliantly than when Cisneros depicts Cleófilas at her kitchen window overhearing in silent horror the men talk their chilling talk.

Violence against women is one of Cisneros's recurrent themes in both the cuento of "Woman Hollering Creek" and the entire collection of cuentos with the eponymous title. She used this theme before the Serbs were publicized as systematically using rape on Muslim women as a means of disrupting and ultimately destroying the fabric of their culture. Muslim men decree ostracism and death to "impure" Muslim women, regardless of how they got that way. This is a severe form of blaming the victim, with which Chicanas and women globally are all too familiar, to say the least. "[S]ome 20,000 Muslim women and girls were raped by Serb men between 1991 and 1995" (Kessler-Harris citing Minow, 16). Rape in such cultures

[I]s like other atrocities in some respects, but it frequently leaves living victims, who cannot speak their shame, to be rejected by the communities to which they return. Unlike victims of prison torture who may return maimed in body but honored by their communities, those who have been sexually victimized often find themselves marginalized. They are tortured by their own nightmares and again by continuing isolation and their inability to return to normal lives. (Kessler-Harris, 16)

In her essay on "The Politics of Rape: Sexual Transgression in Chicana Fiction," Herrera-Sobek, like many other feminist Chicanas, views the concept of rape as "a metaphorical construct" (1988b, 171) skillfully designed by male rulers to perpetuate their hegemony. Chicana writers are primarily concerned about the lower class ranking and oppressive treatment to which they are consigned by men in both their own and the dominant culture. As a way of striking back, they also use rape as the metaphor for the oppressive patriarchy (1988b, 171). From their perspective, both as feminists and as victims, they view rape as an excellent metaphor for their condition. Galvanizing their readers into a sense of what rape feels like, they successfully use this dreadful metaphor with great power.

In Cherríe Moraga's play *Giving up the Ghost* where the protagonist is raped, Herrera-Sobek sees the author as using the rape politically to represent women's oppression through being socialized into putting up with low and liminal positions, or as I term it, being outcast/cast out or "outclassed. " In addition, if Chicanas are only doubly marginalized, as Herrera-Sobek claims, Moraga and women like her are triply marginalized, for she is also a lesbian. Ultimately, Herrera-Sobek's view of women's placement is similar to mine, for she defines it as "absence" from the masculinist culture. However, she concludes that this "absence" is the result of rape. Rape changes women into silent, invisible, nonexistent entities–as nothing more than holes to be filled by males (1988b, 175).[1] In my view women are absented from the culture at birth. Rape, literally or metaphorically, only reinforces the fact of their prior (dis)placement from the world.

Cleófilas's husband throws her book at her and hits her with it in an intertextual moment reminiscent of Thomas Hardy's *Jude the Obscure* when Jude's crude, insensitive wife smears his book with pig grease and then destroys it. Or as in Buchi Emecheta's *Second Class Citizen* when Francis destroys Adah's first draft of *The Bride Price*. In a brilliant juxtaposition of contrasts, Cisneros describes the book that infuriates Juan Pedro as written by the romance writer Corin Tellado. Deprived of TV and the "telenovelas" she loved to watch in Mexico, reading an escapist romance is what Cleófilas, the victim of domestic violence, of battering and abuse, prefers to do with her free time in the United States. Similarly, the hero of Hardy's book is the victim of domestic violence, and in real life, Emecheta's own violent husband burned her first novel (which she rewrote).

Cisneros turns the tables on all the traditional and elitist critics of such works as hers who view them as beneath contempt, too insignificant to warrant inclusion in "the canon." Cisneros uses the scene where Juan Pedro burns the romance novel his wife is reading to expose his sadistic brutality and to reinforce her point about Cleófilas's basically romantic, sensitive, and idealistic psyche. She is similar to Gustave Flaubert's Emma Bovary, Kate Chopin's Emma Pontellier, and Leo Tolstoy's Anna Karenina, all victimized women who had the daring to attempt to overcome their culture's contraints and express their sexuality. They were described by their authors as victims, as subsequently destroyed by the patriarchal system because of their unruly, wayward conduct. Not surprisingly, Chopin's Emma is as convincing as Inés and her unnamed bruja mother and enrages feminist readers equally at the cruelty and barbarism of the culture that deprives a woman so unfairly of her sexual pleasure.

Cisneros, in depicting Cleófilas's stultifying and increasingly frightening existence, underscores Pérez's claim that men as well as women become "addicted" to what is most destructive for them (1993, 66). This is the case in the relationship between Cleófilas and her husband Juan Pedro. A circle of approving male friends, all embodiments of the patriarchy, all like him, surround and support him. They not only condone the violent and self-destructive conduct which cause him to lose his wife and son, they reinforce it. For this reason, Juan Pedro has no motivation to self-reflexivity, to break the cycle of the violence and abuse to which he is habituated as his way of being in relationships with women. Pérez also identifies the root of such an addiction as Juan Pedro's as a pattern in the patriarchal system that he has internalized and that it condones. I believe, however, that the patriarchal system does more. It creates this terrible "dynamic," as Pérez puts it, between the sexes. It is neither "natural" nor spontaneous, but it is permitted by the patriarchy to continue generation after generation on those grounds. Actually, she claims that sex wars are sick and destroy those who engage in them. When are they not? The sexes do not war with each other as some kind of natural order of things.

Nevertheless, Pérez finally does identify the real, the true source of the "dynamic" she perceives between the sexes, not in some essentialist gender binary, but in patriarchal capitalism, in its system of decrees about sexuality that create "the perpertrator-victim dynamic." She then goes on to indict this system as one historically that lives on generation after generation, not only in practice, which is hellish enough, but in the memories of both "Western European conquerors and people of color" (1993, 66). Here she conflates the culprit, patriarchy, as not only the result of capitalism, but as only flourishing in Western European "conquerors." What would she say about Russian, Asian, and African countries that are not capitalistic, but are still patriarchal? Martha Boesing concurs with Blea and others cited previously. In researching male power she and her group found that capitalism caused "a rape culture" (1996, 1019). I would add to her statement that violence against women through rape is also the by-product of a feudal system, of a communist or fascist system, of any system controlled by unchecked patriarchal, hierarchical, inequitable gendered power relations.

Here Ruth Behar's tactful observation about Rebolledo's and Rivero's editing of their anthology, *Infinite Divisions*, applies to Blea's defense of Chicano violence. Behar observes that "[r]ips in the fabric of Chicana identity are carefully avoided" (1993, 19)–by Chicana critics such as Blea et al., even at the expense of the human rights of Chicanas. Every major ethnic group of women writers has this specious pressure applied to them by some of their men, as well as by some women from within their group. These prefer the peace at any price of avoiding confrontation with their men if they step out of line. Maxine Hong Kingston and Alice Walker are only two examples of women who have been subjected to such criticism on these grounds by men from their groups, as well as by gatekeeper women from within their groups.

In "Zapata's Eyes," the concept of saddling a woman is clearly the product of declassification of the female, or as I put it, "outclassing" her, transforming her into a captive animal figure to be hunted, caught, tamed, or worse. Nicaraguan men's discourse about women illustrates my point. Its source lies in the global perception that men's rights are public rights, the rights of citizens, but that women have "different (i.e., lesser) rights to citizenship. Nicaraguan men seem interchangeable with Chicano and Mexican men in this regard:

The motto for the masculine gender–"make a mark on the world"–can hardly be fulfilled by impoverished Third World men. They are, one might say, deprived of their gender prerogative. This fact exacerbates their tendency to violence, a tendency fostered by the war. Even the most deprived male has one or several women at his disposal. One Nicaraguan male imperative is to "put a belly on a woman"; having a child by her is a *sine qua non* of Nicaraguan masculinity. (Leví 1993, 15)

At the historic Beijing Conference of 1995, a new paradigm was attempted for the first time: to maintain that violence against women is a violation of their basic human rights.[2] Aruna Rao of the Bangladesh Rural Advancement Commission who participated in the Beijing Conference, calls for recognition that "violence against women is a public issue, not a private one, demanding public policy response and that freedom from all forms of violence is a basic human right" (1996, 219). Women such as Felice in "Woman Hollering Creek" are depicted as possessed of the extraordinary courage to buck the patriarchal system, while women like Cleófilas finally take action against it, if only to run from it. On the other hand, readers might consider Inés's story, narrated entirely in "introspective personal thoughts in monologue" (Herrera-Sobek 1988a, 28) as expressing the dark underside of Cisneros's perspective. According to Cisneros, men will never give up their oppression of women. It will always be that way. Cisneros's depressing message here is that men will forever prevent women from acting like men in the sense of seeking freedom to express their wishes, as men are free to do, to have free will.

The narrator Flora in the Puertorriqueña Carmen Valle's short, short story "Diary Entry #1," closely resembles the character Marta in Mary Helen Ponce's "The Jewelry Collection of Marta la Güera." Both these stories share similarities with "Woman Hollering Creek" sufficient to warrant their being read in tandem. Cleófilas is from the lower classes, whereas both Flora and Marta are somewhat higher in class. This is the case only because they are married (in)to their husbands' class. Regardless of their supposed class, all women experience astonishingly similar patterns of constraint throughout the classes. Cleófilas is ultimately unwilling to pay the exhorbitant price of enduring a marriage where she is routinely abused and battered. In contrast, neither Flora nor Marta ever achieves her own identity or a decent life.

In "Diary Entry #1," her husband Pedro has just died, and Flora the narrator muses on this as early as the first day of her life without him. As she does so, we come to know Pedro. He could well be interchangeable with Juan Pedro, Cleófilas's husband in "Woman Hollering Creek," or any of the abusive husbands of any patriarchal culture.

Like Cleófilas, Flora would also spend time waiting by the window, many times, all night. She does this, not to commune with nature and empathize with La Llorona, as does the originally idealistic young Cleófilas. She does this in order to pray that her husband will return from his carousing. While she was doing so, she would "maniacally" long for him to "smash his car into a pole'" (135). Like Juan Pedro of "Woman Hollering Creek," her Pedro "punched" her with such ferocity that she "was . . . unconscious for hours" (136) after Flora objected to his staying away from home. Also like Cleófilas's Juan Pedro, Flora's Pedro cried with remorse when his wife regained consciousness. Even more frightening, Flora's Pedro is much like Juan Pedro's friend Maximiliano who murdered his spirited wife. Once after Pedro did not return home until morning and found her furious, he placed a gun to her head and threatened her life if she did not "shut up" (136).

As with Cleófilas's experience of becoming a mother, pregnancy was also a time of terror for the now-widowed Flora. She stopped complaining then, because if she threatened to leave, she was convinced that her husband would come after her and would find her wherever she fled. His justification was that his love for her was too great for him to permit her to leave him. And, in addition, no woman alive could get away with daring to leave him (136). At the end of "Woman Hollering Creek," Cleófilas is carried off to safety across the border to Mexico to her father's home. But a suspicion is left with readers that Juan Pedro will sooner or later come after his wife and small son: like Pedro, he is not going to allow his woman to escape his abuse and live to get away with it.

Cisneros suggests that the presence of Cleófilas's father and six brothers will be sufficient protection for her after she flees Juan Pedro's violence and infidelities. Still, as many well-publicized news events reveal, neither police nor relatives have been able to stop a determined husband who, like Flora's husband Pedro, promises to shoot her and himself in the head if she ever tried to leave him and take their baby with her (136). As law enforcement authorities have finally realized, as the public is now fully aware, Flora was right to believe her husband's threats because he was indeed "capable of doing anything" (136). The culture can no longer place the blame on individual men crazed with jealousy. Their training has inculcated into these men the conviction that they can deny free choice to their women. Forcing women to remain with them is linked with their right, their duty as real men to batter and murder their women if they "dishonor their manhood," their machismo.

Flora has ample reasons to fear her husband, because he gives them to her. Again, as with Cleófilas, she is constrained even from shopping, from any independent movement, without her husband present. However, unlike Cleófilas, Flora has a car. One day, no longer wishing to put up with her marital nightmare, she began to drive away in her car. Pedro immediately "shot out all four tires." He then took over the car and drove it around the farm until it was impossible for Flora to ever use it again–until "there were no tires, no inner tubes, no rims, just those sharpened axles that make the car look like a metallic pig turning on a spit" (136).

Unlike Cleófilas's Juan Pedro who has no redeeming qualities, the narrator's feelings are not all negative toward her Pedro. Sometimes she felt love for him, sometimes hate. For a long time her feelings were mixed, but finally she did stop loving him. There are many reasons for her having loved him as long as she did. He is a more interesting, more complex character than Juan Pedro and does display some qualities that are endearing. For example, Pedro would sometimes "unexpectedly bring home lobster for lunch and cook it up for us in a vinaigrette" (135). He would "do favors" for people out of generosity and never want them to repay him. He was also very generous to Flora on occasion, even "extravagant." On their anniversary he would go with her "to a jewelry store in San Juan" (136) and buy her whatever she wished, regardless of the expense. And he was handsome, even as he aged. Clearly, unlike Cleófilas, the narrator remains with her husband for many years after their son, Augusto, is already grown. She remains, in fact, until Pedro's death.

Now middle-aged, a widow, she justifies not having left Pedro on grounds common to all women of all presumed classes, globally. She was no longer young and attractive. She had no skills, although she had trained to become a pharmacist before marrying Pedro, but he had prevented her from doing so (136–137). In addition, Flora claims that the friends they had were all his and that she was not permitted to have any friends of her own to offer her support and solace. She reasons now that if she had left years before, she could never have paid for her son's tuition. How else could she have paid for "the house, the club dues, and the maid?" Only forty, she is convinced that no other man would look at her any more and that only her grandchildren offer her relief from her "boredom" (136).

Flora imagines what the people who know them are saying to one another now that she is free of Pedro at last: "Now Flora can finally rest, poor thing. You know how he would treat her" (137). Such imagined sympathy from the external community provides a marked contrast to Cleófilas's neighbors who never question her, or seem to be concerned about her, or think anything is unusual about her battered appearance. Flora's neighbors, like a Greek chorus, like Cleófilas's neighbors, are at least sympathetic to her in a passive way, although Flora contradicts herself, first claiming that Pedro's friends were not hers, then showing them as nevertheless aware of his violence. Readers can visualize them shrugging and throwing up their hands, ascribing all Flora's suffering to the ways of men. Their discourse assumes that her tortures are something women have endured endlessly throughout time when certain men have indulged themselves in all the brutality their culture permits their gender.

Cleófilas, more fortunate, is rescued young by allegorical figures embodying both the feminist movement and the sisterhood it ideally provides. In contrast, Flora is starting off the first day of her new life writing her first diary entry alone, isolated, permanently damaged for the rest of her life, and still at the mercy of the patriarchy. She briefly fantasies about making some changes according to her personal liking, for the first time since she was married: "I'll start off with the patio. First I'll get rid of those fighting-cock cages [which represent her husband and his masculinist rule] and replant the hydrangeas [which represent her values] he made me pull out so he could keep an eye on the roosters from the house. I'll get someone to take them away tomorrow morning. I'll even give them away if I have to."

But then she waffles, and the flow of her revisionary tide recedes forever. "Now I'm free and things are going to be different around here. Tomorrow morning I'll start on the garden just as I planned. But maybe I should wait and talk to Augusto first, he might not want to get rid of the fighting cocks right away" (135, 137). Pedro ends up only to be replaced by his son Augusto, just as it is hinted by Cisneros in "Woman Hollering Creek" that Juan Pedro might in time be replaced by his son little Juan Pedro.

Unlike Cleófilas, it is too late for Flora, an ending much more realistic and true to the historical out-placement of women by their culture than that of "Woman Hollering Creek." Still, as is common with other Chicana feminist writers, the home is not described by Valle as men have defined it, as a nest, as a safe space for women, but as a prison, not only metaphorically, as Herrera-Sobek claims, but also literally. It is described as a constraining enclosed cage, "a claustrophobic space" (1995, 165) in which women are oppressed, enslaved, and imprisoned. The father's house is everywhere, and more often than not endlessly perpetuates itself through female enculturation into the same masculine dynasties as have always persisted, down from Pedro to his son Augusto and from Juan Pedro to little Juan Pedro, and so on.

Alas, Flora's mind has been too thoroughly and too long inscribed in her culture's prescriptions for a good woman. She does not have a mind of her own any longer. As she puts it, "I despised him, but I envied him too, because I didn't have half the guts he did" (136). So Valle's is not a revenge tale so much as a feminist cautionary tale, a dystopia, which unfortunately is not imaginary. If the woman puts up with the constraints and goes along with them, she will end up constrained. If the woman does not put up with the constraints and does not go along with them, she might very well end up dead, the way inequitable gendered power relations have traditionally worked and are now currently constructed. There is no constraining factor in the world of inequitable gendered power relations to prevent silencing from occurring if a woman's husband threatens violence, unless she voluntarily imprisons herself in the interior space in which he, his successors, and the past and ongoing culture consign her.

Another story, perhaps the most powerful written on the subject of domestic violence thus far by a Chicana writer is Mary Helen Ponce's "The Jewelry Collection of Marta la Güera." An abusive husband, aptly named Rocky, gives his saintly wife jewelry every time he brutalizes her, just as Pedro does in "Diary Entry #1." Both women, in fact, most women who are also wives in the texts analyzed in this work are trained according to the Catholic cult of Marianismo. Women attempt "to emulate" the qualities that the Catholic Church indoctrinates into Catholic women as like Mary's: "faith, self-abnegation, motherhood, and purity" (Rebolledo and Rivero 1993, 189).

Interestingly, Tey Diane Rebolledo and Eliana S. Rivero add that the Virgin of Guadalupe is also considered a negative role model by many Chicana writers because she is passive–accepting and enduring whatever befalls her (1993, 191). Once socialized into those Catholic values for women that the Virgin represents, women tend to view power as a masculine characteristic, neither natural nor appropriate for women, Bonilla-Santiago argues. For these reasons Hispanic women avoid conflictual situations and abdicate control to their husbands, even unto violence, as in Marta's case.

Bonilla-Santiago came to her conclusions as a result of studying women's conduct in the workplace. She claims that she found that Hispanic women do not like risky situations, want to be secure, in stable situations, do not like change. They valorize "loyalty" to superiors in the workplace. To bargain, to negotiate with employers makes them uncomfortable, and they retreat from such situations. They are not self-confident, do not assert and promote themselves and experience "internal stresses" as a result. When faced with a new task or one without a "structure," they "freeze-up" (1995, 223–224).

This finding perfectly describes many of the female characters found in Chicana texts, not least that of Ponce's Marta La Güera. One of Marta's daughters, the narrator's friend, has internalized her father's attitude toward her mother. She takes the narrator into her mother's bedroom, displays Marta's jewelry collection to her, and tells her the provenance of each gift made "in exchange for the forgiveness she always gave." There are "ruby earrings" for when Rocky punched his wife "in the ribs, cracking two at a time." There is "a silver bracelet" for when he "twisted Marta's wrist until it cracked." There are "diamond earrings" after Rocky "pushed her against the kitchen counter and fractured her collarbone." And in return for the VD she contracted from her husband, she received an "opal ring" from Mexico. Rocky's initial response to her disease was to call his wife "a whore," claiming that she had caught it "from screwing around while he was away," threatening to divorce her until their priest had a talk with him.

Then there is "a string of matching pearls" from Japan that Marta received from Rocky after he broke her nose. Afraid that the doctor would report him, he paid the doctor off in cash. He gave his wife a private room in the hospital and brought her and their daughters flowers. Unfortunately, Ponce adds, with understated irony, Marta's condition at first prevented her from appreciating the beauty and perfect matching of each pearl because gauze covered her purple circled eyes and "swollen nose." But after a while, she did wear them. Not long after that, Rocky gave her a "new" and larger jewelry box with "velvet-lined drawers, one large enough to hold the growing collection of Marta la güera" (150). Much like a be-medalled war veteran, Marta displays these jewels as signs of valor in battle.

Ponce makes another understated ironic insinuation in this story, similar to that of Cisneros's about Cleófilas's son: that the sins of the father may very well be continued into the next generation. In fact, irony deployed to sabotage the violence inherent in the patriarchy is characteristic of most feminist writing. Ponce does this in this instance through critiquing the common masculine custom of bestowing jewelry upon women as signifiers of their love and devotion. By this means Ponce transforms Marta's exquisite jewelry collection into a powerful feminist critique of the sinister source of their existence.

Ponce also uses irony as a further strategy: through increasing and heightening the reader's sense of outrage by describing each more terrifying, supposedly beautiful gift of jewelry as another piece of damning evidence of abuse to the reader. She does this through a translucent sieve: an innocent narrator whose friend is an unsympathetic observer of her mother's oppression. By this means, hitherto fixed signifiers of the patriarchy are effectively transformed into feminist signifiers, proving that masculinist discourse can be destabilized and even transformed. (Bonilla-Santiago 1995, 229). What Ponce here succeeds in doing symbolically is like Dante's technique in *The Inferno* where he depicts thieves shape-shifting continually, changing into serpents, as they are devoured by them, and back again into human form.

Rocky and Marta have two daughters, the narrator's friend, Lina, and her sister, Asunción, who hates her father. Lina, however, has internalized his ways, bullies her mother, and has no sympathy for her. When the narrator asks Lina whether she also hates her father, like her sister, she responds that she does not and justifies his behavior toward her mother, as if in his voice, on the grounds that Marta had "asked for it (150)" by talking back to him.

As was evident from Flora's description of her home and life style in "Diary Entry #1," Marta also lives comfortably in terms of material surroundings. Here is another irony, because from the descriptions of the interior of the couple's home it is evident that Rocky is prosperous. But Marta's fine clothes, elegant lifestyle, gentle, sensitive upper-class manners, the family doctor, and even the priest, all mean nothing when we realize how she lives, the place to which her husband consigns her–a living hell as his slave. Tellingly, their community remains silent, colludes with the husband, attends the couple's frequent parties, and enjoys them. Both these powerful cuentos about domestic violence–Valle's, about a Latina, and Ponce's, about a Chicana, prove my contention that women are totally outside the class system and utterly dependent on their men who control that system of inequitable gendered power relations.

NOTES

1. The latter clause is Herrera-Sobek's paraphrase of the young girl's description in the play of what it felt like to be raped, to be deprived of her intact individual material essence by an elderly school janitor who uses a screwdriver to literally bore a hole into her.

2. This paradigm shift emulates that of Malcolm X when, before his death, he made a crucial, late shift in discourse from civil rights for African Americans in the United States to the violation of their basic human rights by the United States. See *The Autobiography of Malcolm X.*

Part II

Chicana Solutions to Outclassing Women

Chapter 5

Educational, Economic, Individual Solutions

In Cisneros's "My Tocaya," a nameless narrator writes about an adolescent girl who works in her father's small and drab Taco store every day as soon as school is over and on weekends (36). In an effort to bring glamor into her drab and squalid existence, to deny her own skin color, her own identity, Patricia has internalized the master's colonial exploitative racist-ethnic script toward Mexicans and Chicanas by calling herself Trish and attempting to use an English accent. She also adorns herself when she goes to school with imitation "rhinestone earrings and glitter high heels" (36–37). Like Champ, Patricia has a negative attitude toward education because she is treated negatively by Anglo teachers who do not expect much of her and show insensitivity to her as an individual (Segura 1993, 210, 211). Patricia suffers from so low a self-image that it leads her to masquerade as a white girl and ultimately to run away from home in a bid for attention. For she is aware that the odds are that her after-school job will remain her lot all her working life. In this story, as in "One Holy Night," another cuento in *Woman Hollering Creek and Other Stories*, Cisneros captures the young girl's experience of life. She perceives it as an ongoing series of stultifying constraints wherever she turns, while she responds with pathetic attempts to provide exciting alternative possibilities in life choices for herself. Patricia's return to her family represents her depressed and depressing acceptance of the narrow round prescribed for her, into which she is apparently locked forever. This is the same situation as that of the young narrator in "One Holy Night," and of both Arlene and her daughter in Viramontes's "Miss Clairol" and "Tears on Her Pillow."

Alba Rivera-Ramos's analysis of Chicanas has led her to identify economic transformation for Chicanas as one of their major solutions to inequitable gendered power relations:

Chicanas believe that one of the key solutions for transforming gendered power relations, as currently structured, is economic. That is, it is necessary to bring forth a deep change in attitudes in both the male and female populations. It is also necessary to develop new attitudes among employers and employees regarding women's nature, capabilities, roles, and physical, as well as psychological needs in order to optimize women's participation. The optimization of Chicanas' participation not only at the lower level of the labor force but also as leaders, decision makers, and entrepreneurs will contribute significantly to the general well-being of the population. (1995, 195)

Maxine Baca Zinn cites a thirty-year-old study revealing that Chicano families still identified with Mexican family values that taught generations to conform, to be obedient and submissive to authority, and to believe in strictness when raising children. Even at that time, however, Chicano families were Americanizing in that they identified less with Mexican customs where males were the authorities and where the sexes were separated in the home and elsewhere (1995, 238). Nevertheless Zinn feels that Chicano families continue to some large extent their Mexican traditions of familism, their organization of the family around binary gender role distinctions. She justifies such lingering continuity on the grounds that it does not indicate that Chicano families are simply accepting and perpetuating their heritage passively. Unfortunately, because of Anglo oppression Chicano families still need to cling to these Mexican values in order to keep their cultural identity intact, to protect themselves from the destruction of their cultural values by a culture that would destroy both. On this basis she calls this pattern "political familism" (1995, 242) rather than familism, the commonly used term.[1] Beyond that, Zinn makes the ·claim that this new kind of familism not only is due to Chicano families evolving through acculturating or modernizing. Chicanas' "political activity" is challenging traditional inequitable gendered power relations between men and women, women's role in the family, and influencing other Chicanas to be more feminist in their perspective (1995, 243).

Blea offers yet another solution that according to her would be transformative, even revolutionary, if followed. It is based on the contrast between Chicana priorities for success–being respected, having good health, and family values–and Anglo definitions for success–becoming wealthy. She wonders what happened to the idea that merely by being alive human beings were considered worthwhile. Does the question of whether people are "productive" have anything to do with their value? Anglos are responsible for connecting "production, especially production for profit, to human beings as having "value." Increasingly "success is measured by accumulated resources, the result of production" (1991, 94).

Normal, natural, common sense models are designed for the purpose of control and constraint. Like myself, Pérez does not see class as an intersecting issue with gender and race. Instead, she sees the struggle for equality as beginning with an analysis of race and gender issues. In her ranking of priorities, she believes that the granting of sexual freedom to women must be the first element for a successful transformation of inequitable class relations which will

inexorably be followed by the second element necessary for such a change–
"class struggle" (1993, 57). Somehow the struggle for racial equality drops out
of her prioritizing of gender over class struggles. Perhaps Pérez sees race as a
class issue.

Chicana feminists also resist both their original and second cultural
training. Such resistance is linked with their feminist perspective, but it also
includes alert, fully conscious choices to reject as well as to accept certain
ideologies from their country of origin and the United States. They refuse to
either acculturate or assimilate to either or both cultures, doing both, at will.
They all pick and choose very carefully what they wish to expose as detrimental
for women, as well as for men, in either or both cultures. Accordingly, their texts
are organized and structured for the most part in relation to what they are
attempting to expose in terms of inequitable power relations in both cultures, in
terms primarily of inequitable gendered power relations.

Anglo culture reinforces in these women their original culture's
construction of power relations through class rankings by gender and race.
Anzaldúa sees this duality of influence as creating a potentially liberating "split"
in Chicanas. As Chicanas forge a new way of perceiving themelves, it will be
necessary to change their psychic perspective in regard to the "split" between the
two cultures, Mexican and Anglo, in which they are acculturated. She sees the
two cultures as locked in mortal combat. Chicanas could somehow heal the
"split" thus created within themselves by these two cultures so that they might
live simultaneously on both sides, Mexican (the serpent) and American (the
eagle). Or if, having lost all hope, Chicanas decide to separate entirely from
Anglo culture, they could cross over into a wholly new "territory," or even try
another road altogether (1987, 79). As is obvious, Anzaldúa envisions numerous
possibilities of better lives for Chicanas, providing they are self-activating, not
reactive.

With the help of Graciela and Felice, Cleófilas of "Woman Hollering
Creek" crosses back into Mexico, leaving her husband's tyrannical space for safe
haven with her loving father and brothers. By making the safe haven a male one,
however, Cisneros is succumbing to simplistic solutions. True, Cleófilas will be
better treated by her many brothers and her father than by her husband. But hers
is a private, individual solution–to find safe haven within limited cultural
constructs with some decent men who happen to act decently of their own
accord. Nevertheless even if they conducted themselves otherwise, they would
succeed very well in their Mexican culture. They still would never be called to
account.

Here Cisneros again leaves herself open to questions. What if her father
had not offered Cleófilas asylum? What if her father had not been a decent
human being in contrast to his son-in-law, Juan Pedro? What if Cleófilas had had
no father, no relative in Mexico to give her safe haven? She apparently has no
mother. McCracken, in analyzing Cisneros's *The House on Mango Street*, might
provide a clue as to the possible meaning of Cleófilas's flight across the border
from Texas to Mexico. She interprets this move back to her father's home as a

return to her own "ethnic community" which represents Cisneros's rebellion against patriarchy so characteristic of all her work (1989, 70).

However, flight where and when possible does not necessarily render Cleófilas's private, individual solution invalid. There may be another solution embedded within the theme of this story: that of the hollering going on at Woman Hollering Creek. At first, Cisneros links women in their marital suffering and oppression, their rage and pain, to the mythical archetype, La Llorona, the weeping woman. Because her husband betrayed her, she chose to kill her children in revenge. Katherine Rios notes that Cisneros's motive for using La Llorona as referent to Cleófilas is to vent her suppressed outrage at, to rebel against the misogynist discourse involved in the creation and perpetuation of this frightening myth. For this reason she feels that Cisneros is so satisfying to read.

Further, Rios admires the author because she recognizes that her violence is futile and misdirected, but still she admits to it and expresses it in her writing (1995, 207). She does not explain why in her opinion Cisneros's violent feelings would not result in destabilization of any aspects of the patriarchy that the author addresses, such as its mythology about La Llorona. Nor does she explain why Cisneros's violent feelings, which I would define, rather, as powerful feelings, are misdirected. Since Cisneros directs them at oppressive inequitable gendered power relations, in what way is this the case?

With the assistance and support of other women, the contemporary Chicana "hollering" woman is depicted by Cisneros as proud, bold, in command of her actions and her own world, as Tarzan is in command of his world. The problem here is the same as that of Michele's in "'Mericans." The shift Cisneros envisions as a solution is a complete reverse. It therefore replicates masculinist discourse and values for males in the very process of opposing them. As La Llorona forever weeps, replicating the stereotypes for tragic women, "hollering like Tarzan" emulates what a man does, rather than creating a way that is woman's own. Felice, Cleófilas's rescuer, who "hollers," is a courageous, independent individual, a swaggering, loud, crude female version of a Chicano.

By this means, Cisneros is engaging here as elsewhere throughout the text in reverse role modeling as her technique for destabilizing inequitable gendered power relations. Still, by the end of the story, Cleófilas is noticeably not yet fully self-empowered. She is protected by and resituated within a nurturing male circle of power, considered a *consentida* [indulged] by her men, and placed on a pedestal by them. However, through the assistance of a small community of other women whose core members are Felice and Graciela, she has been empowered to leave the dark tower of patriarchal marriage. She has taken the first steps—of transforming what were designed and decreed by the culture to be the hollering of rage and pain into the hollering of laughter, to a whoop of pleasure rather than a cry of pain. [2]

Even so, Anzaldúa's critique of Chicanas here rings true in terms of my critique of Cisneros's solution for Cleófilas. Chicanas are not sufficiently active, she complains. They do not do all they can. They "abnegate." She points to a "crossroads" in front of Chicanas. They can continue to perceive themselves as victims and give over control of their lives to some individual or other authoritative entity to blame for their victimization. They can continue to transfer the blame on their culture, their parents, their lovers, or friends as a way of absolving themselves. Or else Chicanas can become strong women who take "control" (1987, 21) of their lives.

Indeed, Cleófilas in her retreat to her Mexican home is no longer self-destructive, as she would have been had she remained with her husband, stifling her rage and violent feelings of hate and resentment against him, as well as against men in general for the rest of her life. But even during and after Cleófilas's flight to safety, her anger is suppressed. She does not speak it or write it, so that it is not heard, because Cleófilas eschews the venting of anger and outrage, as do most women globally. They are trained that above all else the expression of anger is proscribed, is literally taboo, forbidden to decent, good women. Thus Cleófilas's return home is not a path to self-fulfillment, a rejection of inequitable gendered power relations in patriarchy that feminists would "render impotent" (Rios 1995, 209). It is the best of limited choices available to her: a retreat from patriarchy's worst manifestations to its more benign ones.

As a victim of domestic violence, of wife battering, what are Cleófilas's solutions to her illumination about gender inequality? Cisneros depicts her heroine as beginning that process with herself, with her first small step. She fantasizes a name change because she believes that only women who had jewels for names had exciting and successful lives, whereas the only thing that happened to a woman with a name like hers was that her man would beat her. Her second response is far more nurturing for her own best interests. It is the first realistic step she takes in that direction. When she becomes pregnant for the second time, she begs and pleads with her husband to take her to the doctor for the sake of the new baby, but it is in order to obtain an abortion without Juan Pedro's knowledge. As a further incentive, she swears that she will not mention her battered appearance. Should the doctor wonder about her bruises, she will tell him that she fell or slipped somewhere on their property.

However, a fairy godmother intervenes on her behalf at the doctor's office in the guise of a caring nurse. It is she who observes that Cleófilas is yet one more bride from Mexico who can't speak English and has bruises all over her body. She also observes that Cleófilas has been prevented from calling or writing home to her father and brothers. This nursing woman in the truest sense of the word, kindly calls a friend to help Cleófilas run away. The aptly named Graciela [the spirit of grace or graciousness] makes a different request. She asks her friend Felice [happy one], also aptly named, to take Cleófilas to the bus station. She stresses the vital importance for Felice of getting Cleófilas safely aboard the bus going back to Mexico before her husband finds out when he comes home from work that she has left him.

When Felice asks Graciela what the name Cleófilas means, she responds that she doesn't know, but that she guesses that it is the name of a martyred Mexican saint. If Cleófilas, or, indeed, if women have been anything at all, they have been saints and martyrs. So it is that Cleófilas, through this small network of feminists, finds another, better solution to her plight than changing her name to make it more poetic. It is notable that she does so only after she has taken the first step to self-preservation: getting out of her house and to the doctor's. This, in turn, connects her to the feminist underground network, which, in turn, enables her to flee to shelter in her original birth home with her father and brothers. Minrose Gwin interprets this move back to her Mexican home not as a retreat, but as a "back-and-forthness" because feminist Chicanas, as well as other feminists "keep traveling, negotiating, moving the borders back and forth . . . share, for one reason or another, this negotiation between leaving and coming home. In a sense we are always doing both" (1996, 889).

Yarbro-Bejarano recommends that Chicana critics focus on Chicana writing as emanating at its source from two "crucial axes" (1988, 141) simultaneously: the struggle to define themselves and the need for a sisterhood of mutually shared loving community with other women. Chicana writers, through their characters, courageously privilege and foreground Chicanas' "pivotal relationships" (1988, 144) with other Chicanas historically and in the present. These two drives empower Chicana writers with the courage to continually attempt to intrude themselves into the already existing masculinist scripts. Through revisioning historical and contemporary Chicanas from their own perspective, they seek to disrupt and transform the limited and negative images of Chicanas that pervade Chicano and Anglo literature.

Paradoxically, writing situates Chicanas outside their own community, because in doing so they distance themselves from their culture's time-honored "oral traditions" and from other Chicanas who are not capable of writing and do not wish to write for a variety of reasons. Further, Chicana writers often do not write any longer from within their birth communities. At the same time, Chicana writers also speak for other Chicanas because they are thereby publicly proclaiming their ongoing loyalty in continuing the struggle for equality for their sister Chicanas, even though they are physically no longer participating in their daily struggles. Instead the community Chicana writers thereby create through their written work is one in which they invite participation from their readers who comprise other writers and Chicana critics, as well as the public (1988, 144). She does not tell us how this can be done, however.

Also, to assume that an educated writer or artist is expressing all of Chicana experience may appear essentialist. However, who speaks for whom? Can a Chicana artist speak for her community any more than any other individual artist has ever spoken for hers? As Foucault has maintained, at any given time there is no monolithic regime of domination, but always a complex of countervailing responses and positions. Within any community, there is a dominant external regime. The same goes for the oppressed, in terms of the diversity of responses. Thus variety exists, both on the part of those within the dominant external regime, as well as those groups labelled Other. Given the abstract truth of this conclusion, although contemporary Chicana writers may have diverse styles and approaches, for the most part they do see things alike, for good reason, because they all experience the same oppressions from the same hierarchical patriarchal environment.

Cleófilas is taken away to the bus station in Felice's pickup.[3] After they have crossed the arroyo, safely past Juan Pedro's turf boundary, Felice suddenly emits a loud whoop. This unheard of sound from a woman startles and shocks Cleófilas and her little boy, ominously named Juan Pedrito after his father, doubtless to signify that the oppression of women will go on in perpetuity, because "Little Juan Pedros" grow up to become big ones. Felice informs Cleófilas that she was "hollering" (55) in honor of the creek's name and points out to her that nothing in those parts is named after a woman except for the Virgin, and a woman only achieves fame if she is a virgin.

Felice amazes Cleófilas even further. She drives a pickup truck. When Cleófilas assumes that it therefore belongs to Felice's husband, she replies that she is not married, that the truck belongs to her, that she herself had picked it out, and pays for it. She used to own "a Pontiac Sunbird." But she prefers a pickup now because Pontiac cars are too tame for her. She considers them "Pussy cars" for "viejas" [old ladies] (55), a gratuitous example of unconsciously internalized sexism and ageism on Felice's part, and perhaps the author's, as well. Cleófilas is stunned, but not because of Felice's discriminatory attitude toward her own sex, but with admiration. She loves such talk, such an attitude. She has never heard a woman talk in such a bold, crude manner or make such loud sounds. Felice begins to laugh again, but then Cleófilas becomes aware that it is not the other woman who is doing the laughing. It is herself! Thus Cisneros revises through subversive feminist revision the popular and traditional Mexican myth of the victimized, bereft, lovelorn, desperate La Llorona who is always crying. Similar in crucial ways to the Greek myth about Medea, La Llorona is an abandoned woman who slays her children in revenge and goes howling after them down the centuries.[4]

The message of "Andrea" also finally emerges in the nameless narrator's ultimate resolution of the various perspectives aimed at her by various voices. These voices are personified for the most part as two sisters—Andrea and Consuelo—who have conflicting resolutions for living female lives as they are constructed within the parameters of their culture. In "Andrea," the young narrator's cousin Consuelo and mother, together with other authority figures, advise the narrator to do something practical with her life and not to go in for dancing as her life's vocation. It is hard to believe, though, that the same woman who was Andrea's aunt, who was her most outspoken admirer and supporter, the woman who compiled her historically precious album, could be so inconsistent as to then discourage her own daughter, the young narrator, from following in her cousin's footsteps.

In "Andrea" what all the voices add up to is not just simply where the story ends. Each of the voices is partial or ambivalent in one way or another, compared ultimately with the young narrator's voice. She disagrees with some characters, complies with and takes off from others' moves, corrects others. It is she who represents the sum total, and more, of them all. By the end of the story, the narrator's (re)solution is privileged over all of the other characters. After she realizes that she is an individual within a group, the nameless young narrator encompasses their individual subjectivity and goes on to bond with other women in a feminist project.

What Herrera-Sobek calls "gender over-determination" (1988a, 35) in citing responsibility for women's oppression creates a crisis in self-reflexive Chicanas who chafe against their restricted position in the culture. This crisis serves as the Chicanas' catalyst for self-expression through creative means. The first step that Chicana authors take in their efforts to effect change in terms of how the culture situates women is to become educated and to write, to explore their identities as subjects, especially their sexuality (Yarbo-Bejarano 1988, 142–143). After educating themselves, they begin to write, consciously revisioning Chicana characters in mythology and history as models for future generations of Chicanas, rather than as objects of cautionary tales as has traditionally been the case. They also create fresh and new contemporary Chicana models for their readers, and not only through the valorization of literature. Chicanas depict Chicana creativity, not only in mythmaking and story telling, but in art (Cisneros), dance (Fernández), in home decorating and creative cookery (García, Viramontes), and in the healing arts (Gámez).

Yarbro-Bejarano subtly distinguishes between Chicana writers' source(s) of creativity and those of mainstream feminist writers. At the very least she valorizes Chicana writers for altruism when she observes as a characteristic common to them all that they always intend to return ideologically through their chosen art form to "a community of Chicanas" to whom they are strongly committed. Some escapes are geographic, as well as psychic, as in seeking an education, and some of these Chicana writers are no longer physically part of their birth community. Still they pursue their rocky and torturous path to self-fulfillment and "empowerment," primarily to pay tribute back to their community through the creative discourse they have mastered. In essence, Chicana writers are educating themselves out of their community to ensure that their strength and courage provide a model for other women through publishing their creative work (1988, 143). By and large, for anyone who has read Chicana writers, her tribute to Chicana writers proves as true as it is moving.

In "Andrea," the erasure of the album by Consuelo and its contents allegorizes the historical erasure of in the written and pictorial records of the culture. It stresses, instead, the imposition of cultural training, the lengthy process over many years from infancy, to childhood, to girlhood and young womanhood, into an indoctrination that assures and reinforces the erasure of female existence, their continued invisibility generation after generation. What is invisible in the cultural constructions of power and where power resides can never be present. What is not present does not exist, either in the discourse or the consciousness of the citizenry, because how language is used, a culture's discourse, does not so much reflect the thoughts and actions of its citizenry as Blea claims (1991, 146). Instead the culture we find at birth, into which we are born, shapes us and imposes on our thoughts and actions through its discourse.

Most of us become the unself-reflexive products of our cultures, not the other way around.

At this point in time, Chicana writers generally focus on their own cultures in an attempt to preserve their culture's history, to document their own lives, as well as those of their community. In this context, Roberta Fernández's work can be perceived as her effort to preserve Mexican and Chicana history and to document women's lives from that perspective, which includes a feminist perspective, as well. Sandra Cisneros's *Woman Hollering Creek and Other Stories*, as well as the work of other feminist Chicana writers, is influenced strongly by traditional legends and myths that they use in order to subvert, transform, and even parody them. Often these writers create new genres while engaged in this process. Cherríe Moraga's *Loving in the War Years* could well serve as the model for this new genre in which the lines between poetry and fiction are blurred.

NOTES

1. Her argument here is much like that of Arlene Elowe Macleod's about veiling in Cairo: far from being motivated by regressive or conservative intentions, the young Egyptian women who are insisting upon veiling are doing so as a form of cultural expression of endangered cultural distinctions.

2. As we can see, Cisneros and have much in common in their suggested solutions to gender issues. In both Cisneros and Tan, evil, mean oppressor men play similar and large roles. Good men nurture, cherish, protect and support the heroines. They play very small roles, however. Cisneros creates a gallery of women, different ones in various stories. Tan does this in *The Joy Luck Club*, but in *The Kitchen God's Wife* focuses on Winnie, Hulan, and to a lesser extent, on Pearl. Cisneros works deeper into one major protagonist, working from within her psyche through her personal narration to a listener, but sketches other characters one-dimensionally. With Cisneros, the characters also are oral. Their messages are similar, as are their solutions. It is as if they were fleshed-out characters from newspaper headlines and news clippings on domestic violence, abuse, and murder, as if we were looking at these characters from within and at the sea level of headlines in the news announcements. In addition, the characters also represent their own perspective.

3. Note the symbolism of the term "pickup."

4. Chapter 2 of *Chicana Voices: Intersections of Class, Race, and Gender* (Austin, TX: CMAS Publications, University of Texas Press, 1986), is devoted to a discussion of La Llorona.

Chapter 6

Re-Shaping Religious and Cultural Mythologies

One of the earliest responses to "the monolithic androcentrism" (Pratt 1993, 863) of the La Raza movement was the manifesto *Chicanas Speak Out*. Chicanas called for the destruction of religious and cultural myths that constrain female sexuality. They also maintained that marriage has to be transformed, as well as the Catholic Church, or it should stand aside. Even so, La Raza paid no attention, never including this Chicana manifesto into the archives of the Chicano history of the La Raza movement (Pratt 1993, 861). Nevertheless, in Chicana feminist annals this historic manifesto is memorialized as an extremely significant attempt at "elaborate code-switching," such as Ponce did so successfully in "The Jewelry Collection of Marta La Güera." The Chicana manifesto is significant because it was the first discursive shift of Malinche's image away from that of a traitor to a more accurate historical appraisal of this Chicano cultural icon. It attempted for the first time to revision the normalized patriarchal perspectives, the masculinist discursive codes that outclass women, historically silencing them and excluding them from such discourse. The Chicanas' motive in issuing this manifesto was to make a "testimonio," to finally speak out publicly and claim autonomy as subjects instead of "a dependent space ascribed from the outside by others" (1993, 863). In revising Malinche into "a paradigmatic figure" Chicana feminists, just by "the social act" of insisting upon their own perspective in writing, gave themselves for the first time historically the powers of "speaking subjects" (Torres 1995, 128).

Mary Louise Pratt further identifies a second strategy in this initiative of Chicana writers to question male mythology such as the myth of Malinche. This was to reverse or double "back" on the patriarchy's "politics of blame" (1993, 865) when men depict their female characters such as Malinche as subjects whose characteristics are created and then perpetuated by the culture's male rulers and women who accept their constructions as objective. Male creators of such characters, as well as Chicano culture, assume that what they write is carved in stone by the divinity of masculine opinion presented as objective reality (1993, 866).

Pratt credits the efforts by writers such as Ana Castillo, Cherríe Moraga, Lucha Corpi, Gloria Anzaldúa, and Helena María Viramontes to repudiate masculinist "canonical interpretations" of Malinche. By doing so, these authors work with their own agenda, not anyone else's, to create a specifically female subject in which Malinche's role as mother is made only a small part of her "political and strategical" use by the Spanish. Pratt sees the feminist Chicana writers and critics as attempting through the revision of the Malinche myth to reject patriarchal mythmaking in which women are depicted as "mothers and servants to men" (1993, 869).

Interestingly, Pratt frowns on any authors who would attribute Malinche's "political betrayal" of her people to "religious motivations." She does welcome the possibility that Malinche's conversion to Catholicism was genuine, or that she believed, as did many of her people, that Cortés was the god who had promised to return to them. Pratt also rejects interpretations of Malinche's conduct as stemming from passion or love for Cortés. Instead she lauds those Chicana writers who have not seen Malinche in any of these ways. They have courageously chosen to provide complex and diverse descriptions of the experience of women that serve as alternative conceptualizations of Chicano culture. They do this by avoiding the polarizing nationalism of the Chicano leaders and members of the La Raza movement, as well as assenting to the damaging depictions of Malinche (1993, 871).

I submit that as wholeheartedly as I agree with Pratt, we have no absolute knowledge of Malinche's motives for her conduct. It is only interpretation. Adding positive interpretations of this historic character is a worthwhile project because it opens up the possibility that she was not a supine dupe or traitor or a willing convert to Catholicism, turning her back against her own religion and culture. Still, we can leave room for negative interpretations, or mixed ones, of her conduct. Why should we replicate the methods and strategies of intransigently negative masculinist interpretations? They leave no room for her motives and conduct to be interpreted other than negatively, so that they can fit into their misogynistic iconography and mythology. Why should we fall prey to their simplistic binary thinking and replicate it?

In masculinist discourse, the Mayan princess Malinche serves a dual purpose. Already enslaved by Montezuma, she served as the interpreter for and mistress of Cortés and thus is traditionally conceived of as an arch-traitor. On the other hand, in becoming mother to his (mestiza) children, she thus functions as the originating source for La Raza, a symbol of that which comprises Mexico and Mexicanness. Traditionally, also, Malinche is seen as somehow both a passive victim as well as a collaborator. This perspective is illustrated in Elizabeth Ordoñez's insight that the rape motif in Chicana poetry is connnected with Malinche. Chicanas' consciousness is influenced more by rape trauma than other women because of the first rape, that of Malinche, by the Europeans. Further it impacts on their view of themselves as sexual beings and by all the "sexual violence" surrounding them today in their "immediate environment" (Herrera-Sobek citing Ordoñez 1988b, 180). Notice that the term "Europeans" is used by both critics, instead of the term "Spanish Europeans," probably because of their acute discomfort involved in calling their own Spanish ancestors into account.

Nevertheless, Herrera-Sobek takes issue with Ordoñez, not so much because the use of rapes in Chicana literature resonates metaphorically from the Malinche-Cortés relationship. She also observes Chicana writers, unlike other women writers, using their experiences of being raped economically, socially, and politically as metaphors. She admires Chicana writers for their courage in adding rape as "an important literary motif in American literature" (1988b, 181). To buttress this insight, she uses the example of other women of color writers who incorporate rape in the same way into their work: African American women writers such as Alice Walker, Maya Angelou, and Toni Morrison. Perhaps she is only familiar with this "minority" group. The fact is that as a major theme rape is common to most ethnic and women of color writers, as well as to women writers in every "economic and socio-political" category. It is a major problem for all women globally, whatever their race and class. In addition, Herrera-Sobek adds a mystifying disparity with my analysis here when she concludes that Chicana writers, unlike their Mexican sisters, do not as a rule write about rape or use it as a major "motif" (1988b, 180). However, she does not offer any explanations for this surprising anomaly.

In her role as translator, as mediator between two cultures, Malinche attempted to do the best she could in an almost impossibly oppressive situation.[1] Hernán Cortés, a Spaniard, led the conquest of the Aztec civilization. Malintzin, gave birth to his son and therefore of Mexicans, also converted to Catholicism, and therefore has always been defined as a traitor.

Alarcón sees Chicana writers' attempts at mythological and stereotypical recuperation of Malinche as resulting in no less than five "sexual political themes" in their works. First, they show that for women to choose among patriarchal systems (Indian, Chicano, Anglo) is no choice, as Anzaldúa argues. Second, Chicana writers describe their characters as being lost, abandoned, orphaned, and psychically and emotionally starved even when they have families. Fernández's Consuelo and Cisneros's Chayo and Patricia provide sad examples of this theme. Third, Chicanas are depicted as enslaved and exploited within the patriarchal political and economic organization of gendered power relations. The authors and critics I have analyzed in this text all bear out the validity of this point, for example, in Viramontes's works, not only "Miss Clairol" and "Tears on My Pillow," but in *Under the Feet of Jesus*, most powerfully. Fourth, Alarcón sees as another characteristic theme of Chicana writers the pitfalls of women who rely on an unquestioning religious faith. Alarcón illustrates this theme brilliantly when she calls readers' attention to the fact that there are very few poems written by women to the Virgin of Guadalupe but many written by men. Finally, Chicana writers describe their female characters' love for men as "at best deeply ambivalent" (1981, 187) as we have seen illustrated in "Zapata's Eyes" and Patricia Preciado Martín's "La Virgen de la Soledad."

In "La Fabulosa, a Texas Operetta" in *Woman Hollering Creek*, Cisneros takes on Bizet's opera *Carmen*. She does a hilarious feminist send-up, or, rather, a feminist revisioning, much as she has done of the Chicano cultural myth of La Llorona, and, again, with an up-beat twist, but with more humor. She de-males masculinist cultural mythology merrily away as she goes. Like Felice of "Woman Hollering Creek," Cisneros's Carmen Berriozabal is a spirited and sassy woman. Her Jose is a corporal at Fort Sam Houston who has a girl waiting for him to return and marry her "and buy that three-piece bedroom set on layaway. Dream on, right?" the nameless narrator adds sarcastically. Cisneros's Carmen has a worldly, cynical independent spirit. Jose was not Carmen's one love, just a passing fancy. But men are strange, the narrator muses. The worse a woman treats a man the more he loves her.

After Carmen takes up with a well-known politician who keeps her in style, Jose attempts to murder her and commit suicide. But the senator, who is married, with children, is ambitious for the governor's position and successfully keeps the scandal from the media. Some people claim that Jose carved his initials into Carmen's breasts, but the narrator claims that this story might just be a rumor. She has heard that Jose left the army without leave and took up bullfighting in order to die honorably according to the rules of machismo. She has also heard that Carmen does not want to live, either.

Here Cisneros is showing the ambiguity of reality, of actual history, going beyond simplistic binaries of characterization. But then the narrator interpolates her suggestion for changing the culture's gendered relations of power. Interestingly, in this case, the model is traditionally European but her twist is feminist Chicana. This move by Cisneros seems here, and, in fact, in all her work, to be a response to Pérez's "challenge" to Chicanas. In view of the fact that global patriarchy in the form of white colonizing male father figures affects all women, Pérez challenges all women to rebel against this system, separate ourselves from all its oppressive ideologies and, instead, "create life-affirming *sitios*" (Pérez 1993, 63).

First, Chicanas should try to get at the source of their addiction to the group that is responsible for their oppression. They must ask themselves why, even though they are fully aware of the destructive results for themselves and their menfolk, they nevertheless obey and perpetuate Anglo patriarchal laws. Pérez places the blame on Chicanos who have internalized Anglo men's worldviews and then imposed them on Chicanas, making themselves "caricatures" (1993, 63) of the colonizers in the process. Instead I would define such Chicanos as being reinforced in their machismo by the Anglo conqueror. Since Indians and then Chicanos were hierarchical and patriarchal oppressors of women before, during, and after the advent of Europeans, her claim is based more on blaming the colonizers for Chicano machismo than on historical accuracy. She further goes on to indict those Chicanos, like Cisneros's Eddie, who quickly emulate Anglo men when they enter mainstream institutions. They exclude Chicanas and other women of color from those institutions and all seats of power within them.

Cisneros is devoted throughout *Women Hollering Creek* to altering such masculinist assumptions of female subordination as expressed in its discourse and hegemonic plot lines. She takes on the traditional operatic reading of Carmen as having a death wish, using her narrator to advise her presumptive auditors not to believe that rumor. She knows for a fact that Carmen ran away with "King Kong Cardenas, a professional wrestler from Crystal City and a sweetie" (62).

Carmen lives! Or at least her spirit lives: her right to enjoy herself sexually, to change men as she pleases when she pleases—just as men have traditionally had the right to do in Chicano culture, and in all cultures, as well. She is, after all, only twenty. This is the other solution to the problem of a culture's constraining models for women: maintaining an intellectual and spiritual independence of spirit, especially maintaining a distance from the myriad cultural ties and gags that bind and constrict in male-female entanglements.

In the cuento "Woman Hollering Creek," Cisneros exposes the folk myth of La Llorona as perpetuating the myth's essential message that men betray women. Cisneros conveys an enormous grief, combined with rage, over that chasm between women's conduct in relationships and men's, especially between women's unfulfilled expectations of reciprocity in terms of mutual respect from men. The reader grieves with the young, romantic, idealistic Cleófilas as she suffers disillusion, then beatings, infidelity, and finally near-martyrdom from her Juan Pedro (Everyman) husband. Clearly, Cisneros's solution to the myth of La Llorona is to reject this myth as an example of Chicano culture's myths about women that it has developed and propagated within its masculinist discourse and perspective, its inequitable gendered power relations. She shifts the stereotypical definition for woman embedded in the discourse associated with the La Llorona myth from that of a nonentity and victim to active agency, to choice, and thence to triumph.[2] Cisneros displaces the myth constructed by patriarchal male discourse in order to perpetuate inequitable gendered power relations through ideology. Instead she shapes it to further women's agenda. The woman "hollering" at the end of "Woman Hollering Creek" is "hollering" empowerment "like Tarzan," Cisneros's trope for the natural, uncivilized, but somehow intuitively gentle man.

Cisneros, in reversing Cleofilas's traditionally predictable fate, is also creating an alternative response to the Mexican corrido "Delgadina." In that corrido a father jails his young daughter in a tower for refusing to allow him to commit incest with her. During her imprisonment, he deprives her of food and drink as punishment for daring to disobey him. Although she pleads with her mother, her brother, and her sister for sustenance to keep alive, as well as to be free, she is unsuccessful. Every member of her family fears what will happen to them if they disobey their father's authority: his decisions, his judgment, his rules and regulations, including his sexual abominations. They prefer to betray Delgadina and permit her to suffer and die alone, isolated from her loved ones.

Her mother and her sister, unwilling or not, serve as collusive gatekeepers of the patriarchy and betray her. Yet what else can they do? Delgadina, like Malinche, archetype of the Indian, then Chicana predicament, with no one to help her, has nowhere to turn and dies from hunger for nourishment, for freedom.

Cisneros, in her best work, such as "Woman Hollering Creek," positions herself as a kind of witness behind and above her heroines, testifying to injustices against them. She writes as if in concealment, a guerrilla in a literal and cultural landscape: a war zone of power in which girl children and women have been captured ideologically, discursively, and socially by occupying forces. Although they never succeed in entirely escaping their cultural prisons, only in sometimes going from maximum to minimum-security prisons, they nevertheless experience illumination at some point. They realize that they are prisoners in a hostile world for no rational, sane reason, but entirely because of cultural oppression caused by a patriarchal power setup of inequitable gendered power relations. Other women, their gatekeepers, act as implacable wardens.[3]

In "Bien Pretty Lupe" in *Woman Hollering Creek*, Lupe explains yin and yang to her model Flavio as the totality of all paired forces. The relationship between men and women illustrates this complementarity. The male force is heaven, the female force is earth. When men and women interact, the result is "the whole shebang." And if one force is present without the other, then "shit is out of balance." Flavio's response is to relate yin and yang to the Mexican term for the world–"sky-earth" (1991, 149). He had learned this concept from his grandmother Oralia whose name pays tribute to the orality of historical culture transmission in Mexico. Again we see in this incident how foremothers serve as gatekeepers for the cultural regime, training the new generations in their worldviews, but this time, unlike gatekeepers who keep their charges in blindfolds, the gatekeeper perpetuates Chicana and Indian (oral) traditions. Cisneros views women such as Oralia as "cultural practitioners," perpetuators of oppositional traditions. Like her, they produce oppositional "discourses" (Dernersesian 1993, 45). In all likelihood, Oralia is either a curandera or a bruja:

Curanderismo consists of a set of folk medical beliefs, rituals, and practices that seem to address the psychological, spiritual, and social needs of traditional . . . people. It is a complex system of folk medicine with its own theoretical, diagnostic, and therapeutic aspects. *Curanderismo* is conceptually holistic in nature; no separation is made between the mind and the body, as in western medicine and psychology.

Negative healers . . . *as brujas* (witches) have an extensive command of malevolent techniques of witchcraft and can cause great harm in the form of illness. They also analyze dreams, have premonitions, read cards, and indulge in other areas of the black arts. (Perrone, Stockel, and Krueger 1989, 86, 92)

Like Oralia, a major characteristic of curanderas is that they

have challenged the normal female roles within their culture and have assumed the authority and leadership traditionally reserved for men. Even as youngsters, the healers never accepted the submissiveness and passivity that is the fate of nearly all traditional females in their societies. As a matter of fact, even in their earliest years, most *curanderas* knew they were different. They broke the rules in their own ways. . . . These women represent the traditional ways, but they refused to be molded into stereotypes because they believed their destiny could not be determined by cultural standards that were designed on earth. Quite the contrary: *las curanderas* know their lives had been guided by God, and that reality is the only permission they need. (Perrone, Stockel, and Krueger 1989, 96)

Rocky Gámez writes a powerful story about a traditional curandera, Doña Marciana García. Like her sisters, she carries a "burlap bag . . . with an assortment of medicinal herbs, votive candles and the clay statuette of the virgin de Guadalupe." These are the things "she believed in and held sacred. These were the tools of her trade" (1983, 11). Lost on the road, "she couldn't really tell how far away from home she was" because she "had left her rosary beads" (1983, 13) at her last patient's bedside. She habitually prays as she walks and knows how long each prayer takes according to how many steps she makes. As she dies, she sighs "Que sea lo que Dios quiera."[May it be as God wills it] (1983, 14). The irony is that her last moments are spent in torment, convinced that the young nurse trained in a modern Anglo school and now working in the area, will accuse her of malpractice because she has just lost a patient in labor. In reality, the nurse and the whole village admire her work without reservations and mourn her death as a great loss.

In keeping with the demand that Chicanas adhere to their own cultural experience, past and present, Teresa Palomo Acosta would have the "Chicana Poeta" create revisionist poetry. Instead of wandering in a fog of confusion and ignorance caused by subjugation, being colonized to Anglo ways of doing things, she should learn about her own culture's time-honored ways of doing things. Then the Chicana poet should disseminate those traditional ways that are her cultural inheritance in order to counteract the influence of alien Anglo customs and institutions. One example of traditional ways is the treatment and healing of physical and spiritual ills by Chicana curanderas such as Doña Marciana García. In her poem "They Are Laying Plans for Me–Those Curanderas," Palomo Acosta imagines the curanderas as digressing long enough from their work to discuss her plight as a typical colonized contemporary Chicana. First they mourn that the Chicana no longer remembers their ways of healing. Then, convinced that Chicana poetry is another form of healing equivalent to theirs, they make Palomo Acosta a poet in order to reconnect her to their healing mystique through her use of poetic discourse about her Chicana sisters. Through poetry she will be able to find herself, to become spiritually whole again, although she is now wandering, ignorant and mentally colonized, lost as in a fog. By linking with her past and present cultural women's traditions, she (and other contemporary Chicanas whom she represents, as well) will become her "own curandera" (1993, 296–297).

Flavio, an exterminator, becomes Lupe's lover and leaves her suddenly to return to Mexico to his two wives and seven children. In her sorrow she takes to watching telenovelas, the form of entertainment that had provided surcease from her bleak existence for Cleófilas, the protagonist of "Woman Hollering Creek."

Interestingly Resnik recommends that women accept and embrace these idealistic and romantic dreams about how life might be for them, which the masculinist discourse and most men hold in the utmost contempt. Resnik is in sharp disagreement with Alarcón who, although seeing this type of literature as universally appealing to women, still internalizes a derisive attitude toward it. She complains that at the present time what is considered the traditionally valorized form of love is the erotic and romantic love disseminated "*ad nauseam* through romance novels, or in the case of Mexico and Latin America, *fotonovelas*" (1996, 965). Undoubtedly, this genre attracts and unites women of all kinds and classes, causing them to become "sisters under the skin, daughters of patriarchy" (Alarcón 1989, 103). However, instead of being ashamed at what the culture mocks and invalidates as cheap, unreal, stupid, and trivial, at what it scorns and trashes as women's illusions, Resnik suggests adhering to them as subversive models for the culture to live by, even in the face of mockery.

Lupe starts dreaming of the major female characters of these telenovelas. In these dreams, she is in a rage, beating them up. She demands that they be proactive, not victims all the time, nor always tormented in love. She is fed up with the depictions of men in the telenovelas as "powerful and passionate," whereas women are depicted as either passive and humble, or fiery and bad. She wants these heroines to be like the proud and independent women she has known and loved all her life: girlfriends, comadres, mothers, and aunts. These are women who tell men to love them or leave them, women who are strong, filled with power and passion, bravery and ferocity, and who are simultaneously also "tender and volatile" (161). But such women are not depicted in literature or on the telenovelas.

In a hilarious and heretical twist by means of her twin volcano painting, Lupe also reverses the culture's prevailing construction of inequitable gendered power relations. Reversing traditional postures, she paints Princess Ixta gazing down at the sleeping Prince Popa [Popocatepetl] lying flat on his back, not the other way around as is traditional. When all is said and done does anyone have the right to maintain that "the sleeping mountains" are female rather than male? Once having made this change, Lupe then makes some necessary "anatomical adjustments" in the mountains and is going to call the painting *El Pipi del Popa* (163). Here Cisneros, through humor, is expressing her position relative to the ongoing discussion by feminists about the situatedness of the gaze. Whose gaze is it? What difference does it make when the gaze is male or female? If readers are outraged by this reversal, why are they outraged? What in their training has led them to believe that only the male gaze is appropriate in sexualizing females?

In her analysis of Bernice Zamora's "Notes from a chicana Coed," Dernersesian could well be describing Cisneros's answer. She contrasts the major elements of Chicano discourse as nationalist abstractions that make no reference whatsoever to gender, whereas Chicana discourse is primarily concerned with specific statements about inequitable gendered power relations that reflect the reality of being oppressed in those relations that Chicanas actually experience (1993, 51). Hererra-Sobek gives credit to the source for this consciously female sexual perspective as "the advent of the feminist movement." Since then, both men and women have acknowledged the extent and intensity of female sexuality [because] in our patriarchal culture [female sexuality] has been denied, kept a dark secret up until recent times" (1988a, 27).

However, the drawback to Cisneros's solution in this cuento and others is that she is not simply affirming women's sexuality, but reversing the male scopic and discursive perspective. Women, according to Lupe's argument, will literally and figuratively stand upright whereas men will lie down with their body parts available for women's examination. Women will be in power, will control the terms of the discourse, whereas men will be vulnerable to women's judgments and definitions. Lupe's choice of perspective is nothing more than a reversal, a replication in reverse of the oppressor's mentality. Women objectifying male body parts as men objectify women's is like replicating the abuses of the oppressor when the oppressed come to power, as in the classic case of the French Revolution, where the revolutionaries became the brutal oppressors of the aristocrats in their turn. As I have noted in "'Mericans" and elsewhere, Cisneros illustrates in her characterizations a belief that women are not different from men when allowed full, free self-expression. I contend, however, that there are more constructive feminist solutions that do not merely replicate or imitate the way the hegemony does things and acculturates women to do so, namely, by equating "subject and object" (Piper 1995, 174).

"Little Miracles, Kept Promises," one of Cisneros's most delightful cuentos, is written in the form of "milagritos" [little miracles]–missives, notes, or testimonios. These are "safety-pinned to effigies of the Virgin and of name-saints, in which the deities involved point back through time and Christianity to the dark presence of Aztec cosmology" (Lee 1992, 22). This format gives Cisneros room for full expression of her panoply of talents which range from conveying the most tragic human experiences of suffering to the humorous, silly, and trivial, simultaneously.

Unlike Felice or Lupe, Chayo appropriates power without reversal. One of Resnik's key solutions to the problem of masculinist religions and myths is to subvert the deities already created by male religions. She would have this done by modifying, changing, adding, shaping, and in general modelling them on what women would want them to be, not on imitations of how men are trained to conduct themselves. The closest illustration to her prescription is the magnificent monologue by Chayo at the end of this cuento.

Throughout readers hear the discordant external voices of Chayo's culture, as troped by her family and neighbors who all unite against Chayo in acting as her gatekeepers. They insist upon guarding her against "the corrupting influence of U.S. ways on Mexican women" (Ruíz 1993, 119). What Alarcón observes about Viramontes's young protagonist Naomi in "Growing" applies just as well to Chayo here, except Chayo does not attempt to deviate from her culture's demands on her as a Chicana girl by following Anglo ways. Chayo follows her own talents.

Naomi is correct in her perception of the difference in social experience between girls due to the relatively different cultural/racial codes (perhaps class-rooted codes as well). She is too young, however, to understand that in a patriarchy such as she has been born into virtually all women will sooner or later reach a limit with regard to the speaking position that they may take up as women. How rapidly that limit is reached and how women may/may not express themselves after that point may vary according to what is deemed permissible discourse for women in her specific culture. Often that boundary line is drawn by her father (and assenting mother), because they perceive her body as always that of a woman and therefore always limited to her sexual/maternal function. (1988, 149)

Cisneros conveys the pitfalls and dangers of familism to young Chicanas who seek their identity by exposing the continual disruptions Chayo is subjected to in her attempts to find and express herself. Further, Chayo's letter serves as vehicle for Cisneros's proposed solutions to the unequal gender relations of her broader culture. She attempts to shift the masculinist discourse, to change its language and meaning in such a way as to expose its injustice and artificial constraints on women–in Herrera-Sobek's vivid metaphor, "the multiple shackles imprisoning women." The latter lists "restraints imposed by patriarchal society" first, and then the restraints of "tradition, poverty, censorship, social mores" (1995, 148). Chayo, like Tere of Ana Castillo's *The Mixquiahuala Letters*, is "trapped" by having internalized the patriarchal "ideological nexus" (Alarcón 1989, 95) indoctrinated into her that all women must continually guard against by being vigilant. They must question and disrupt the oppressive messages at every turn.

Characteristic of Cisneros's work, as with all the writers analyzed in this text, is the quality of seeing the tragic in the comic and the comic in the tragic. To cite only a few among numerous examples in this story, there is the letter acknowledging a donation as promised because of a disaster when the bus skidded and overturned in which the Familia Arteaga was travelling. The accident killed a woman and her little girl, but by some miracle the family in question was not hurt at all. However, from that time on they avoided riding in buses. Then there is the missive in which the author's unique tone of sprightly sarcasm is nowhere more evident or more delightful as when Barbara Ybanez of San Antonio writes to Saint Anthony of Padua. She begs the saint to assist her in getting a man who does not bring pain to her *nalgas* [ass] like the educated ones who leave Texas to find a job in California. She also does not want a man who can't speak Spanish, or a man who doesn't define himself as "Hispanic," unless he needs to apply for federal funding.[4] Instead, she wants a man who is unashamed to cook, or clean, or take care of himself, who can buy his clothing himself, who can iron himself, not a man like her brothers whom their mother spoiled outrageously. She justifies her order on the grounds that she has endured frustrating relationships with inferior men too long, that she deserves better.[5]

Katherine Rios sees Cisneros as recuperating "the Malinche/Guadalupe/ Llorona triad–the three icons that supposedly structure the psychic and material basis of Chicana identity–throughout her stories." Rios perhaps sums up the meaning of Malinche best in a pointed anecdote. When she informed "a Chicana friend" that she was reading Cisneros's "Never Marry a Mexican" as "a revision of the Malinche myth," the friend "countered, 'Is there any *other* way to read the story'" (1995, 204). To her mind, Lucha Corpi's poems about Malinche (in *Fuego de Atlán: Palabras de Mediodía*) finally "put Dona Marina to rest," gave all the interpretations to Malinche that are possible, so that now we can "move on to something else" (as cited in Pratt 1993, 872). To my mind, however, it is Sandra Cisneros who has finally achieved this goal by adding mocking laughter to the artillery that other authors have used to besiege the traditional masculinist myths of Malinche, La Llorona, the Virgin Mary, and the Virgin of Guadalupe, as well.

Chayo links herself with Malinche by using the term "traitor" when she confides her problems to the Black Virgin of Guadalupe. Eventually she grows strong enough to cut her braid off as a gesture of liberation, to become a painter, to go to school. Cleófilas, after great suffering from her abusive husband, comes to believe in and act upon a very different feminist version of La Llorona than does her society. Chayo, also after great suffering from her abusive family, creates for herself a very different feminist version of Malinche, one opposed to her society's masculinist version. Chayo is called a traitor, too, and by her own mother, every time she attempts to explain to her mother and her grandmother why she does not intend to turn out as they did (128).

She even transforms a traditional religious icon, the Virgen de Guadalupe, by destabilizing the masculine discourse around her myth. She does this by changing the deity's image from mediator to one of agency and power. For many Chicanas the Catholic Church should serve as a refuge, but, unfortunately, when those like Chayo turn to it, they find it "oppressive and hostile." This is because the Catholic God (and I might add, from personal experience, the Hebrew God) is resolutely male and does not seem to them "a benevolent comforting figure . . . Instead, it is yet another male, terrifying and oppressing women." True, "women can identify and receive solace" from the Virgin. Nevertheless, "her direct connection with institutionalized religion transforms her into an inaccessible figure" (Herrera-Sobek 1988a, 29).

Chayo, in doing her own research about the "Virgencita de Guadalupe," as she calls her, does not refute Alarcón's observation that the saint lacks attractiveness for females. Instead she tries to recuperate her for feminist purposes. As a result of this research, Chayo discovers that indeed the saint can be recuperated. She can be interpreted in such a way as to undo the threads that masculine discourse has so tightly woven around her. As masculinist discourse would have it, Chayo has always previously identified the Virgencita de Guadalupe with her own mother "with her folded hands." She permitted her continually drunken father to always blame any and all of his problems on her. She and her mother and all her mothers' mothers endured this treatment "in the name of God" (127).

But now Chayo refuses to create a new Virgin in her mother's and foremothers' image, a saint who would replicate and valorize and perpetuate their culturally prescribed lives of endless self-abasement and suffering in silence. Instead she creates a new Virgin, or rather recreates her from pre-Columbian mythology. She is nude, holding snakes. She jumps over "the backs of bulls." She swallows "raw hearts" and rattles "volcanic ash" (127). She is "our mother Tonantzin. Your [male Catholic] church at Tepeyac built on the site of her temple. Sacred ground no matter whose goddess claims it" (128). This is not quite true. For when the male hegemony, which is the Catholic Church in this case, claims a goddess for its own and turns her into a saint, then she gets filtered through its mystifying essentialist sacred guidelines so as to naturalize and normalize her in the masculinist discursive mold. Such a saint is the Virgin Mary, the meek and mild archetypal mother.

In a lengthy epiphany, in marked contrast to the lists Cleófilas had made of women's potentially deadly relationships with their male guard(ian)s, Chayo finally undertakes to revise the traditional masculinist myths. From her feminist perspective, she expands the pantheon of deities to include Aztec goddess figures and syncretized female Catholic saints. By so doing, Cisneros, through Chayo, creates a space for contesting and demystifying patriarchal religious hegemonic discourse for hitherto culturally naturalized religious icons. Cisneros realizes that our unconscious naturalization of intensively prescribed masculinist religious icons must be destabilized first, for "the [so-called] 'natural' . . . underpins the power of hegemony" (Kim 1996, 221). Once Chayo "learned" about and began to worship Coatlaxopeuh, "She Who Has Dominion over Serpents," and "Tonantzin . . . Teteoinnan, Toci, Xochiquetzal, Tlazolteotl, Coatlicue, Chalchiuhtlicue, Coyolzauhqui, Huixtocihuatl, Chicomecoatl, Cihuacoatl," only then could she understand and accept the Catholic versions of "the great mother": "Nuestra Senora de la Soledad, Nuestra Senora de los Remedios, Nuestra Senora del Perpetuo Socorro, Nuestra Senora de San Juan de los Lagos, Our Lady of Lourdes, Our Lady of Mount Carmel, Our Lady of the Rosary, Our Lady of Sorrows" (128)."[6] Now Chayo is no longer ashamed to be the daughter of any of her foremothers.

Chayo moves even further away philosophically from this stunning integration. She moves out to a bold subsummation of male gods, then moves even further out into visualizing a female totality composed of facets of a "many-in-one" female goddess that includes male facets, as well, such as Buddha, Christ, and Jehovah. She also now can love "the Heart of the Sky, the Heart of the Earth, the Lord of the Near and Far, the Spirit, the Light, the Universe." Learning to love this "many in one" (128), she finally learns to love herself.

So it is that when Chayo comes to write her own little miracle to place beside all the others, she calls the saints "Mighty Guadalupana Coatlaxopeuh Tonatzin" (129) which bears no reference whatsoever to male gods and masculine discourse. Cisneros is here suggesting that from historically viable precedents women can create their own female deities to worship. Using the Virgin of Guadalupe in a nontraditional, transformational way is a common strategy to both contemporary Chicana writers and artists such as Yolanda López. The latter's well-known *Serie Guadalupe* seeks freedom from the imposition of male image-making of Chicanas and from the constraints imposed upon Chicana creative artists by the crippling power of a hostile system imposed upon their sensibilities (Dernersesian 1993, 42–43).[7] This is reminiscent of the medieval Catholic Church's historic imposition of brutal censorship on artists to the point where they could not depict their wives or mistresses, but had to pretend that they were the Virgin with Child.

Rebolledo and Rivero say of Cisneros's work and the efforts of other Chicana writers in this regard that they have consciously used their culture's own "myths and archetypes" and shaped and recreated those that did not suit them. They feel that the "myths and archetypes" they then create are not carved in stone, but rather evolve from a constant movement and flow "of Chicana ideology, ideals, and desires" (1993, 24). In this way "Malinche is an archetype redeeemed and changed through Chicana literary discourse" and "the Virgin of Guadalupe acquires tennis shoes, a sewing machine, a suitcase, and whatever other implements she needs to increase her activism" (1993, 24).

Cisneros and López, as well as many other Chicana writers and artists, emphasize the subversion of masculine discourse through the creation of a transformative discourse of a female-identified deity. A goddess or saint may be given female qualities physically by the culture, but the possession of such attributes does not necessarily mean that she functions for feminists as a female/female-identified icon. The goddess Athene in Homer's *Odyssey* is an example of a supposedly female goddess who is not female-identified. She confers directly with her favorite Odysseus and with his son Telemachus. She does this both in disguise and as an extraordinary dispensation to these males. She also spends all of her time busying herself on behalf of Odysseus.

Rarely does Athene appear to the female protagonist Penelope. Yet it is the latter who is most in need of consolation, of female community. Athene never consoles Penelope, nor works on her behalf, or even thinks of her at all, except that once she dries her tears–in order to make her look younger and prettier for the suitors! These young men hound Penelope nearly to death for three years without Athene giving emphasis to her plight. Instead she focuses her attention entirely on Telemachus and Odysseus.

What assistance Athene does give Penelope is given only to forward the goddess's agenda for Odysseus. And neither Athene nor Penelope herself takes into account, as if it did not exist, Penelope's sexual needs and frustration. She goes twenty years uncomplainingly without sex, the last three surrounded by 108 young men. As much as they are her enemies, as much as they badger her continually, as much as they eat her out of her husband's house and home, as much as they are arrogant and obnoxious, still Penelope would have felt some physical attraction and lust for the more decent of them, if nothing more.

Only the product of a patriarchal culture, only a male mind with a masculinist phallocentric perspective on gender, as well as a male's agenda, could have so Othered Penelope, so distanced himself and all he knew about his own sexual needs as to create a female and depict her devoid of such needs. Only a male could have created such a sexless deity as Athene, or indulged in imagining and forwarding the misogynistic myth that she was born from her father's brow. The myth about the Virgin Mary's impregnation by the Holy Spirit also resembles in reverse the myth of Athene's birth from Zeus's forehead.

Margarita Cota-Cárdenas worries about Penelope with good reason. In many cultures over many centuries she has been valorized as a female ideal for role modeling by those who run those cultures. The way this has been done is clearly to reinforce and perpetuate their position of complete gender control and power over women. What is most disturbing about Penelope is that she is created without any regard to female biological reality, to human biological reality in fact, but entirely in regard to enforced acculturated standards for ideal females— first and foremost, sexual and psychic fidelity to their men at all costs. There are still cultures extant where women never remarry, such as Chicano culture, where women are expected to become and remain faithful widows without recourse to male companionship. If they do remarry, if they do see men after widowhood, they are ostracized, as we have seen illustrated in Anzaldúa's "The Ghost Trap."

In the poem "Gullible," Cota-Cárdenas first exclaims over the contrast between husband and wife in terms of Penelope's patience at performing her lonely duties, as troped in the weaving of her "tapestries." The poet grieves most, however, for "how lonely" Penelope is, when compared with her husband Odysseus. In fact, Cota-Cárdenas is so alienated from the patriarchy Odysseus represents that she refuses to name him. She calls him only "he" when she contrasts him to his long-suffering wife.

While "he's over there Circeing himself/ taking his sweet time," Cota-Cárdenas asserts that Penelope's work and conduct has been made, at least for gullible women, "a symbol now of patience." Circe is the sorceress, the bruja, with whom Odysseus dallied for three years, until one of his men pointed out that no one could any longer believe that his relationship with Circe was enforced.

Cota-Cárdenas's solution to such a sadistic imposition on women is to stress that we would be fools if we believed that Penelope spent all that time pining away before her husband returned to her for one night and then left again. Penelope provides an excellent "example," but only for men to impose on gullible females. Furious at the sadism that deprives Penelope of sexuality, she concludes sarcastically that Odysseus must have "satisfied" Penelope by means of "egotistical telepathy" (1993a, 266–267), or perhaps, she wonders, Penelope had another man all those years. But, then, *The Odyssey* would be a different work altogether if that were the case.

This decision to modify or transform patriarchal religion and myths is a common project with most Chicana writers and artists. Unfortunately it is tantamount to maintaining that Mary had a human lover when she became pregnant with Jesus, as Angela de Hoyos does in her "Fairy Tale." She depicts the Virgin as an innocent, sensitive princess born into an age of cynicism and materialism. Not surprisingly, Mary dreams that a Prince Charming will sweep her off her feet and they will live happily ever after. After she has met him, however, she discovers that he is cheating on her. When she prays to God to do something, he remains aloof on "his throne" up in the heavens, without blinking "an eye." Like Cota-Cárdenas, de Hoyos ends on a distinctly separatist note, describing the Virgin as no longer blind, no longer a believer either in gods or men (1993, 267–268).

One can imagine the response outside of feminist circles to such iconoclastic poems and other similar revisionary efforts. The power of patriarchal religion and myth is simply too strong to modify or break, reinforced by church and state alike over centuries and in most known cultures globally.

In "Protocolo de verduras/The Protocol of Vegetables," Lucha Corpi reinforces de Hoyos's insight, as well as suggests an alternative to handling impossible constraints in the form of myths. She shows that a woman's daily life and work make all the myths ludicrous. Between her vegetable gardening and her housework, she has no time to feel forlorn or melancholy, or even lonely about her lover's absence. She has too many household chores to do. With great irony, she powerfully contrasts the ridiculous masculine pretensions/conventions, resonating with/ricocheting off, burlesquing, high-flown Shakespearean sonnets in the face of a woman's cramped reality. The woman can only create her poetry in the brief spaces of time between the spaces in the winds in the laundry tempest, or recollect her beloved in "wash water," or while watering "thirsty houseplants," or picking the "cabbage and pepper" (1993, 281).[8]

Anzaldúa believes in head-on confrontation, however, not subtle opposition, like Corpi. She envisions opposition and insurrection against "the rock," that is, masculinist culture. Not only will her rage and rebelliousness crack the rock, but "hope" will, as well. Then "*la Coatlicue*" within her will emerge triumphant. She will take control over all aspects of her own life, the positive and the negative. She will take control over her own material essence, her own sexuality, her own psyche, define for herself what are her weak and strong points, as will her Chicana sisters. She does not want "the heterosexual white man's or the colonized man's or the state's or the culture's or the religion's or the parents" (1987, 51) to do this for her and her sisters.

Cisneros represents men as dangerous, violent, brutal, incorrigibly unfaithful, murderous, and in continual conflict with one another about one thing or another. Emiliano Zapata, in her cuento "Eyes of Zapata," perhaps best epitomizes this model. According to Cisneros, the culture reflects only the way men are because only men run the culture. It is not surprising therefore that the Mexican hero Zapata is one of Cisneros's "heavies" (Dernersesian 1993, 51) because he represents those men who promoted exploitation of women in the household while enjoying sexual privileges and leadership positions outside the home.

Cisneros devotes her work to giving voice to characters in situations that would otherwise be best described as "the hidden, the concealed, the repressed": victims of "domestic violence, aging, poverty, mental retardation," who question "the power relations inherent in affairs of love" (Ordoñez 1995, 180). She also gives voice to women in all the "affairs" between men and women, not only in "the master narrative of love." In most of her stories, Cisneros depicts a devastating contrast between the world as run by men and what her female protagonists envision as the way to live. Alarcón shrewdly perceives that this solution is dangerous for women. They live on expectations and fantasies about romantic love created by the patriarchy and "*re*-presented in all manner of popular literature," as well as in other media. This myth is a maneuver on the part of the male-run culture to destroy women's "subjectivity" and prevent them from exploring and knowing the nature of "their own desire" (1989, 104).

Another modification we can make to the Penelopean and Marianismo clichés for women is to exaggerate through "metaperformance" reading. For example, we could interpret Penelope as only outwardly in conformity to her culture's mythology about the nature and condition of the ideal woman. Penelope might be seen as subverting this myth by forwarding her own agenda. Appearing to conform to its dictates by day, she nevertheless subverts it by night. It is then that she unravels the threads of the tapestries that comprise the masculine decree. She might be interpreted as unravelling the work her culture deems as appropriate for her in order to covertly pursue her personal preference as a woman: to wait for the man she has chosen and to ignore all others whom she perceives as nuisances. In gender trouble, it is possible to mock/battle through metaperformance–outfeminizing feminine models through outsized exaggeration rather than through direct confrontation.

Tragically, female models in myths such as Penelope and La Virgen de Guadalupe, La Llorona, and Malinche for Chicano/as are always aggressively conceived by the patriarchy in masculine terms for masculine purposes: controlling the power in inequitable gendered power relations. Many alternatives have been suggested by Chicana writers, so far without success, because they are reactions based on an already firmly entrenched system of cultural models. Nevertheless, many Chicana writers and critics (Fernández, Cisneros, Corpi, Cota-Cárdenas, Anzaldúa, and others) continue their efforts to modify or transform, to challenge "paternal discourse" with a "reassessment of inherited knowledge" (Ordoñez 1995, 180).

NOTES

1. Nancy Saporta Sternbach in "'A Deep Racial Memory of Love': The Chicana Feminism of Cherríe Moraga," gives a complete summary of the history of the diversity of responses to Malinche, which focuses primarily on the reassessment by Chicana writers. Some see her as a "metaphor for the silencing of the Indian voice and stress her victimization, as exemplified by Rosario Castellanos and Lucha Corpi. Stressing "vindication" of Malinche, on the other hand, Sternbach enumerates "a Chicana tradition of writers, critics, and historians such as Norma Alarcón, Cordelia Candelaria, Adelaida del Castillo, and Marcela Lucero-Trujillo. All "have written about how painful it is to be Malinche or her daughter . . . or to finally speak in her own voice" (1989, 53). Margarita Cota-Cárdenas illustrates this difficulty in "Malinche's Discourse." She sarcastically mimics the voices and perspective of La Raza critics of feminism who argue that "the chicano/mexican/latin family has to maintain itself intact, that traditions are more important for the good, for the future . . . that all this stuff about women's liberation is just bourgeois women's junk, those women that have idle time to write and to draw and to . . . discombobulate themselves" (1993b, 205). Cherríe Moraga, Sternbach asserts,

expected, the mother who is also socialized by the culture, does not always reciprocate" (1989, 53). Moraga directs "her analysis toward Malinche's mother, likening her to her own" (1989, 53). In this text, readers have seen that Moraga's stance toward a mother who has acted as what I have termed a "gatekeeper" or "collaborator" by perpetuating the culture's models for women onto her daughter is prevalent, if not universal, contrary to Sternbach's assertion. That the mother's position in Chicano culture is very complex is also noted in relation to "the legacy of Malinche . . . for any woman with the audacity to consider her own needs before those of the men of her family. By placing herself (or any woman, including her daughter) first, she is accused of being a traitor to her race (Moraga 1983b, 103). "By fulfilling her daughter's desire and need for love, the mother is also labeled la chingada. Her 'Mexican wifely duty' means that sons are favored, husbands revered. 'Traitor begets traitor,' Moraga warns: like mother, like daughter. Malinche's mother, then, was the first traitor (mother) who begot the second one (daughter)" (Sternbach 1989, 55). Irene Blea in *La Chicana and the Intersection of Race, Class, and Gender* (1991) also gives a complete summary of both La Malinche and La Llorona (25–29, 36).

2. La Llorona is also used as a scare tactic for children to keep them in line, to keep them inside the house after dark. Ofelia in Helena María Viramontes's short story "Tears on My Pillow" exemplifies this use: "You could hear her crying for reals, I swear. When you hear her crying far away that means she's real close so don't go out at night. She's as close as your bed, so don't sleep with your feet to the window cause even she can pull them out. She'll get you. I swear" (1992, 110–11).

3. This is much like the situation in Margaret Atwood's dystopian *The Handmaid's Tale*.

4. The federal government began to use the term "Hispanic" in the seventies as a blanket category to which many Chicanos and Chicanas object. Guillermo E. Hernándezdiffers from other scholars in arguing that the term "has been used to include the post-1970s emerging urban middle-class professionals who, as had some of their Mexican American predecessors, sought total integration into diverse areas of the American cultural mainstream" (1991, 7). Elsewhere, however, he reinforces Barbara's observation about some Chicano grant applicants. He notes "the contradictions of internalizing the normative values of a dominant group that relegates [Chicanos] to a status of marginality–denying prestige to Chicanos who assert their cultural background while rewarding those who demonstrate social and cultural disloyalty" (1991, 38).

5. Segura informs us that "the experiences of upwardly mobile Chicanas" are generally unpleasant. They experience "inner turmoil" because "their achievements contradict ethnic, gender and class traditions." Sadly, "emotional support from their families" which she believes "is critical to the success" of such "high achieving Chicanas" (1995a, 123), is not usually forthcoming, nor, according to Cisneros, is it forthcoming from the men with whom the Chicanas are in relationship. Segura reports, on the other hand, that men do get this support from the public and their family. She also considers "the acquisition of a high degree of knowledge of the dominant culture" as well as family support, as equal in value to family support. Cisneros's female characters, such as Ms. Barbara Ybanez, seem to be living in isolation, unlike Cleófilas.

6. Blea spells "Coyolxauhqui" what Cisneros spells as "Coyolzauhqui" and defines her as "goddess of the moon, who was sister of Huitzilopochtli, the god of war. Coyolxauhqui is known as 'she of the face painted with rattles.' This gives rise to her Nahuatl name. Coyolli signifies rattles in Nahuatl, the language of the Mexica, or Aztecs" (1991, 24). She further identifies Coatlicue, goddess of the earth and of death, as depicted in a large sculpture in the Museum of Anthropology, Mexico City. "She is

represented as a decapitated woman from whose neck springs two serpent heads symbolizing streams of blood. She wears a necklace of hands and hearts. Her hands are shown as serpent heads and her feet as eagle claws. Women were represented in Aztec religion as spiritual and mythological figures on earth and in other worlds. The universe was divided into male and female counterparts, and all things were based on male-female elements" (1991, 25). Rebolledo and Rivero assert that Coatlicue was not acceptable to the Catholic Church, the emissary of European culture, because her characterisitcs were not what they wanted perpetuated. "She was independent, wrathful, competent, her power to create and destroy was autonomous, as was that of most of the Nahuatl deities; it was a power not emanating solely from a central male figure" (1993, 190). Sosa Riddell makes no bones about the role of the Catholic Church in relation to Mexico and women. It subjected natives to the conquistadors, and made women "subjects of the subjects *and* the subjugators." It guards and perpetuates the conviction that women were inferior to men and needed constant watching. Mexican culture was not unique. Every other culture controlled by the Spaniards was controlled by the Catholic Church and its perspective on women and Indians. Spanish women were believed embodiments of the Virgin Mary in their qualities, whereas Mestizas and Indian women were "heathens, women in need of redemption, loose women, thus women who could be exploited without fear of punishment" (1995, 404).

7. Sternbach alludes to a study of "cultural stereotypes" which has shown "that the figures most often used–Malinche, La Llorona and the Virgin of Guadalupe–have historically been models to control women. . . ." (1989, 57). Cherríe Moraga places the blame, not on the influence of historical "cultural stereotypes," but rather on "the institution of obligatory heterosexuality" (1983b, 132). The places or sites for pointing to blame, however, are all located in the hegemony that controls the culture, which prescribes and mandates its systems of power relations–masculinist patriarchy. Blea states that those Chicanas "active in the Catholic church are quick to point out that Nuestra Señora de Guadalupe (Our Lady of Guadalupe) is a significant female deity with both Indian and Spanish-European characteristics." Most interestingly, because not previously publicized, these Chicana Catholic activists "would like this holy image to be more fully incorporated into religious services outside the Chicano community" (1991, 112). Anzaldúa, for example, believes that "[t]he first step is to unlearn the puta/virgen dichotomy and to see *Coatlapopeuh-Coatlicue* in the Mother *Guadalupe*" (1987, 84).

8. Emily Dickinson, unlike Queen Elizabeth I or Corpi, seems to have incorporated household imagery and items like brooms and teacups into her passionate poetic metaphors of undying love without rancor or resentment, such as Corpi's, or defensiveness about being a woman, like Elizabeth. Unlike Corpi's, these pathetic responses to the declassing of females out of the hierarchical systems of ranking and meaning in the culture are far more common.

Chapter 7

Transforming Inequitable Gender Success Models

That a man wins if he possesses a woman, that she loses everything overdetermines female corporeality because it links ideological abstracts to it. Postcolonial critics like Homi Bhabha refer to colonized people's "mimicry" in the sense that what they do is done "imperfectly or overly perfectly." They do this so as to expose a situation with conscious irony, to retell "stories otherwise forgotten . . . a process that discovers or recovers the discredited histories of groups circumscribed by regimes of repressive discursive practices" (Pérez Torres 1993–1994, 185–186). But sadly, as Richard McCormick has pointed out, just "the mere existence of . . . subversive or resistant perspectives in a text cannot undo the power of what is socially 'dominant'" (1993, 662).

Strength is strength, whether it is male or female. To link both female and male sexuality to concepts about corporeal strength and weakness is to mix apples and oranges. To be strong or weak, whether male or female, is simply a physiological condition.

It is specious, Chicanas believe, to link weakness with sexuality, to conflate sexuality prior to, during, or without marriage as weakness in females. Such linking also leads to differentiations in class ranking, not only between men and women, but women and women. Some women are situated as inferiors in class and status relative to other women, ranked according to how acceptable/unacceptable they are politically and socially in terms of their sexual morals and behavior (Castañeda 1993, 33).

It is also specious to maintain, on the other hand, that strong sexuality (to the point where they "can't help it") is deemed a natural characteristic only of males at all times: prior to marriage, during marriage, and outside marriage. If the women's body is violated, or known and used outside of legal marriage, then she has lost the battle, lost her virtue, or purity, or honor. This is the currency of respectability to men for listing a woman as a bona fide member in the ranks of culturally acceptable, decent women.

In this regard, whether in Chicana or American models for gendered power relations, the linking of the concept of moral weakness in terms of male corporeality together with men's sexuality is comparatively rare. Whenever such a linkage is described, men are invariably depicted as victims hypnotized, then distracted into sexuality by women. Under the spell of a witch, a vixen, a female goddess, a femme fatale, and the like, men just cannot help themselves: "The devil made them do it."

From the Chicana writers' perspective, it never seems to occur to obedient women that such gender discourse for defeat and victory are male definitions that serve to reinforce church and legal decrees and therefore their control over women. A Catch-22 situation is thereby created, because these are all male models for women created by the same males who then created the restrictive discourse for women and the scripts and plots to match. On the other hand, they allocated freedom for themselves from these restrictive rules and regulations within which they constrained women, thereby signifying that they were a higher class of beings than women and the ones in power in that culture.

It also never seems to occur to the majority of women that these religious and legal models are often tied to their economic wellbeing. Unlike men, women who do not marry will generally know poverty unless they remain in birth families headed by a male. Nor does it ever seem to occur to most women that these models are political: who controls the power controls the culture. In general, it never seems to occur to most people in a given culture that somehow different rules apply according to individuals' gender roles by which men always win and women are always defeated.

Women might choose to refuse to perpetuate only male fantasies. They could laugh them out of existence. They could stop taking them so seriously as sacred decrees from on high cast in stone and heretical to disobey. They could view them, instead, as the unfair and inequitable fantasies of petty minds:

[A] woman excluded from . . . property/inheritance . . . *is consequently excluded from the corresponding concepts and structures of social legitimacy.* The woman who is defined out of social legitimacy because of the abrogation of her primary value to patriarchal society, that of producing heirs, is considered without value, without honor. . . . A woman (women) thus devalued may not lay claim to the rights and protections the society affords to the woman who does have sociopolitical and sexual value. (Castañeda 1993, 27–28)

Unthinking reinforcement of the culture's masculinist models for unequal gendered power relations through institutionlized ostracism declasses any woman acccused of sexual misconduct, even though she may have thought herself to be in the same class as those who ostracized her. Christopher Lane calls this "social disaffiliation" (1994, 37), and Jutta Brückner calls this "social exclusion," that is, an exclusion not based on lack of money, but one in which women and people of color are excluded from the class structure and are considered separated from its organization of class hierarchy. Such exclusion brings with it a sense of "shame" that is used by "capitalist society . . . as a disciplinary measure" (as cited in Kosta and McCormick 1996, 350). Gatekeeper women assist the culture in turning out future generations of women exactly to fit given specifications.

So long as women accept the conventions of constructed female conduct necessary for their acceptance into the culture, so long as they do not rebel against those conventions that decree women deviant by male standards, then no change can take place. No destabilization, no transformation of the culture's prevailing conceptions of gendered power relations is possible. In most cases, as in Chicano culture, this is done by the patriarchy in terms of inequitable gendered power relations by constructing differing and constraining gender role success models for women. As Foucault stated so brilliantly about sex, it is not a fixed entity, but cuturally deployed and manipulated by "cultural regimes" of power:

The central issue, then . . . is not to determine whether one says yes or no to sex, whether one formulates prohibitions or permissions, whether one asserts its importance or denies its effects, or whether one refines the words one uses to designate it; but to account for the fact that it is spoken about, to discover who does the speaking, the positions and viewpoints from which they speak, the institutions which prompt people to speak about it and which store and distribute the things that are said. . . . What is at issue, briefly, is the over-all "discursive fact," the way in which sex is "put into discourse." (1980, 111)

Quintana provides an alternative–through the use of words also. She consciously uses words as bridges "reaching out to other women, linking them to one another so that no woman with a free spirit will feel the world has forgotten her, so that women who have felt trapped or imprisoned by the word can also begin to look to the word for its reviving and liberating force" (1995, 215). This is what Cisneros is doing in "Zapata's Eyes" by writing Inés's story in Inés's words from Inés's perspective, not as has previously been the case. Historically Inés has been noticed only because of her relationship to Zapata, as women in all cultures are noticed, according to their relationship to their men. As Ruth Behar muses:

So often I have wondered: Where are the women among those gigantic looming shadows of the male liberators, tyrants, generals, colonels and revolutionaries who have ruled the countries of Latin America and the Caribbean for the past century? Did women not fight alongside Simón Bolivar and Jose Martí? Have women not shared beds with revolutionaries like Emiliano Zapata and Pancho Villa, or dictators like Batista and Duvalier? Were there no women in the Sierra Maestra with Fidel Castro? The history textbooks tell the story of Spanish America's bloody national struggles for independence, decolonization and freedom as if women were never there, as if women had no place in the nation and in history. Is there really no story for those women other than the romance? (1995, 6)

Blea blames men for consciously or unconsciously distorting history in order to make it seem as if only they have performed significant accomplishments. Further she blames the mainstream Anglo culture for working in binaries, for being responsible for making men significant, whereas women and especially women of color are made insignificant (1991, 132). Yet, in truth, this dichotomizing or binarism in gendered power relations is a global one, as well as a characteristic of Chicana culture. Of many examples to prove this global proclivity on the part of male rulers, I point to a better known one than Cisneros's Inés, at least in American culture–to Pocahontas, in relation to English history and literature. Like the mass of women everywhere, named in history or unrecorded, she "did not produce her own narrative, and the documents written by Englishmen display a remarkable indifference to her opinion of them" (Robertson 1996, 553).

Although Cisneros titled her cuento "Zapata's Eyes," Inés is looking at Zapata while *his* eyes are closed. As she did in "Bien Pretty Lupe," Cisneros is reversing "the specular economy of patriarchy" (Scheman 1993, 152) where women serve as eternal students to men in the classroom of life, always dutifully taking notes while their professors lecture. Only what their male professors feel, do, think, and value as they strut in front of the classroom has meaning. For women to raise their hands and question their professors, to speak up from their perspective would be considered disruptive. Inés does more than gaze at Zapata while he is sleeping. Her doing so gives rise to silent musing to herself about the nature of their relationship.

In detailing historical accounts of Mexican women from their own silenced perspective, Cisneros is challenging the perspective of male historians, which hitherto prevailed unchallenged. She is also obliquely referring to a second nationalist movement, the La Raza movement in the United States, approximately half a century later than the period when the events in "Zapata's Eyes" occur. In all the published histories of Mexico and biographies of Zapata, male scholars wrote only from a perspective of nationalistic ideology which excluded women from their histories as a (sub)class apart. In the La Raza movement, as well, Chicanas were outclassed, and masculinist discourse and perspective prevailed. Gendered power relations were still seen through "Zapata's Eyes." For years, as in the black power movement, their men and other Chicanas attacked Chicana feminists. They were accused of being divisive, of weakening the movement, of acting as dupes of white feminists whenever they attempted to use a "Chicana-centered" (Cohen 1996, 711) perspective and discourse, whenever they dared to question the blatant sexism of the movement's male leadership. If they continued to see things as through "Zapata's Eyes," through the masculinist perspective of the leaders of La Raza, if they accepted their exclusion as females and concerned themselves only about their common cause with Chicanos, then Chicanas would be included in the movement–as handmaidens and followers to the movement's male leaders in an extension of familism.

Inés has previously been seen only through "Zapata's Eyes." She is still reflected by what Zapata sees through his eyes when he looks at Inés and other women. Such a "gaze" in Freudian terms, according to Toril Moi, is "phallic activity linked to the anal desire for sadistic mastery of the object" (1985, 134). Luce Irigary's psychoanalytic critique of the male gaze in terms of Freud's essentialist construction of an Oedipus which he applied generically to all males, applies here also to what Zapata and his kind see when they gaze at Inés– generically all women. Oedipus who has "the ability to make capital out of ideals and out of mothers, wives-mothers, laws, gazes. . . . Oedipus will have all the mothers he wants, all laws in his favor, and the right to look at anything. . . . all or most, mothers, laws, views (or at any rate points of view). . . . As long as his love of looking is satisfied, his domination is secure" (1985, 81).

Notice, however, that Cisneros's Zapata is sleeping. His eyes are closed. By seeing events neither through "Zapata's Eyes" nor through Chicano eyes, Cisneros, through Inés, is taking a subject's position that reverses the male gaze where Chicanas are viewed as objects. Cisneros is not depicting Inés as thinking that her man is "sadly tender and vulnerable" as Behar imagines that Inés "imagines" (1995, 6) him to be. Rather, Cisneros is changing the perspective of the viewer when she has the woman in question speak to readers while the man sleeps. The man is silent for a change, a drastic shift from all previous historical representations of women's situation, especially because Zapata in male texts is a figure identified as a kind of "epic hero" in the Mexican Revolution, in the annals of male history. Inés gives her daughter, María Elena, as the reason for her desire to continue to live, whereas María Elena objects to being identified with her mother, the outcast Indian mistress of her father,. Again we see the motif of invalidating discourse used by men to control women, the masculinist discourse of the culture run by men who *man*ipulate the discourse and its meanings. Cisneros weaves this motif into so much of her work–in "'Mericans," in "Holy Night," in "Woman Hollering Creek," and other stories like "Zapata's Eyes," where the author epitomizes Inés as her symbol for all women not given their due.

Zapata is the symbol of the man in control, of the men who create the inequitable gendered power relations, the ones who have started it all, even ongoing external warfare between men and men, nations against nations. While Zapata sleeps, Inés attempts to reason him out of his machismo through appealing to his feeling for his daughter. Would he want his daughter to be treated by another man as he has treated Inés and still continues to do so? All that Inés has asked for, all that would make a difference is decent discourse– words–words spoken, or words written to reflect respect for herself and other women; not Othering, diminution, and even invisibility. Respectful words to her would be almost magical. They would bring her some peace, but he has never spoken such words to her because the Chicana's very "subjectivity is . . . *overridden* at the linguistic level by a gender referent that centers a Chicano masculinity and denies the Chicana an independent subjectivity" (Dernersesian 1993, 55). Although Inés and Emilio Zapata are historical Mexican characters, Cisneros extends them to trope the current Chicana-Chicano relationship, as the Chicana experience with the La Raza movement exposed. This is the major reason why Cisneros used Inés's story from Inés's perspective. Josefina López, the playwright, for one, has made it her business to make herself the protagonist in most of her plays:

By making myself the protagonist I am saying to the world that my experience, that of a woman and a Latina, is important and valid. I put myself as the protagonist in my writing and in my life because I refuse to allow a "white man" or any man to rescue me. I, like my characters, am in control of my destiny. By writing about myself and Latinos I am reclaiming my humanity that was taken away from me not just when the Spaniards raped Mexico, but when the first man raped the first woman. (1993, 45)

Cisneros's project in "Zapata's Eyes," as well as in all the cuentos of *Woman Hollering Creek*, is nothing less than monumental in its sweeping attempt to resolve so many Chicana issues.

Afterword: Chicanas and the Feminist Movement

The current rejection of the second-wave movement as essentialist because it saw all women (but really only white middle-and upper-class women, like themselves) as victims of a global masculinist *man*olith is equally essentialist. It dismisses this movement out of hand as dated, ahistoric, nonspecific, racist. Further, when feminists object to the abuses against ethnic women and women of color and Third World women as founded in patriarchal, hierarchical oppressions, they are dismissed by some Chicana feminists as Anglos–code for white and mainstream.

I agree with Martha Boesing, a second waver like myself, that "this kind of simplistic analysis" divides and conquers us, makes the second wavers appear to be "political New Age flakes," which embarrasses our daughters and causes them to reject us out of hand. This is a mistake on their part that probably dooms "them to repeat all our mistakes instead of learning from and building on our experience" (1996, 1020).

The refusal of certain contemporary Chicana critics to either look back at the past realistically or to look around at who is walking beside them–still–illustrates Boesing's view of what our "daughters" are doing to us. I wonder what makes any new feminists assume that second-wave feminists still now functioning, past and present are fixed forever in the past? Why can't we be assumed as also growing as we go, as some younger feminists are assuming for themselves, but not for us whom they imagine as frozen forever in those moments of time known as the second wave? Are all feminists of the same generation in any given time period, or even when they are from different generations identical according to generation, ethnicity, color, and class? Such narrow thinking replicates the essentialism they both fear and continually use as a discursive coded weapon against second wavers.

I for one am still very much alive and still believe–more strongly than ever–that feminists err when we concentrate solely on particularities, on differences within systems. Valorizing pockets of resistance through guerrilla warfare evades the necessity of focusing on the source, the roots of the system. These are very deep, very tangled and complex, very strong. They emanate from one source, globally, whether in feudal, communist, democratic, or socialist regimes. To focus on research that says, "You see, certain groups, classes, races of women at certain times and in certain places were not oppressed," is as if to point out oases in a vast desert of historical times and places. I disagree with Brian Massumi when he asserts about the "late-capitalist" system of power relations that ideology although still around and often very "virulent" is no longer a global, all-encompassing monolith of power. Now it is only one of many modes "of power" in a much "larger field" that cannot contain any one ideology. For this reason Massumi feels it is vital to "connect ideology to its real conditions of emergence. For these are now manifest, mimed by men of power" (1995, 104). Feminists have always been suspicious of patriarchal hegemonies for situating them not "at the bottom tier" (Resnik 1996, 969), but even further, outside the playing fields of the world. This is why we should never forget that in all cultures all over the globe women have never been and are not now where the seats of power are. That is, if we would even have a hope of instituting change in the system of inequitable gendered power relations.

Certain Chicana feminists and other feminists of color practice essentialism themselves when they valorize those feminists who practice particularism and identity politics over those feminists who prefer a global picture of oppression, and when they define the latter group as racists for attempting a more inclusive theory. The Chicanas do this when they perceive their group as valiant women of color struggling against stereotypes imposed on them by mainstream white feminists. Chicanas always depict these Anglo feminists as racists themselves, or tools of their racist menfolk, never imagining that they themselves could be practicing reverse racism. As a solution to either dread possibility, Teng advocates self-reflexivity, continually being consciously aware of our situatedness, or what special interests we might be supporting when we frame our questions for research (1996, 142–143).

We should continually use self-reflexivity, whoever we are, rather than insist on showing preferentiality by specific skin, gender, and class identities only. In a conversation with Nicholas Luhmann, Katherine Hayles agrees with me, at least in describing an earlier period in science studies "when you couldn't write an article without including a brief autobiography on who you were (1995, 33). In my more recent experience, if a feminist who is not visibly ethnic or a woman of color dares to write on topics about ethnic and women of color, she is dismissed out-of-hand by those who practice "identity politics" as a "privileged" woman presuming to "speak for" that group. She is denounced as "silencing the authoritative voices of experience" of that group. Thus anyone not by birth, race, ethnicity, or class from any special interest group is herself silenced.

Hayles also speaks to more current practice. She courageously points out that many publishers are wary of publishing work that does not originate "from within specific groups." She also speaks to current practice, as I myself observe it, of "college and university administrators" who "would hire only members of certain groups to teach courses which are connected to those groups" (1995, 33). This is again essentializing, to make the assumption that only members of a given group have the appropriate genetic makeup and experience to qualify as experts on given cultures in that field and then to validate and certify them only on those grounds. Whereas "identity politics" does provide critiques of the racism and sexism of traditional critics who valorize Enlightenment universalism, the advocates of "identity politics" in focusing only on differences among feminists reject the possibility of unification, identification, and collaboration with each other and across groups. As Peck warns, engaging in "power struggles between different collectivities in a world defined by scarcity . . . contributes to further polarization" (1994, 118).

Such is the thinking of black power advocates, whom Charles Hersch critiques for demanding that African Americans unite on the grounds of common interests, while also demanding that they act as if they march in lock-step, subordinating themselves entirely to the group leadership as though they were "interchangeable parts." He defines this choice of "order over individuality" as characteristic of "mainstream group politics" (1996, 115, 116). I view it instead as a style of leadership characteristic of traditional African chiefs historically. Like him, feminists believe that individualism in a group can deteriorate into anarchism whereas rigid "group solidarity" more often serves as a threat to individual expression than otherwise. Hersch's practical suggestion is that we be supportive of others, but not yield our identities in favor of others, "to contribute to the whole of which both [self and others] are a part" (1996, 119).

As Rhoda Lois Blumberg points out in her discussion of social movement theory, the problem is that such theory

concentrates on the sense of grievance of a disadvantaged group but generally fails to explain the paths to involvement of outsiders, persons from the dominant [or simply another] group whose sense of justice is outraged by perceived inequalities. By assuming that people join movements only because of a narrowly conceived self-interest, such theory overlooks white people in the civil rights movement, men in the women's movements, and Christians who saved Jewish lives during the Holocaust, to cite three examples. (1990, 167)

Some Chicana feminists I have discussed previously in this text assume that white women are distant, aloof, and condescending aliens. Those who lump all white women together as Others may well be losing opportunities to view as allies those who would walk beside them, who would support them. For a variety of reasons, there are women who might feel deeply about Chicana issues. Chicanas might view these women as allies, as resources (Beckwith 1996, 1055). They could be viewed as constituting "'a vertical class' that can coalesce around a 'column of injustices'" (Koelsch 1995, 21). Chicanas also miss out when they ignore men who are feminists who would ally themselves with them.

Like Katie King, who prefers to view simultaneous oppressions as "reductive" but "overlapping necessities" (1990, 86), Moraga argues powerfully and eloquently on the "danger" of even "ranking the oppressions." "Without an emotional, heartfelt grappling with the source of our own oppression, without naming the enemy within ourselves and outside of us, no authentic, non-hierarchical connection among oppressed groups can take place" (1981, 29). She critiques the male oppressor on the basis of "*externalizing*" his fears and "projecting them into the bodies of . . . whoever seems most 'other.'" Her most acute perception is that it is not really our being different that the oppressors of women fear, but that they are like women whom they have "shitted on" (1981, 32). They fear many things, especially the violent responses of those whom they have oppressed. Beyond this, Moraga believes, those whom men have oppressed have the same fears because "each of us in some way has been both oppressed and the oppressor" (1981, 32). It is not enough to complain about what men have done to women because we have failed to support each other by internalizing oppression and then reversing it upon ourselves. We are afraid to admit how deeply inscribed in all of us are inequitable gendered power relations and its masculinist discourse in all its forms.

Moraga speaks from personal experience on several counts, about the necessity to "recognize privilege" in a culture that would elide it. In relation to the major topic of my text, the outclassing of Chicanas, she speaks with most relevance to this issue of "privilege." She experienced it when it was used as a weapon against her, as well as when she herself used it. The white skin she inherited from her father gave her one privilege where in every other way she was oppressed, as are many ethnic women who appear white.

Why assume disagreement among groups of feminists on such matters? Why not assume that such a world is not any woman's, ideologically, that many women become feminists because they want no women to be victimized? Castillo refuses to be part of a world in which women are considered "prey." She asserts that in the world that she would have, no one would be treated as women are in Arab cultures when they are forced to "cover their faces" and forced to submit to clitoridectomies and infibulations, to "allow their sexual parts to be/torn out" (1995, 90). But when feminists from Third World countries defend their patriarchal, hierarchical cultures by pointing out some isolated examples historically where some women in those cultures had decent lives, then they do not define themselves as gatekeepers of their culture, or as cultural apologists, but as nationalists. Particularism, identity politics, and ethnic Balkanization all play into this distracting of feminists away from the source of oppression.

Those who complain about second-wave feminists as having excluded them, themselves exclude second wavers and the many great achievements we made and continue to make. These objections perpetuate the inequitable gendered power relations of the oppressive hierarchy that they are supposedly working to end (Harding 1995, 144). Some Chicanas' favorite complaint is that second wavers were narrow and racist in our attempts to make sweeping changes for all women based on our situatedness and that therefore our definition of "women" too often included ourselves only–privileged, white, middle- and upper-class women. Pérez, for example, argues speciously that Chicana protest against Chicano machismo is due solely to their being influenced by ignorant Anglo feminists to echo their antagonism to their menfolk. Again, the truth is that when other feminists express and emphasize their distaste for machismo, Chicanas are told by Chicanos that Anglo feminists criticize machismo in order to distract Chicanas so that they do not notice that the Anglo feminists are really racists. Pérez is in a bind here. She cannot and will not define other Chicanas as guilty of racism when they join Anglo feminists in criticism of Chicano machismo. So she conveniently ignores the fact that although many Chicanas do deplore machismo, she only accuses Anglo feminists of being racist and heterosexist, as well. It is they who have prevented linking between themselves and Chicana feminists, not only because they are racist, but also because they focus primarily on phallocentrism (Pérez 1993, 68).

There is much controversy on the meaning of machismo both within the Chicana community and outside of it. In all cases, in all the writers and critics analyzed in this text, machismo "connote[s] arrogance and male pride and emotionality" (Knouse et al. 1995, 3), although Knouse et al., like Pérez, maintain that this "particularly important yet highly misunderstood Hispanic value" is misunderstood by "many Anglo Americans." It is Knouse's position, like that of many apologists, that "[I]n reality . . . true machismo signifies duty and loyalty and strong bonds of honor in all Hispanic cultures" (1995, 3). García and Sosa Riddell, like Pérez, see Anglo conspiracy as the source for the bad press about the myth of Mexican and Chicano machismo. According to their interpretation, the Anglo capitalist colonizers manipulate the negative public impression of this myth as a tool of ideology, as just one more excellent reason out of many for them to oppress and exploit Mexican men and Chicanos as inferiors. In propagating this myth, the Anglo colonizers and oppressors also create and perpetuate damaging stereotypes about Mexican men and Chicanos (García 1995, 402–403, 364–365; Sosa Riddell 1995, 411). What bothers Sosa Riddell even more is that Chicanos then have to justify themselves–their culture, their customs, all their ways. They are positioned by the Anglo rulers so as to have to be defensive about their traditions and themselves, apologetic, believing that they would be better in some way if they imitated Anglos. She also suspects that if more Chicanos ever rose to administrative levels, they would discriminate against Chicanas even more than Anglo males (1995, 408). Like Eddie, in Cisneros's "Bien Pretty Lupe," some Chicanos feel that to achieve success they should emulate Anglos in every way they can, thus denying, casting aside their heritage and identity.

So it is that the machismo myth is used to socially control Chicanos by the Anglos. But it doesn't stop there. At the same time, the Anglos perpetuate and re-create complementary stereotypes of machismo–passivity and docility–onto Chicanas. Reasoning in this way, Sosa Riddell then concludes that the Anglo myth of machismo led to and perpetuated the images of Chicanos and Chicanas as inferior and "subordinate" (1995, 411) in status to Anglos.

I fail to see how white and Chicana feminists both complaining about machismo makes Chicana feminists the dupe of either the Anglo male rulers, or the racist white feminists, or how this exposes their racism. It seems, rather, that cheap shots are being taken against any Anglo feminists who are negative about machismo, because Pérez doesn't give the benefit of the doubt to them or to the Chicana feminists who make the same complaints. Or else, it doesn't occur to Pérez or Knouse, et al. that both groups critique machismo because it is indeed nothing more nor less than an unjust use of power in gender relations. In fact, it is such thinking as Pérez and Knouse et al. here reveal, such an assumption of racism *a priori* that itself illustrates precisely what they are complaining about.

Pérez and many other critics I have analyzed in this text lump together all other feminists than women of color as Anglo feminists, despite the fact that they are not a monolithic group. In fact many ethnic feminists who appear Anglo do not ordinarily identify with Anglo women so much as they do with women of color. Some of these women even define themselves as women of color, despite their external appearance. They are unnecessarily put on the defensive by a divisive and essentialist discourse that subsumes their historic and current experiences of oppression under the rubric of Anglo. Some Chicana critics use the terms Anglo/European/Anglo/American for any and all feminists not visibly women of color, and, specifically in this instance, not visibly Chicana.

Like Pérez, Sosa Riddell distinguishes between white feminists and Chicanas, making the same charge as has now become so common that it is not even questioned. White feminists only demand equal access to the "American pie," whereas Chicanas primarily desire the "restoration" (1995, 409) of their own traditional historical customs where they had "control." By the term "restoration," Sosa Riddell is implying that before the Spanish Conquest of what is now Mexico, women had such "control." Given the fact that the princess Malintzin/Malinche was sold into slavery by her own mother and new stepfather, such a conceptualization seems to stretch credibility. This claim is similar to those that some feminists make when they theorize a time before patriarchy in Western civilization when women had such "control." In reality, this did occur, but rarely, and in only a few scattered social groupings globally–such as in some Native American societies on the North American continent, in Hawaii, and Africa. Patriarchy has been the prevailing model for power and control throughout recorded history and in all cultures globally.

With admirable courage, Moraga has defended white or Anglo feminists from what she calls this "alongside-our-man-knee-jerk-phenomenon" (1981, 30) by many Chicana critics when they contend that the white feminists and their movement are irrelevant to their needs. By the same token, the particularists who today critique second wavers as a (wo)monolithic mass, all of the same class and race, all thinking white, seem to have the same failing as the Anglo feminists they excoriate. They are convinced that by virtue of their being ethnic and women of color, racism can only go one way, directed only at them, and that they are guiltless of that stain themselves. Castillo, for example, essentializes all white women into one generic white woman who by inheriting her "father's library" and "her brother's friends," inherits the great white father's discourse and codes, as well as his protection. With "Nahua eyes" from her Indian ancestry, with a "Spanish surname," which may indicate enforced Spanish conquistador/colonizer relations she has inherited, she speaks Spanish as her primary language. "English syntax" is foreign to her and so difficult for her to enunciate that she likens the sounds she makes to walking "with the grace of a clubbed foot" (1995, 63). She and other women of color have never had such privileges as the privileged white woman of the dominant U.S. culture.

It is impossible for me to relate to Castillo's first argument, addressed to an essentialist idea of white woman. My people/I had no library to inherit, nor could we/I afford one. My foremothers were not allowed to read and write. In the United States, they themselves, as well as mainstream culture, oppressed and harassed me exactly as Chayo was harassed by family and community, although in Yiddish/English because I disobeyed them and pursued an education, instead of marriage.

And like Castillo, I also speak "with the grace of a clubbed foot" because I am the first generation of my family to have been born on American soil and learned to speak by emulating their foreign accents, sounds, gestures, and hand movements. All my professional life I was called "dumb and stupid." I was made the object of mockery, of educational and job discrimination because of my "crude, lower class Brooklyn Jewish" accent, sound, gestures, hand movements, and loud, strident, grating, voice, especially when under stress. Such examples of discrimination, based entirely on difference in sounds and movements are exactly what Chicanas and Asians experience.

Nevertheless, because of my outer appearance I am automatically included by too many women of color feminists in their definitions of Anglo feminists. This is ironic, because it does not take my experience and that of my ancestors into account, but lumps all apparent whites together by racial appearance. These melting pot chefs for everyone but themselves and their own group must have no knowledge of historical and contemporary oppressions, except as suffered by their own group. My ancestors have only known peace and plenty in pockets of time and isolated places. Anti-Semitism is a global phenomenon lasting over millennia, historically and currently, a global oppression enduring far longer than theirs, if they insist upon comparing and ranking oppressions.

I deeply resent this essentialism and reverse racism by the practitioners of Afrocentrism or any other centrism, and I write as a long-time, respected professor of Africana Studies, as well as a pioneering expert in ethnic studies. To take the external shell of an identity, a human envelope, to box it in as being the representative of all they are angry at, the object of whatever gripes they have against a person who is not of color is reverse racism. No one has a right to define anyone else's identity.

I do understand Chicana reasons for stressing apparent differences rather than commonalities with Anglo feminists whom they consider privileged under the patriarchy. However, this is the case only if these Chicanas would be willing to consider such feminists as trustees in a prison, or as "house" slaves compared with "field" slaves. As Isabel in Denise Chávez's play *Novena Narratives*, proclaims: "As far as I'm concerned, when you're a woman, no time is easy. And when you're an artist, it's worse. Those born rich suffer as much as those born poor" (1988, 88).

The argument, as Castillo's poem illustrates, goes that white women are privileged, apparently all white women. In our case, Jewish feminists, we are privileged here and now, regardless of the past. Today we are not discriminated against if our skin color is fair, if our religion and ethnic identity is not publicized, if our features and coloring are Anglo. Nor are we discriminated against if our accents and ways of moving do not evidence any traces of Jewish ethnicity, or if we become invisible ethnics, as many Jewish women have chosen to become.

However, if we do "pass," merge in with the mainstream population, then we appear like any number of light-skinned and Anglo-Saxon-featured Chicana, Asian Americans, Native Americans, and African Americans who have passed and continue to choose to do so. The most popular argument by centrics is that we Jewish women *could* pass any time we wanted to do so. We have choice in the matter, whereas most women of color do not. They cannot pass. For many Jewish feminists, however, as for Rios, "crossing-over" or becoming a "*Vendida* or Sell-out*" through rejection of "one's class or cultural identity" (1995, 210) is not a viable choice. It is not even a possibility.

Passing comes with a very high price to pay, exactly as other ethnics and people of color who have done this realize. Many Jewish feminists do not wish to pass as Anglo, to fit into such a category, even if we could and even if we appear interchangeable, visually. There would be no Jews then. In fact, our very identity as Jews is based on the fact that we could have assimilated into certain cultures historically and did not or were denied any opportunities to do so. That we are still Jews means that our ancestors did not choose to or were not permitted to pass. To pass as Anglo in the Chicana sense of that term is to deny our very identity as Jews.

Therefore it is an insult to Jewish feminists when women of color feminists point to our whiteness of skin and maintain that it privileges us, because such a privilege can only ever come at the expense of our Jewishness, the denial of our ancestry, our culture. For many reasons and in many ways, we relate far more to Chicana, other Latina, Asian American, Native American, and African American women than to mainstream white feminists. This is why many Jewish feminists, like myself are scholars of multiethnic American literature and ethnic literature globally–not because we are latching onto fads, but because we have, with good reason, always identified with other ethnic women and women of color.

Women of color might question themselves more, show more self-reflexivity, if they feel they have no grounds for identification with Jewish feminists. They should not automatically assume that they themselves lack bias. They should not automatically assume that they don't identify with certain of their sisters only because of their sisters' problematic attitudes and situatedness, rather than the other way around.

Some women of color do read histories about Mexico, the slave trade, or the deplorable Japanese internment camps in the United States. They might in addition see films such as *Life Is Beautiful*, *Schindler's List*, or *Europa, Europa*, familiarize themselves with Jewish history, or read Holocaust memoirs. They might also read and dialogue with other ethnic and women of color feminists from other groups.

Chicana separatists respond with great anger when non-Chicana feminists tell the truth about their cultures. Simultaneously, they dismiss Chicana feminists from their own groups whom they vilify for being Aunt Tómasas if they dare to make the same critiques about Chicano culture as the white feminists. These Chicanas might stop censoring and ostracizing and policing feminists like Moraga and Anzaldúa from within their own groups who disagree with them when they wish to talk about some commonalities with white feminists, to express sisterhood, to hold out hands across the ethnic fences and fences of color.

Moraga and Anzaldúa share my vision and serve as examples in this regard:

[W]e women on the bottom throughout the world can form an international feminism. For separatism by race, nation, or gender will not do the trick of revolution. *Autonomy*, however, is *not* separatism. We recognize the right and necessity of colonized peoples throughout the world, including Third World women in the U.S., forming independent movements toward self-government. But ultimately, we must struggle together. (1981a, 196)

Moraga and Anzaldúa, both Chicanas, write exactly what I write and feel exactly as I do about white mainstream feminists. Anzaldúa writes that she refuses to exclude whites when it comes to those she loves in order to take a "politically correct stance." She refuses to allow "barriers" to be erected between herself and "kindred spirits" whatever their differences of "color, class, and gender" (1981b, 206) from herself. She deplores the ever higher walls, the ever widening gulf, the ever more profound silences between groups of women. She conceptualizes her role as that of "a bridge" between whites and other races as extremely difficult. This is the case because by speaking out she feels she has to "be hard" on her own people who view themselves as "victims" of oppression by whites. She also has to call them "on a lot of shit like our own racism, our fear of women and sexuality" (1981b, 207).

Anzaldúa also makes the common claim that when she associated with white women in the Feminist Writers' Guild, the latter would wonder about why women of color did not come to their meetings and readings and that she knew the reason. They did not appreciate tokenism, or being made invisible, or treated as inferiors and not being engaged in dialogue as equals (1981b, 206). In deploring this gap between feminists and women of color, Anzaldúa and some women of color inadvertently place white feminists in a no-win situation. If white feminists do not cite or relate to women of color, then they are called to task for ignorant racism. If they do, they are excoriated for having the unmitigated gall to speak for women of color, to appropriate their voices. Anzaldúa vividly describes this insensitivity as "a rape of our tongue." Women of color who permit white feminists to get away with this are complicitous with that rape (1981b, 206).

What's a feminist, to do, then? A feminist who is not "white" in the sense that Anzaldúa and other women of color mean, but who is presumed to be so on the basis of appearance? Or even if a feminist is white, who is not intending to speak for anyone else white or of color, but is attempting to speak *to* her sisters? To silence white feminists on the grounds that they are presuming to speak *for* their sisters of color whenever they so much as express their opinions is reverse racist practice. Rios suggests revising Gayatri Chakravorty Spivak's suggestion that feminists should learn to speak to (rather than listen to or speak for) other kinds of women than mainstream women. She suggests, instead, that we dialogue with one another. Of course, as both Spivak and Rios point out, this is to go on the assumption that other women wish to speak to and with mainstream feminists (Spivak 1988, 295; Rios 1995, 210).

Like Anzaldúa, I believe that patriarchy and its enforced naturalized heterosexism have held ultimate power too long. Like her, I feel both women of color and white feminists see me as alien to them and their worldview, that I also have had to construct my own "universe." I also felt for a long time that I had to "belong to myself and not to any one people" (1981, 209), nor to any one culture. Like her, I continually plead in all my work for all women as well as like-minded men to come together globally:

Only *together* can we be a force. I see women as a network of kindred spirits, a kind of family; that not all of us have the same background, but we empathize and identify with each other's oppressions. We do not have the same ideology, nor do we derive similar solutions. . . . But these different affinities are not opposed to each other. . . . I with my own affinities and my people with theirs can live together and transform the planet. (1981b, 209)

I am heartened by Anzaldúa's galvanizing idea of a "mestiza consciousness." It suggests ways for different identity categories to produce new subjectivities that define their identity not by remaining within racial, class, and gender group borders but by crossing them or revisioning them (O'Driscoll 1996, 33; Yarbro-Bejarano 1994, 25).[1]

My reading of Chicana works does not bear out Nancy Sternbach's contention that feminist priorities are different from those of Chicana and other ethnic and women of color feminists. Further, my reading of white feminists does not bear out her second contention, that their priorities were only sexism and that they were not concerned with any other aspect of inequitable power relations such as issues of class and ethnicity. In fact, from the very beginnings of the second-wave feminist movement, these issues were indeed considered interconnected by most feminists, white, ethnic, and of color. Rather, Sternbach, in essentializing white feminists, is herself guilty of what she is accusing them: taking only one aspect, namely that of Chicana writers, into account (1989, 48-61). Certainly people who lacked sensitivity to the situations and experiences of others participate(d) in the feminist movement. Insensitive people obsessed only with their own agenda, their own concerns and issues exist in all movements, in all areas of life. Far more so than Sternbach would grant. In reality, the themes and perspectives of Chicana writers and white feminist writers, as well as other ethnic and women of color feminists are similar. In fact, the concerns and issues of feminists globally throughout all cultures of the world are similar. This is the case because women around the globe have concerns and issues in common.

Unlike Sternbach, Norma Alarcón situates herself within the feminist movement, as well as in Women's Studies. However, she dismisses Women's Studies. She conflates this discipline with white feminists for the same reason as does Sternbach. Women's Studies, they both believe, is deeply entrenched in the liberalism and individualism of "Angloamerican bourgeois feminist theorists." Alarcón dismisses their worldviews as outmoded, albeit still of interest historically. Her major complaint against these theorists, like Sternbach's complaints against the simplistic essentialism of "white feminists," is that "they are not complex enough to explain our diverse sociosymbolic formations, positionalities or heterogeneous histories" (1995, 189). Perhaps this was the case to some extent with certain leading voices in the second-wave feminist movement of the late sixties, all throughout the seventies, and into the mid-eighties. These voices were not by any means the only ones, as some second wavers, such as myself, are testifying in an attempt to set the record straight. Calling attention to a blatant, fundamental weakness in the theory of the few white mainstream second-wave feminists who achieved notoriety does not mean that the feminist movement did not include other groups of women than our own birth groups in our theory and activism, then and now.

I ask then, in all due respect, of Alarcón and Sternbach, in relation to their critique of white feminists as parochial, simplistic, and racist, are you yourself not exposing the same qualities when you do that? Also, is it not about time to stop concentrating on your differences from white mainstream feminists? They have been whipped now for their sins of omission for nearly fifteen years. How long can you beat the dead mare of token second wavers? Especially in view of the fact that such omissions were and are also still being routinely made by some ethnic and women of color feminists in terms of white women and in terms of other ethnicities and races than their own? A focus limited to their own group and their own priorities is by no means unique only to white feminists. This is evidenced by the examples of parallel insularity on the part of Chicana critics that I have cited, as well as recognition of that insularity by other Chicanas who disagree with Alarcón's and Sternbach's position.

Just as we would not expect all Chicanas to take one monolithic stand on any issue, especially to take cheap and easy shots against second-wave feminists, we should not stereotype second wavers as one united mass of selfish insularity. Most critics of any group are broader in their perspectives, agendas, and sensibilities than those figureheads the ethnic and women of color critics drag out over and over again to use as examples of typical feminist ethnocentricity. In fact, they are no longer bothering to specifically identify the offensive white feminists by name, just as a generic group–as white feminists–or as Anglo feminists. The litany of their sins has been so often repeated that it has become gospel about a movement, the second-wave movement that inspired millions of women of all races and classes throughout the world, including many men. The feminist movement is one of the two greatest movements of the second half of the twentieth century. Many Asian American, Chicana, and African American feminists wince when they read their sisters' arguments that they should ignore the calls of white feminists to fight sexism on the grounds that there was a white female conspiracy against their men. And they wince at the argument that they should stand (well) behind their men during the revolution in a united battle against racism. Period. And forget all about sexism until after that battle is won.

I for one am not one of those feminists that Anzaldúa resents for being "boarders in the borderlands" (1987, 194) whom she claims speak for, instead of, to Third World feminists because they romanticize Chicana lives, envy them, or feel guilty about being privileged white women. Since when is human curiosity and learning to the point of becoming expert enough to write and speak about matters outside of one's own little square of birth situatedness a quality to be deplored? Humans have pursued an enormous range of interests *outside* and beyond their own narrow birth turf since the dawn of humankind. Such a phenomenon is widely defined as becoming educated.

Cornel West, the African American philosopher shares my continuing anxiety about the identity politics that Sternbach and Anzaldúa expose in the statements I have cited above. He fears that if its advocates do not accord recognition to universal human experiences, then "parochialism, provincialism, narrow particularism" will ensue (1993, 122). Without "an understanding of human universality" he maintains, "there cannot be significant social movements" (1993, 124). I wonder how ethnic and women of color critics and writers can fail to perceive that a global male hegemony oppresses all women and that its enormous power "erase(s) difference" (Robertson 1996, 577) between women?

A variety of ethnic writers and critics have made the same complaints about similar problems for years now. Yet they complained and still complain, as though unaware that anyone else from any another group than theirs was also complaining, and about the same problems! Alarcón rightly deplores this ignorance of other groups' literature as limitations, but only for students and only because they are taught about groups "in isolation from each other" (1995, 193). However, she directs her complaint only against mainstream feminist academics, not against women of color or ethnic feminists, as well. She writes as if the latter groups are somehow free from limitations in their knowledge and understanding of other women from other groups and that white feminists alone are limited in their knowledge and understanding of other women from other groups.

True, like some women of color feminists, some mainstream Anglo feminists were unaware of any other groups having similar complaints as theirs and thus failed to include them, or did so at best, by subsuming them within their theory. For a long time and too often into the present, the only other group they ever took into consideration was African American women writers. Indeed, it sometimes appears to many of us ethnic feminists that mainstream feminists are wearing blinders in terms of all groups other than African American women. They gesture toward and even sometimes actually cite African American writers and critics. But rarely, if ever, do they include any other ethnic and women of color writers and critics, even in their gracious nods and waves.

Lately, however, more mainstream feminists, who are by far the greatest number of feminists in and outside of academia, have begun to read other groups of women than their own and African American writers and critics. Still, as I write these words there is little evidence that ethnic and women of color feminists are reading each other and are knowledgeable about our commonalities, although they never fail to emphasize our differences. Indeed, my position is akin to Ann Taylor Allen's, that "[t]o establish a new basis for the discussion both of commonalties and differences is the most important challenge facing both feminist movements and the field of women's studies" (1996, 172–173). This text is my attempt to put that position into practice.

I believe that we must work toward including each other's groups without yielding to the temptation to fragment on an ethnic and national basis, a tendency that Allen sees increasing globally. To avoid both pitfalls, Allen suggests creating "alliances" built on "respect for difference and recognition of commonality" (1996, 174). Perhaps the first feminist to envision such a possibility and use that term politically, I called for a "rainbow" more than twenty-five years ago in a Middlesex County (N. J.) N.O.W. publication, *The N.O.W. Sound*. For many years I issued this call in my classroom, as well, replete with statistics on the blackboard, showing to my students how many votes all women and "minorities" could amass if only we could unite, at least on shared experiences as women. This was long before the Rev. Jackson's concept of a "rainbow coalition" and long before my own position was more widely distributed than in an editorial in a N.O.W. newsletter in the early seventies (Kafka 1997, 155–171).

As M. Rivka Polatnick points out, my long-held appeals to unify around "women's common differences" (1996, 680) rather than on our differences is now the major goal of feminism and Women's Studies programs and departments. She believes, as I do, that from a scholarly perspective, this effort enables us to better understand the relationship of inequitable gendered power relations with other inequitable power relations under patriarchy, such as the gendering of class structure which is my chosen topic in this work. However, whereas I view our commonalities as providing a bridge across women's differences globally, Polatnick sees our differences as providing a bridge that will increase our comprehension of our situatedness in that vast network of systems under patriarchy, rather than serving as a wedge for heightening our differences (1996, 704).

For millennia my birth group has suffered and endured an entirely different history from that which (too) many ethnic and women of color critics and writers seem to have learned about when they lump us in with American white mainstream groups. Our history, one of almost universal global oppression, led to the Holocaust in our time. First-generation American Jews like myself are still alive. We are still close to our very different history of genocide and persecution in another world and time from that of the Miss Anns that ethnic and women of color writers, including Chicanas, imagine they are addressing when they critique the white mainstream feminist movement. Many of us protest being lumped together with WASP American men and women, with mainstream groups with whom we have no shared history, no prior knowledge of, nor participation in events in the United States or Western or Eastern Europe.

Yes, we have a shared skin color, but nothing else–not religion, not ethnicity, and, above all, not history. We were the oppressed, the Other, throughout history, on a scale lasting so long in time and so broadly in terms of our affected populations, such as no other group has ever experienced. I include in this claim even the natives of what is now the Caribbean, Mexico, and parts of the Southwestern United States under the onslaught of the conquistadors. I include in this claim, even enslaved Africans under the onslaught of the Europeans. The oppression, slaughter, and injustice that these groups as groups experienced lasted several centuries. Only Native Americans suffered comparably to Jews and comparatively briefly. The Native Americans were defined as "enemy aliens" and, as such, became the objects of an official governmental policy to exterminate them all as a group, which is genocide. By 1890, there were very few Native American males left alive over the age of eleven in what is now the United States. Similarly, by 1945, official Nazi governmental policy, had exterminated European Jewry, whose population comprised the majority of Jews.

In addition, I identify with women whose writing matches my own experiences in life, not only because of persecution and oppression of my ethnic group, but by class. My maternal grandmother was illiterate, my mother was a sixth grade graduate. All three of us experienced the greatest of difficulties in the pursuit of a decent life: my foremothers, just to survive in the face of pogroms and anti-Semitism in Europe, and myself to survive and succeed, by the most tremendous exertions of endurance and strength of will. All throughout my life sexism has been directed against me by my own family, my relatives, my friends, my colleagues, my students, my employers, the general public, in every institution, and combined with anti-Semitism, as well, everywhere.

At this stage in my life, most of my adult years have been spent in the academy as a student first and then as a professor and administrator. I fervidly hope that the time will come very soon when scholars do not have to justify themselves when they choose a subject. I would like to live to see the day when it will not automatically be assumed that a white-skinned ethnic feminist scholar who presumes to write about ethnic and women of color writers and critics other than her own birth group is therefore acting as a voyeur or a tourist. I would like to see this knee-jerk assumption come to an end. I would like to see this belief that women from white-skinned groups who write about women of other groups position these Others as "a nonspeaker (a silent subaltern) because the privileged linguistic practices cannot hear, translate or transcode (with a residue of non-equivalence) what is said" (Alarcón 1995, 191).

Why does this argument run only one way? Why is it not considered possible for ethnic and women of color writers and critics to have difficulty hearing *me* because they speak from "privileged linguistic practices" from within their own group, which excludes *their* presumed Others? They make the unexamined assumption that a white woman's voice is automatically more "privileged" and insensitive than theirs. Does belonging to and speaking from some inner group that gives a safe space from which to take cheap shots at mainstream feminists make some women of color writers and critics any more deserving than mainstream feminists? Unfortunately, the current generation remembers only the "self-righteous, privileged atmosphere," the "airy cheerfulness" of second-wave feminist leaders when women of color critiqued "the whiteness of their organizations" (Wilson 1999, 4). On the other hand, many members of the latter group bend over backward to try to make amends, to try to understand, to try to link with their sisters, even though clumsily? Is embittered separatism from and mockery of their presumed ignorance, insensitivity, or guilt tripping mainstream feminists a positive and productive solution to our mutual problems?

Why can't any of our voices be considered as just another voice joining in with like voices in a common struggle, a common goal? I fervidly hope that a writer's passionate interest in a subject will suffice some day. She will not be immediately subjected to the knee-jerk assumption that a white writer can write only through the lens of uncomprehending and insensitive condecension because she is not a woman of color, or the assumption that she writes only as the result of a fad. She must be pursuing a sleazy, easy interest in an area that she thinks is "hot" to study, or she must be a "politically correct," "bleeding heart liberal."

Since I entered ethnic studies (as a pioneer in the field in 1976), my research and interest in ethnic literature is hardly new. Rather, because of my background and personal experience of oppression and because of my feminism, I identified with other ethnic and women of color writers and critics. I do agree, however, as I have stated above, that many traditional theorists and many feminist theorists have indeed failed to expand the heritage and ideas of Chicanas into their theories and practices. In addition, many feminists are justifiably accused of failing to include all women in their organizations with respect (Bonilla Santiago 1995, 217). In this regard, Blea contends that African American and Hispanic women were the first to form and build coalitions to confront their oppression in terms of specific issues for themselves as women of color (1991, 81). Further, she deplores the lack of sisterhood between Chicanas and Anglo women, although she concedes that nationwide some women from these groups are attempting to make up for this lack (1991, 102).

I am neither Anglo nor Chicana. My family was persecuted in their countries of diaspora to the point of Holocaust for those members who remained. Once here, we learned only about Anglo history and Anglo male life on this continent from school and the media. In the early sixties I was "traditionally" trained to specialize in English (specificially, Victorian) literature at a time when there was no other training available or even yet conceived of in graduate schools. In 1976, I became one of the first scholars in the nation to offer a course in higher educaion in ethnic American literature The course I developed then covered only Other ethnic American writers than those previously taught in the traditional American literature canon. For the first time in their lives students had the opportunity to read the works of African American, Asian American, Native American, Chicana/o and Latina/o writers. Since then, I have been engaged with many other mainstream, ethnic, and women of color feminists in a ferocious, ongoing struggle in the American academy to include ethnic and women of color authors on a global basis into the higher education canon. Recently, I have begun to publish appeals to Anglo mainstream feminists to routinely include the works of ethnic American women, women of color writers, and women writers globally, into the feminist canon, in their courses and in their research, as I myself have done for so many years.

I also include myself in the small number of women whom Blea notes as working to fill in the lack, not only of a sense of community with each other, but of knowledge, one of the other, of writers from groups other than our own. African American women writers are unfamiliar with other women writers. Asian American writers seem familiar only with the works of African American women writers, besides their own. Meanwhile, many Chicana and other Latina writers talk disparagingly only about Anglo women writers and scholars. As I have pointed out, they rarely cite from specific works to anchor their critiques, either from works by other groups of women of color or from Anglo feminists. Blea, for example, focuses only on Anglo women, scolding them for their failings in relation to Chicanos and Chicanas. Evidently she writes from her own personal experience and anecdotal evidence, but like too many others, she does not point to specific instances of omission to prove her point, nor does she indict any other ethnic and women of color writers for their sins of omission.

Such omissions are due, either to ignorance of other groups' literature, or to a desire to protect their own group, as well as women from other ethnic and women of color groups from charges for which they wish to accuse only white mainstream feminists. If they read across the ethnicities and the color lines, they would perceive that very few writers and critics are aware of what writers and critics in other groups are writing. In fact, they all have the same complaints, all stated with the same outrage, as if the oppression were limited only to themselves and their own group, or at most, one other group, such as the same few iconized African American critics and writers being referred to with respect over and over again.

I also include myself on Blea's short list on the basis of my activist praxis as a second waver , as well as lengthy academic experience in ethnic studies, and my previous theoretical feminst projects, including this current one. Through it all, I have been thrilled to join and participate in one of the most powerful movements of my time. I have celebrated my life as an ethnic, bicultural woman with outrage at the seemingly endless cycle of oppression of all women, with joy in the struggle to end that oppression, with passionate commitment to the feminist movement and to feminist scholarship.

At one point Blea does clearly separate Jewish women from Anglo women. Still she lumps them both together as distinct from Chicanas when she tells readers that she has herself entered into "international Chicano-Jewish dialogues and political and cultural exchange trips" (1991, 138). She also knows of there being a dialogue between women internationally and American members of the Board of the *YWCA*. She complains about the Anglo women in that organization for wanting to control and direct the latter organization. However, in any grouping, men within those groups would consider certain members of those groups of a lower order than themselves. For example, Anglo men would still claim their superiority over Anglo and all other women members of socially subordinated groups by class according to their gender, race, and ethnicity.

What has been Blea's experience with Anglo women? She complains bitterly about their contribution to Chicano and Chicana disempowerment by taking work and other perqs away from Hispanics because of the privileging of Anglo women over them. Further, Anglo women have not yet confronted their sense of racial and class superiority to Chicanas. They are rude to Chicanas, interrupting them while they are talking and sometimes walking past them as if they don't exist. Anglo women have also absorbed the racist perspectives of their male counterparts. Consequently they not only want the same privileges as white men, their "power, status, and prestige," but they confine their efforts only on their own behalf and that of other "Anglo women" (1991, 139). This has been my personal experience, as well, and with individuals in all groups of women.

Finally, and for me her most telling charge, is that Anglo women hungry for upward mobility have treated Chicanas in "degrading and "condescending" ways. For example, they "mistreat Chicano children in classrooms, where they far outnumber Chicanas as teachers, principals, administrators, and professors" (1991, 102). This is an issue of grave concern among Chicana critics and writers, addressed in several of the works analyzed in this text.

Anzaldúa courageously goes against the grain of most Chicana critics, refusing to defend any culture, even her own, from injustice to women, although she will defend her birth culture from attacks by "non-*mexicanos*." Cherríe Moraga, providing an even greater contrast to Blea and other centric critics than Anzaldúa, lets chips fall where they may. She prefers her truth to the defense of one's group at any cost. She perceives that women, because of their varying origins and "sexual orientations" have forged weak links, at best. We have failed to unite because we are afraid to confront "some very frightening questions." Is there the possibility that women of color not only have experienced oppression but have themselves been guilty of some reverse oppression, as well? Have women of color "let rhetoric do the job of poetry" (1981, 30)? Moraga sees as a solution a different and fresh discourse that will better convey "women's fear of and resistance to one another" that will not come across as "dogma" (1981, 30).

Chicana literature and critism is not material for mainstream feminists and postmodern, postcolonial, or any other kind of literary theorists to take into consideration solely in order to be multicultural, global, inclusive. Nor is it a literature and criticism to study in order to somehow subsume yet another Other into a mainstream analysis, or to be shunted off into Women's Studies, which too often is "happy to take her [Chicana] text but not her, except as a seasonal worker" (Alarcón 1995, 192). Chicanas should not be placed in some kind of subordinate position in an outline within which mainstream feminist literature or postmodern literature serves as the invisible heading. Chicana feminist criticism and literature is not material to be "assimilated" into canonical mainstream American literature as one Other voice amidst a multitude of ethnic and women of color voices.

Hopefully my project will bring attention to the works of Chicana writers, providing that mainstream and other ethnic and women of color feminists are willing to include feminists other than their own group in terms of race and class gendered power relations. Hopefully they will not want to just rest on their previous training and background as being sufficient in this day and age. Hopefully my project will address these groups and play a part in the effort that has begun to redress these failures of omission in traditional and mainstream feminist theory, as well as in other ethnic and women of color feminist theories. Alas, the only difficulty in pursuing a global linkage is too often considered to be entirely the fault of mainstream feminists, never other women.

Bonilla-Santiago repeats the same charge that Anglo feminists are patronizing to black feminists and neglect other ethnic and women of color whom she lists as Chicanas, Puerto Ricans, Asians, and American Indians.[2] She locates the source for Anglo feminists' sole concentration on African American writers and critics as in Anglo feminists who come from the East, where African American women predominate as a minority and are consequently more visible than other women of color. Still, when women of color were included in feminist activities, commissions, clubs, or organizations, it was always under the title of committee or subcommittee on minority women and never as president or chairwoman (1995, 229).

Tey Diana Rebolledo, as a former director of the Women's Studies Program at the University of New Mexico, and a highly respected and prominent Chicana writer and scholar, also reports the same difficulties. She puts them in the form of the two most crucial questions in my experience, which I believe all mainstream white Women's Studies directors and feminist scholars should routinely answer: Have the white mainstream feminists included Chicana and other women of color fully and routinely? Are they included from the very beginning of any white women's agendas in order for them to be included fully in them (1995, 386)? Without affirmative responses to both questions, neither Women's Studies programs, nor scholarship about women can be validly defined as feminist. Rebolledo claims that during her tenure at the University of New Mexico, Chicanas and women of color became visible there, as well as students of other ethnicities. After she left, however, she noticed that there was a very obvious decline in both groups. On the basis of this observation, she feels that one of the solutions to racism, at least in the universities, is for Chicana writers and critics to keep up the pressure on their "Women [*sic*] Studies Programs" (1995, 386).

Whether or not this is done, Rios argues that Chicanas should join the feminist movement and not refrain from doing so. Participation with all women in the struggle to end inequitable gendered power relations in every area of patriarchy will benefit Chicanas, as well. Conversely, however, mainstream feminists should not be let off the hook, but be expected to take up other issues besides gender, to work for the improvement of the lives of Chicanas and other ethnic women, and women of color, and not just for their own piece of the pie. White women should pay equal attention to other issues besides gender, which are of equal, if not more concern to other women, if not to themselves–issues such as poverty and racism (1995, 209). Sternbach and others go further. They tell white feminists to limit their obsession with sexism and simultaneously deal with issues of "class, ethnicity, cultural norms, traditions, and the paramount position of the family" (Blea 1991, 125, 126) as if white feminists did not do so and indeed had only one agenda.

Here Blea's attack on Anglos who write about Chicanas and Chicano family life is germane. In her view, such writers offer nothing but stereotypical view of Chicanas in their roles as wives and mothers. Chicanas are portrayed by Anglos as inert, masochistic sufferers who forgive all the ills of their lot, especially their victimization at the hands of freely adulterous, brutal men. In fact Chicanas are no more mistreated by their men than Anglo women are by theirs. Furthermore, she proclaims that the small number of Anglo women who have written about or researched Chicanas have done so from "white, Anglo, male-dominated paradigms" (1991, 131). Aren't Chicana-centered writers like Cisneros, who also critique Chicanos and use the same discourse as "Anglo, male-dominant" women, using the same paradigms? Isn't it possible that the critiques are simply telling it the way it is?

My scholarship is committed to listening to the voices of all women globally, to dialoguing with them, and to bringing them to the attention of mainstream feminists and traditional critics in order to expand their paradigms beyond the "underlying [discriminatory] premise of [their] traditional disciplines." I also hope to challenge these scholars' smug and complacent certainty, their "Eurocentric male bias of 'detached,' 'value-free' inquiry" (Facio 1996, 16), even when these scholars are female by external appearance. I view such a perspective as gatekeeping at the least, and global myopia at the worst, as most disturbing in a hierarchy of mistaken perspectives, because it is held by scholars around the world who are blind to the parochialism and elitism of such Enlightenment theories. They are not just Eurocentric, though. They cling to an underlying class elitism in which race and gender are two major elements that de- or underclass (and yes, undercut women) out of consideration from their worldview.

The consciousness of oppression is triple on the part of Chicana critics and writers. For they are neither Anglo women, nor Chicanos, but Chicanas. Alarcón distinguishes different strands of Chicana critics, ranging from assimilationists to those advocating a "less fractured" (1995, 196–197) segmentation of selfhood. By this she means "a bi- or multiethnicized, raced and gendered subject-in-process [who] may be called upon to take up diverse subject positions which cannot be 'unified' without double-binds and contradictions" (1995, 199). She fails, however, to distinguish that there are also different and complex strands of feminists of other kinds. Each and every group in Women's Studies and elsewhere in academia, as well as in communities outside academia, can be similarly characterized as she characterizes only Chicana writers and critics.

Rios critiques traditionalists for linear thinking, for conceptualizing race, class, and gender issues as separate and fixed integers. Like Alarcón, she calls instead for three-dimensionality in the use of our models that would not foreground and prioritize any single problem. Instead, valid theory would attempt to replicate the complex realities beyond the hitherto rigid limits of tradition (1995, 205). Rios's reasoning may well grasp a wider reality than that of tradition-bound theorists. There is no question that in the past the theories of the mainstream feminist movement have failed many Chicanas because they perceived the movement's theories as treating them as tokens and marginalizing them because of racial and class bias. Nevertheless, as I have argued, it is time to move on.

Quintana approaches the issue from a somewhat different angle. She sees Chicana writings as simultaneously offering alternatives to traditional thinking in her field of social science, as well as serving as reinforcements to unthinking acceptance of hidebound, outmoded paradigms. Because, after all is said and done, Chicana experiences are experiences of females, like other females (1986, 209). Unfortunately, she essentializes women writers as "ethnographers" on the grounds that they "focus on microcosms within a culture, unpacking rituals in the context of inherited symbolic and social structures of subjugation" (1986, 209–210). I would contend, instead, that women writers reinforce their own perspectives through the most powerful medium of exposure: their texts.

The Chicana authors describe themselves as, or convey a perspective about inequitable gendered power relations different from any of their characters, male and female. Theirs is a perspective that is current at the historical moment in which they are writing their texts, as opposed to that of their troubled characters. Theirs is also a perspective that is feminist. It is informed by a conscious, feminist critique of inequitable gendered power relations in terms of class as grounded in and emanating from cultural gender and race constructions. As Foucault puts it, although only in terms of men on men, these constructions are based on "the self-affirmation of one class [men] rather than the enslavement of another: a defense, a protection, a strengthening, and an exaltation . . . as a means of social control and political subjugation" (1980, 123).

From their present feminist perspective, the Chicana authors critique their past: their original Chicana and then later Anglo American cultures, which have constrained women, ethnic women, and women of color from full expression of their humanity. Both cultures practice what even recent American legal reports define as "systemic discrimination, disparities in treatment [that] do appear to correlate with membership in minority groups and 'even' with gender" (Resnik 1996, 959).

Even if all that these authors are aiming at in their works is to oppose gendered and raced power relations, at the very least, to oppose them is to make a first step in the direction of transformation. It is a mistake, as I have argued elsewhere, for groups of women in any and all cultures to separate and distance from each other on the basis of frightening arguments that our assorted, diverse, miscellaneous, complex, and complicated differences are so enormous that they cannot be sorted out.[3] On the basis of these hitherto compelling, but ultimately superficial rationalizations, we have been divided and conquered everywhere to the delight of our oppressors. We should continually expand our perspective until it encompasses and incorporates the global oppression of women, until we experience and focus on our commonalities as women, regardless of divisions along lines of privilege, or apparent privilege, until push comes to shove.

NOTES

1. In this regard and relevant to the project of my text, O'Driscoll writes that "Anzaldúa and de Lauretis, among others, recognize the mutual interdependence of sexuality with class, race, and gender" . . . that "sexuality functions differently, and therefore constructs identity differently, in different classes" (1996, 44).

2. See Preface and Conclusion in Phillipa Kafka, *(Un)Doing the Missionary Position: Gender Asymmetry in Contemporary Asian American Women's Writing* for a lengthy discussion of this problem and attempt to resolve it. For a valuable history of the Chicana feminist movement, also see Alma M. García, "The Development of Chicana Feminist Discourse, 1970–1980," in *Latinos in the United States: History, Law and Perspective.* Vol. 2. *Latina Issues: Fragments of Historia (Ella) (Herstory).* ed. Antoinette Sedillo López, 359–380 (New York and London: Garland Press). See pp. 362–63, 366, 373, especially. García also makes the only feminist analysis, to my knowledge, besides my own, to include other ethnic and racial groups, even citing their own critics (specifically Asian American and African American, but not Native American critics). She concludes that "[a]mong the major ideological questions facing all three groups of feminists were the relationship between feminism and the ideology of cultural nationalism or racial pride, feminism and feminist baiting within the larger movements, and the relationship between their feminist movements and the white feminist movement" (1995, 363).

What Grindstaff remarks about African American men can be extended to the men of other ethnic and racial groups: "If black women do not support black men unconditionally, they too get positioned as part of the white conspiracy" (1994, 39). These are relationships that I explore at great length in the Conclusion to *(Un)Doing.* Like myself in that text, García believes that "Future dialogue among all feminists will ·require a mutual understanding of existing differences as well as the similarities" (1995, 375).

3. See Conclusion, Phillipa Kafka, "Asian American Women and the Feminist Movement" in *(Un)Doing the Missionary Position: Gender Asymmetry in Contemporary Asian American Women's Writing* (Westport, CT: Greenwood, 1997).

Works Cited

Acosta Palomo, Teresa. 1993. "They Are Laying Plans for Me—Those Curanderas." In *Infinite Divisions: An Anthology of Chicana Literature*, ed. Tey Diana Rebolledo and Eliana S. Rivero, 296–297. Tucson: University of Arizona Press.

Alarcón, Norma. 1995. "Cognitive Desires: An Allegory of/for Chicana Critics." In *Chicana (W)Rites on Word and Film*. Series in Chicana/Latina Studies, ed. María Herrera-Sobek and Helena María Viramontes, 185–200. Berkeley: Third Women Press.

———. 1993. *Displacement, Diaspora and Geographies of Identity*, ed. Smadar Lavie and Pat Swedenborg. Durham, NC: Duke University Press.

———. 1989. "The Sardonic Powers of the Erotic in the Work of Ana Castillo." In *Breaking Boundaries: Latina Writing and Critical Readings*, ed. Asunción Horno-Delgado, Eliana Ortega, Nina M. Scott, and Nancy Saporta Sternbach, 94–110. Amherst: University of Massachusetts Press.

———. 1988. "Making *Familia* from Scratch: Split Subjectivities in the Work of Helena María Viramontes and Cherríe Moraga." In *Chicana Creativity and Criticism: Charting New Frontiers in American Literature*, ed. María Hererra-Sobek and Helena María Viramontes, 147–159. Houston: Arte Publico Press.

———. 1981. "Chicana's Feminist Literature: A Re-vision through Malintzin/or Malintzin: Putting Flesh Back on the Object." In *This Bridge Called My Back: Writings by Radical Women of Color*, ed. Cherríe Moraga and Gloria Anzaldúa, 182–190. Foreword by Toni Cade Bambara. Watertown, MA: Persephone Press.

Alcalá, Kathleen. 1992. *Mrs. Vargas and the Dead Naturalist*. Corvallis, OR: Calyx Books.

Allen, Ann Taylor. 1996. "The March through the Institutions: Women's Studies in the United States and West and East Germany, 1980–1995." *Signs: Journal of Women in Culture and Society* 22(1): 152–180.

Andrade, Susan Z. 1994. "White Skin, Black Masks: Colonialism and the Sexual Politics of *Oroonoko*." *Cultural Critique* 27: 189–214.

Anzaldúa, Gloria. 1993a. "By Your True Faces We Will Know You." In *Infinite Divisions: An Anthology of Chicana Literature*, ed. Tey Diana Rebolledo and Eliana S. Rivero, 81–82. Tucson: University of Arizona Press.

———. 1993b. "El dia de la chicana." In *Infinite Divisions: An Anthology of Chicana Literature*, ed. Tey Diana Rebolledo and Eliana S. Rivero, 82–83. Tucson: University of Arizona Press.

———. 1993c. "Linguistic Terrorism." In *Infinite Divisions: An Anthology of Chicana Literature*, ed. Tey Diana Rebolledo and Eliana S. Rivero, 293–295. Tucson: University of Arizona Press.

———. 1992. "Ghost Trap." In *New Chicana/Chicano Writing*, ed. Charles M. Tatum, 40–42. Tucson: University of Arizona Press.

———. 1987. *Borderlands/La Frontera: The New Mestiza*. San Francisco, CA: Aunt Lute Books.

———. 1981a. "El Mundo Zurdo." In *This Bridge Called My Back: Writings by Radical Women of Color*, ed. Cherríe Moraga and Gloria Anzaldúa, 195–196. Foreword by Toni Cade Bambara. Watertown, MA: Persephone Press.

———.1981b. "La Prieta." In *This Bridge Called My Back: Writings by Radical Women of Color*, ed. Cherríe Moraga and Gloria Anzaldúa, 198–209. Foreword by Toni Cade Bambara. Watertown, MA: Persephone Press.

———. 1981c. "O.K. Momma, Who the Hell Am I? An Interview with Luisah Teish." In *This Bridge Called My Back: Writings by Radical Women of Color*, ed. Cherríe Moraga and Gloria Anzaldúa, 221–231. Foreword by Toni Cade Bambara. Watertown, MA: Persephone Press.

———, ed. 1990. *Making Face, Making Soul–Haciendo Caras: Creative and Critical Perspectives by Women of Color*. San Francisco: Aunt Lute Books.

Beckwith, Karen. 1996. "Lancashire Women against Pit Closures: Women's Standing in a Men's Movement." *Signs: Journal of Women's Culture and Society* 21(4): 1034–1068.

Behar, Ruth. 1995. "Revolutions of the Heart: Review of *In the Time of the Butterflies*, by Julia Alvarez." *Women's Review of Books* 12(8): 6–7.

———. 1993. "North of the Border: Review of *Infinite Divisions*." *Women's Review of Books* 11 (2): 16–19.

———. 1993. *Translated Woman: Crossing the Border with Esperanza's Story*. Boston, MA: Beacon Press.

Blea, Irene J. 1991. *La Chicana and the Intersection of Race, Class, and Gender*. Westport, CT: Praeger Publishers.

Blumberg, Rhoda Lois. 1990. "White Mothers as Civil rights Activists: The Interweave of Family and Movement Roles." In *Women and* Social *Protest*, ed. Guida West and Rhoda Lois Blumberg, 166–179. New York: Oxford University Press.

Boer, Inge E. 1996. "Despotism from under the Veil: Masculine and Feminine Readings of the Despot and the Harem." *Cultural Critique* 32: 43–73.

Boesing, Martha. 1996."Rushing Headlong into the Fire at the Foot of the Mountain." *Signs: Journal of Women in Culture and Society*." Special Issue Edition: *Feminist Theory and Practice* 21(4): 1011–1023.

Bonilla Santiago, Gloria. 1995. "Hispanic Women Breaking New Ground through Leadership." In *Latinos in the United States: History, Law and Perspective*. Vol. 2. *Latina Issues: Fragments of Historia (Ella) (Herstory)*, ed. Antoinette Sedillo López, 217–235. New York: Garland Press. Orig. ptd. in *Latino Studies Journal* 2(1991): 19–37.

Bourdieu, Pierre. 1979. *La distinction: Critique sociale du jugement*. Paris: Editions de Minuit.

Broyles, Yolanda Julia. 1986. "Women in El Teatro Campesino: 'Apoco Estaba Molacha La Virgen de Guadalupe?'" In *Chicana Voices: Intersections of Class, Race, and*

Gender, ed. Teresa Córdova, Norma Cantú, Gilberto Cardenás, Juan García, and Christine M. Sierra, 165-185. Albuquerque: Univesity of New Mexico Press.

Bruce-Novoa, Juan. 1995. "Sheila Ortiz Taylor's *Faultline*: A Third Woman Utopia." In *Chicana (W)Rites on Word and Film*. Series in Chicana/Latina Studies, ed. María Herrera-Sobek and Helena María Viramontes, 225–243. Berkeley: Third Women Press.

Butler, Judith. 1991. "Imitation and Gender Insubordination." In *Inside/Out: Lesbian Theories, Gay Theories*, ed. Diana Fuss, 13–31. New York: Routledge.

———. 1990. *Gender Trouble: Feminism as the Subversion of Identity*. New York: Routledge.

Castañeda, Antonia I. 1993. "Sexual Violence in the Politics of Conquest: Amerindian Women and the Spanish Conquest of Alta California." In *Building with Our Hands: New Directions in Chicana Studies*, ed. Adela de la Torre and Beatríz M. Pesquera, 15–33. Berkeley: University of California Press.

Castillo, Ana. 1995. *My Father Was a Toltec and Selected Poems 1973–1988*. New York: W.W. Norton.

———. 1994a. *So Far From God*. New York: Plume/Penguin.

———. 1994b. *Massacre of the Dreamers: Essays on Xicanisma*. New York: Plume/Penguin.

———. 1986. *The Mixquiahuala Letters*. Binghamton, NY: Bilingual Review Press.

Chávez, Denise. 1992. "Saints." In *Mirrors Beneath the Earth*," ed. Ray Gonzales, 38–51. Willimantic, CT: Curbstone Press.

———. 1988. "Novena Narratives." In *Chicana Creativity and Criticism: Charting New Frontiers in American Literature*, ed. María Herrera-Sobek and Helena María Viramontes, 88-100. Houston, TX: Arte Publico Press.

Cisneros, Sandra. 1992. "Divine Providence." In *New Chicana/Chicano Writing*, ed. Charles M. Tatum, 76–78. Tucson: University of Arizona Press.

———. 1991. *Woman Hollering Creek and Other Stories*. New York: Vintage.

———. 1987. *My Wicked, Wicked Ways*. Bloomington, IN: Third Woman Press.

———. 1983. *The House on Mango Street*. Houston, TX: Arte Publico Press.

Cixous, Hélène. 1983. "The Laugh of the Medusa." *The Signs Reader: Women, Gender and Scholarship*, ed. Elizabeth Abel and Emily K. Abel, trans. Keith Cohen and Paul Cohen. Chicago: University of Chicago Press.

Cohen, Philip N. 1996. "Nationalism and Suffrage: Gender Struggle in Nation-Building America." *Signs: Journal of Women in Culture and Society* 21(3): 707–727.

Córdova, Teresa, Norma Cantú, Gilberto Cardenas, Juan García, and Christine M. Sierra, eds. 1986. *Chicana Voices: Intersections of Class, Race, and Gender*. Albuquerque: University of New Mexico Press.

Corpi, Lucha. 1993. "Protocola de verduras/The Protocol of Vegetables." Trans. Catherine Rodriguez-Nieto. In *Infinite Divisions: An Anthology of Chicana Literature*, ed. Tey Diana Rebolledo and Eliana S. Rivero, 280–281. Tucson: University of Arizona Press.

———. 1980. *Palabras de Mediodía/Noon Words*. Berkeley: El Fuego de Aztlán Publications.

Cota-Cárdenas, Margarita. 1993a. "Gullible." In *Infinite Divisions: An Anthology of Chicana Literature*, ed. Tey Diana Rebolledo and Eliana S. Rivero, 266–267. Tucson: University of Arizona Press.

———. 1993b. "Malinche's Discourse." In *Infinite Divisions: An Anthology of Chicana Literature*, ed. Tey Diana Rebolledo and Eliana S. Rivero, 203–207. Tucson: University of Arizona Press.

de Hoyos, Angela. 1993. "Cuento de Hadas/Fairy Tale." In *Infinite Divisions: An Anthology of Chicana Literature*, ed. Tey Diana Rebolledo and Eliana S. Rivero, 267–268. Tucson: University of Arizona Press.

Del Castillo, Adelaida R. 1995. "Malintzin Ténepal: A Preliminary Look into a New Perspective." In *Latinos in the United States: History, Law and Perspective*. Vol. 2. *Latina Issues: Fragments of Historia (Ella) (Herstory)*, ed. Antoinette Sedillo López, 2–27. New York and London: Garland Press. Orig. ptd. in Rosaura Sanchez, ed., *Essays on La Mujer*. Anthology No. 1 Chicano Studies Center Publiction, UCLA, 1977: 12–149.

Dernersesian, Angie Chabran. 1993. "And, Yes . . . The Earth Did Part: On the Splitting of Chicana/o Subjectivity." In *Building with Our Hands: New Directions in Chicana Studies*, ed. Adela de la Torre and Beatríz M. Pesquera, 34–71. Berkeley: University of California Press.

Dewey, Janice. 1989. "Doña Josefa: Bloodpulse of Transition and Change:" *In Breaking Boundaries: Latina Writing and Critical Readings*, ed. Asunción Horno-Delgado, Eliana Ortega, Nina M. Scott, and Nancy Saporta Sternbach, 39–47. Amherst: University of Massachusetts Press.

Dietz, Mary G. 1992. "Introduction: Debating Simone de Beauvoir." *Signs: Journal of Women in Culture and Society* 18(1): 74–88.

Disch, Lisa, and Mary Jo Kane. 1996. "When a Looker Is Really a Bitch: Lisa Olson, Sport, and the Heterosexual Matrix." *Signs: Journal of Women in Culture and Society* 21(2): 278–308.

Domino, George. 1995. "Acculturation of Hispanics." In *Hispanics in the Workplace*, ed. Stephen B. Knouse, Paul Rosenfeld, and Amy L. Culbertson, 56–74. Newbury Park, CA: Sage Publications.

Ebert, Teresa L. 1991. "The 'Difference' of Postmodern Feminism." *College English* 53(8): 886–904.

Eisenstein, Zillah. 1998. *Global Obscenities: Patriarchy, Capitalism, and the Lure of Cyberfantasy.* New York: New York University Press.

Facio, Elisa. 1996. *Understanding Older Chicanas.* Sage Series on Race and Ethnic Relations. Vol. 14. Thousand Oaks, CA: Sage Publications

Ferdman, Bernardo M., and Angelica C. Cortes. 1995. "Culture and Identity among Hispanic Managers in an Anglo Business." In *Hispanics in the Workplace*, ed. Stephen B. Knouse, Paul Rosenfeld, and Amy L. Culbertson, 246–277. Newbury Park, CA: Sage Publications.

Fernández Roberta. 1988. "Andrea." In *Chicana Creativity and Criticism: Charting New Frontiers in American Literature*, ed. María Hererra-Sobek and Helena María Viramontes, 106–128. Houston, TX: Arte Publico Press.

Feyder, Linda, ed. 1992. *Shattering the Myth: Plays by Hispanic Women.* Selected by Denise Chávez. Houston, TX: Arte Publico Press.

Fiske, John. 1996. "Black Bodies of Knowledge: Notes on an Effective History." *Cultural Critique* 33: 185–212.

Foucault, Michel. 1980. "Truth and Power," In *Power and Knowledge*, ed. and trans. Colin Gordon, et al., 109–133. New York: Pantheon Books.

Fregoso, Rose Linda. 1993. "The Mother Motif in La Bamba and Boulevard Nights." In *Building with Our Hands: New Directions in Chicana Studies*, ed. Adela de la Torre and Beatríz M. Pesquera, 130–145. Berkeley: Universtiy of California Press.

Frye, Marilyn. 1996. "The Necessity of Differences: Constructing a Positive Category of Women." *Signs: Journal of Women in Culture and Society* (21) 4: 991–1010.

Gámez, Rocky. 1983. "Doña Marciana García." In *Cuentos: Stories by Latinas*, ed. Alma Gómez, Cherríe Moraga, and Mariana Romo-Carmona, 7–15. New York: Kitchen Table Women of Color Press.

García, Alma M. 1995. "The Development of Chicana Feminist Discourse, 1970–1980." In *Latinos in the United States: History, Law and Perspective*. Vol 2. *Latina Issues: Fragments of Historia (Ella) (Herstory)*, ed. Antoinette Sedillo López, 359–380. New York: Garland Press. Orig. prtd in *Gender and Society* 3(1989): 217–238.

———. 1986. "Studying Chicanas: Bringing Women into the Frame of Chicano Studies." In *Chicana Voices: Intersections of Class, Race, and Gender*, ed. Teresa Córdova, Norma Cantú, Gilberto Cardenas, Juan García, and Christine M. Sierra, 19–29. Albuquerque: University of New Mexico Press.

Gaspar de Alba, Alicia. 1993. "Literary Wetback." In *Infinite Divisions: An Anthology of Chicana Literature*, ed. Tey Diana Rebolledo and Eliana S. Rivero, 288–292. Tucson: University of Arizona Press.

Gómez, Alma, Cherríe Moraga, and Mariana Romo-Carmona. 1983. *Cuentos: Stories by Latinas*. New York: Kitchen Table Women of Color Press.

Gonzales-Berry, Erlinda. 1995. "The [Subversive] Mixquiahuala Letters: An Antidote for Self-Hate." In *Chicana (W)Rites on Word and Film:* Series in Chicana/Latina Studies, ed. María Herrera-Sobek and Helena María Viramontes, 115–124. Berkeley: Third Woman Press.

Gonzalez, Ray, ed. 1992. *Mirrors beneath the Earth*. Willimantic, CT: Curbstone Press.

Grindstaff, L. A. 1994. "Double Exposure, Double Erasure: On the Frontline with Anita Hill. *Cultural Critique* 27: 29-60.

Gwin, Minrose. 1996. "Space Travel: The Connective Politics of Feminist Reading." *Signs: Journal of Women in Culture and Society* 21(4): 870–905.

Haaken, Janice. 1996. "The Recovery of Memory, Fantasy, and Desire: Feminist Approaches to Sexual Abuse and Psychic Drama." *Signs: Journal of Women in Culture and Society* 21(4): 1069–1091.

Harding, James M. 1995. "Adorno, Ellison, and the Critique of Jazz." *Cultural Critique* 31: 129–158.

Hartmann, Heidi, Ellen Bravo, et al. 1996. "Bringing Together Feminist Theory and Practice: A Collective Interview." *Signs: Journal of Women in Culture and Society* 21(4): 917–951.

Hayles, Katherine, and Niklas Luhmann. 1995. "Theory of a Different Order: Conversation with Katherine Hayles and Niklas Luhmann." *Cultural Critique* 31: 7–36.

Hernández, Guillermo E. 1991. *Chicano Satire: A Study in Literary Culture*. Houston, TX: Arte Publico Press.

Herrera-Sobek, María. 1995. "The Street Scene: Metaphoric Strategies in Two Contemporary Chicana Poets." In *Chicana (W)Rites on Word and Film*. Series in Chicana/Latina Studies, ed. María Herrera-Sobek and Helena María Viramontes, 147–169. Berkeley: Third Women Press.

———. 1990. *The Mexican Corrido: A Feminist Analysis*. Bloomington: Indiana University Press.

———. 1988a. "Introduction." In *Chicana Creativity and Criticism: Charting New Frontiers in American Literature*, ed. María Hererra-Sobek and Helena María Viramontes, 9–39. Houston, TX: Arte Publico Press.

———. 1988b. "The Politics of Rape: Sexual Transgression in Chicana Fiction." In *Chicana Creativity and Criticism: Charting New Frontiers in American Literature*, ed. María Herrera-Sobek and Helena María Viramontes, 171–188. Houston, TX: Arte Publico Press.

Herrera-Sobek, María, and Helena María Viramontes, eds. 1995. *Chicana (W)Rites on Word and Film. Series in Chicana/Latina Studies*. Berkeley, CA: Third Women Press.

———. 1988. *Chicana Creativity and Criticism: Charting New Frontiers in American Literature*. Houston, TX: Arte Publico Press.

———. 1985. *Beyond Stereotypes: The Critical Analysis of Chicana Literature*. Binghamton, NY: Bilingual Review Press.

Hersch, Charles. 1996. "'Let Freedom Ring!' Free Jazz and African American Politics." *Cultural Critique* 32: 97–123.

Hofstadter, Douglas R. 1980. *Godel, Escher, Bach: An Eternal Golden Braid*. New York: Vintage Books.

hooks, bell with Tanya McKinnon. 1996. "Sisterhood: Beyond Public and Private." In "Feminist Theory and Practice," Barbara Christian, et al., ed. Special issue of *Signs: Journal of Women in Culture and Society* 21(4): 814–829.

Horno-Delgado, Asunción. 1989. "Introduction." *In Breaking Boundaries: Latina Writing and Critical Readings*, ed. Asuncion Horno-Delgado, Nina M. Scott, and Nancy Saporta Sternbach. Amherst, MA: The University of Massachusetts Press.

Horno-Delgado, Asuncíon, Eliana Ortega, Nina M. Scott, and Nancy Saporta Sternbach, eds. 1989. *Breaking Boundaries: Latina Writing and Critical Readings*. Amherst: University of Massachusetts Press.

Irigary, Luce. 1985. *Speculum of the Other Woman*, trans. Gillian G. Gill. Ithaca: Cornell University Press.

Kafka, Phillipa. 1997. *(Un)Doing the Missionary Position: Gender Asymmetry in Contemporary Asian American Women's Writings*. Westport, CT: Greenwood Press.

Kessler-Harris, Alice. 1999. "From Retribution to Restoration." Women's Review of Books 16.6: 15–16.

Kim, Helen M. 1996. "Strategic Credulity: Oz as Mass Cultural Parable." *Cultural Critique* 33: 213–233.

King, Katie. 1990. "Producing Sex, Theory, and Culture: Gay/Straight Remappings in Contemporary Feminism." In *Conflicts in Feminism*, ed. Marianne Hirsch and Evelyn Fox-Keller, 82–101. New York: Routledge.

Knouse, Stephen B., Paul Rosenfeld, and Amy L. Culbertson, eds. 1995. *Hispanics in the Workplace*. Newbury Park, CA: Sage Publications.

Koelsch, Patrice Clark. 1995. "Art for Activism's Sake?" *Women's Review of Books* 12(8): 21.

Kosta, Barbara, and Richard W. McCormick. 1996. "Interview with Jutta Brückner." *Signs: Journal of Women in Culture and Society* 21(2): 343–374.

Kutzinski, Vera M. 1993. *Sugar's Secrets: Race and the Erotics of Cuban Nationalism*. Charlottesville: University Press of Virginia.

Lane, Christopher. 1994. "The Drama of the Impostor: Dandyism and Its Double." *Cultural Critique* 28: 29–52.

Lee, A. Robert. 1992. "Latin Sights." *American Book Review* 14(3): 22.

Leps, Marie-Christine. 1995. "Empowerment through Information: A Discursive Critique." *Cultural Critique* 31: 179–196.

Leví, Lillián. 1993. "La Mano Vuelta [a hand extended]: A Letter from Lillián Leví." *Women's Review of Books* 10(10–11): 15.

Levinson, Marjorie. 1995. "Pre-and Post-Dialectical Materialisms: Modeling Praxis without Subjects and Objects." *Cultural Critique* 31: 111–127.

Límon, José E. *Mexican Ballads, Chicano Poems: History and Influence in Mexican American Social Poetry*. Berkeley: University of California Press.

Lomas, Clara. 1986. "Reproductive Freedom: The Voice of Women in Margarita Cota-Cardenás's 'A una Madre de Nuestros Tiempos.'" In *Chicana Voices: Intersections of Class, Race, and Gender*, ed. Teresa Córdova, Norma Cantú, Gilberto Cardenás, Juan García, and Christine M. Sierra, 194–201. Albuquerque: University of New Mexico Press.

López, Antoinette Sedillo, ed. 1995. *Latinos in the United States: History, Law and Perspective*. Vol. 2. *Latina Issues: Fragments of Historia (Ella) (Herstory)*. New York: Garland Press.

López, Josefina. 1993. "On Being a Playwright." *Ollantay Theater Magazine* 1(2): 43–46.

Lopez-Garza, Marta C. 1986. "Toward a Reconceptualization of Women's Economic Activities: The Informal Sector in Urban Mexico." In *Chicana Voices: Intersections of Class, Race, and Gender*, ed. Teresa Córdova, Norma Cantú, Gilberto Cardenás, Juan García, and Christine M. Sierra, 69–89. Albuquerque: University of New Mexico Press.

López Springfield, Consuelo. 1994. "'I Am the Life, the Strength, the Woman'": Feminism in Julia de Burgos' Autobiography and Poetry." *Callaloo* 17(2): 701–720.

Luke, Timothy W. 1995. "On Environmentality: Geo-Power and Eco-Knowlege in the Discourses of Contemporary Environmentalism." *Cultural Critique* 31: 57–81.

Maranda, Pierre. 1980. "The Dialectic of Metaphor: An Anthropological Essay on Hermeneutics." In *The Reader in the Text: Essays on Audience and Interpretation*, ed. Susan R. Suleiman and Inge Corsman, 183–204. Princeton: Princeton University Press.

Martín, Patricia Preciado. 1996. *El Milagro and Other Stories*. Tucson: University of Arizona Press.

Martínez, Demetria. 1995. "Power." In *Chicana (W)Rites on Word and Film: Series in Chicana/Latina Studies*, ed. María Herrera-Sobek and Helena María Viramontes, 49. Berkeley, CA: Third Woman Press.

Martinez, Virginia. 1995. "Chicanas and the Law." In *Latinos in the United States: History, Law and Perspective*. Vol. 2. *Latina Issues: Fragments of Historia (Ella) (Herstory)*, ed. Antoinette Sedillo López, 204–216. New York: Garland Press. Orig. ptd. in *La Chicana: Building for the Future* (National Hispanic University, 1981), 134–146. National Hispanic Center for Advanced Studies and Policy Analysis. Courtesy of Antoinette Sedillo López.

Massumi, Brian. 1995. "The Autonomy of Affect." *Cultural Critique* 31: 83–109.

McCormick, Richard W. 1993. "From Caligari to Dietrich: Sexual, Social, and Cinematic Discourses in Weimar Film." *Signs: Journal of Women in Culture and Society* 18(3): 640–668.

McCracken, Ellen. 1989. "Sandra Cisneros' *The House on Mango Street*: Community-Oriented Introspections and the Demystification of Patriarchal Violence." In *Breaking Boundaries: Latina Writing and Critical Readings*, ed. Asunción Horno-Delgado, Eliana Ortega, Nina M. Scott, and Nancy Saporta Sternbach, 62–71. Amherst: University of Massachusetts Press.

McLaren, Peter. 1996. "Paulo Freire and the Academy: A Challenge from the U.S. Left." *Cultural Critique* 33: 151–184.

Miller, Beth, ed. 1983. *Women in Hispanic Literature: Icons and Fallen Idols*. Berkeley: University of California Press.

Minow, Martha. 1998. *Between Vengeance and Forgiveness: Facing History after Genocide and Mass Violence*. Boston: Beacon Press.

Moi, Toril. 1985. *Sexual/Textual Politics*. New York: Routledge.

Moore, Henrietta L. 1986. *Space, Text, and Gender: An Anthropological Study of the Marakwet of Kenya*. Cambridge: Cambridge University Press.

Moraga, Cherríe. 1994. *The Last Generation: Poetry and Prose*. New York: South End Press.

———. 1993. *Heroes and Saints & Other Plays: Giving Up the Ghost, Shadow of a Man, Heroes and Saints*. Albuquerque: University of Mexico Press.

———. 1986. *Giving Up the Ghost: Theatre in Two Acts*. Los Angeles: West End Press.

———. 1983a. *Cuentos: Stories by Latinas*, ed. Alma Gómez, Cherríe Moraga, and Mariana Romo-Carmona, xiii. New York: Kitchen Table Women of Color Press.

———. 1983b. *Loving in the War Years: Lo que nunca pasó por sus labios*. Boston: South End Press.

———. 1981. "La Güera." In *This Bridge Called My Back: Writings by Radical Women of Color*, ed. Cherríe Moraga and Gloria Anzaldúa, 27–34. New York: Kitchen Table Women of Color Press. Foreword by Toni Cade Bambara. Watertown, MA: Persephone Press.

Moraga, Cherríe, and Gloria Anzaldúa, eds. 1981. *This Bridge Called My Back: Writings by Radical Women of Color*. New York: Kitchen Table Women of Color Press. Foreword by Toni Cade Bambara. Watertown, MA: Persephone Press.

———. and Gloria Anzaldúa, 1981. " El Mundo Zurdo: The Vision." In *This Bridge Called My Back: Writings By Radical Women of Color*, ed. Cherríe Moraga and Gloria Anzalduúa, 195–196. New York: Kitchen Table Women of Color Press. Foreword by Toni Cade Bambara. Watertown, MA: Persephone Press.

Naiman, Eric. 1995. "When a Communist Writes Gothic: Aleksandra Kollontai." *Signs: Journal of Women in Culture and Society* 22(1): 1–29.

Nin, Anais. 1966–1980. *The Diary of Anais Nin*, ed. Gunther Stuhlmann. 7 vols. New York: Harcourt, 2: 233.

O'Driscoll, Sally. 1996. "Outlaw Readings: Beyond Queer Theory." *Signs: Journal of Women in Culture and Society* 22(1): 30–51.

Olmos, Margarita Fernández, and Lizbeth Paravisini-Gebert, eds. 1993. *Pleasure in the Word: Erotic Writings by Latin American Women*. Fredonia, NY: White Pine Press.

Ordoñez, Elizabeth J. 1995. "Webs and Interrogations: Postmodernism, Gender, and Ethnicity in the Poetry of Cervantes and Cisneros." In *Chicana (W)Rites on Word and Film*. Series in Chicana/Latina Studies, ed. María Herrera-Sobek and Helena María Viramontes, 171–184. Berkeley CA: Third Woman Press.

Orozco, Cynthia. 1986. "Sexism in Chicano Studies and the Community." In *Chicana Voices: Intersections of Class, Race, and Gender*, ed. Teresa Córdova, Norma Cantú, Gilberto Cardenás, Juan García, and Christine M. Sierra, 11–18. Albuquerque: University of New Mexico Press.

Ortega, Eliana. 1989. "Poetic Discourse of the Puerto Rican Woman in the U.S.: New Voices of Anaconian Liberation." In *Breaking Boundaries: Latina Writing and Critical Readings*, ed. Asunción Horno-Delgado, Eliana Ortega, Nina M. Scott, and Nancy Saporta Sternbach, 122–135. Amherst: University of Massachusetts Press.

Peck, Janice. 1994. "Talk about Racism: Framing a Popular Discourse of Race on Oprah Winfrey." *Cultural Critique* 27: 89–126.

Pérez, Emma. 1993. "Speaking from the Margin: Uninvited Discourse on Sexuality and Power." In *Building with Our Hands: New Directions in Chicana Studies*, ed.

Adela de la Torre and Beatríz M. Pesquera, 57–71. Berkeley: University of California Press.

Pérez Torres, Rafael. 1993-4. "Nomads and Migrants: Negotiating a Multicultural Postmodernism." *Cultural Critique* 26: 161–189.

Perrone, Bobette, H. Henrietta Stockel, and Victoria Krueger. 1989. *Medicine Women, Curanderas, and Women Doctors*. Norman: University of Oklahoma Press.

Piper, Karen. 1995. "The Signifying Corpse: Re-Reading Kristeva on Marguerite Duras." *Cultural Critique* 31: 159–177.

Polatnick, M. Rivka. 1996. "Diversity in Women's Liberation Ideology: How a Black and a White Group of the 1960s Viewed Motherhood." *Signs: Journal of Women in Culture and Society* 21(3): 679–706.

Ponce, Mary Helen. 1993. "The Jewelry Collection of Marta la Güera." In *Infinite Divisions: An Anthology of Chicana Literature*, ed. Tey Diana Rebolledo and Eliana S. Rivero, 146–150. Tucson: University of Arizona Press.

Pratt, Mary Louise. 1993. "'Yo Soy La Malinche': Chicana Writers and the Poetics of Ethnonationalism." *Callaloo* 16(4): 859–873.

Quintana, Alvina E. 1995. "Beyond the Anti-Aesthetic: Reading Gloria Anzaldúa's *Borderlands* and Maxine Hong Kingston's *The Woman Warrior*." In *Chicana (W)Rites on Word and Film*. Series in Chicana/Latina Studies, ed. María Herrera-Sobek and Helena María Viramontes, 125–145. Berkeley: Third Woman Press.

Rao, Aruna. 1996. "Engendering Institutional Change." *Signs: Journal of Women in Culture and Society* 22(1): 218–221.

Rebolledo, Tey Diana. 1995. "Chicana Studies: Is There a Future for Us In Women Studies?" In *Latinos in the United States: History, Law and Perspective*. Vol. 2. *Latina Issues: Fragments of Historia (Ella) (Herstory)*, ed. Antoinette Sedillo López, 382–387. New York: Garland Press. Orig. prtd. in *Chicano Studies: Critical Connections between Research and Community* (National Association of Chicano Studies, March 1992): 32–37

———. 1995. *Women Singing in the Snow: A Cultural Analysis of Chicana Literature*. Tucson: University of Arizona Press.

———. 1988. "The Poetics of Politics: Or, What Am I, A Critic, Doing in This Text Anyhow?" In *Chicana Creativity and Criticism: Charting New Frontiers in American Literature*, ed. María Hererra-Sobek and Helena María Viramontes, 129–138. Houston, TX: Arte Publico Press.

———. 1985. *Beyond Stereotypes: A Critical Analysis of Chicana Literature*. Binghamton, NY: Bilingual Review Press.

———. 1983. "Abuelitas: Mythology and Integration in Chicana Literature." *Revista Chicano-Riqueña* 11(3): 148–158.

Rebolledo, Tey Diana, and Eliana S. Rivero, eds. 1993. *Infinite Divisions: An Anthology of Chicana Literature*. Tucson: University of Arizona Press.

Resnik, Judith. 1996. "Asking about Gender in Courts." *Signs: Journal of Women in Culture and Society* 21(4): 952–990.

Rios, Katherine. 1995. "'And you know what I have to say isn't always pleasant': Translating the Unspoken Word in Cisneros' *Woman Hollering Creek*." In *Chicana (W)Rites on Word and Film*. Series in Chicana/Latina Studies, ed. María Herrera-Sobek and Helena María Viramontes, 204–224. Berkeley: Third Woman Press.

Rivera-Ramos, Alba N. 1995. "The Psychological Experience of Puerto Rican Women at Work." In *Hispanics in the Workplace*, ed. Stephen B. Knouse, Paul Rosenfeld, and Amy L. Culbertson, 194–207. Newbury Park, CA: Sage Publications.

Robertson, Karen. 1996. "Pocohontas at the Masque." *Signs: Journal of Women in Culture and Society* 21(3): 551–583.

Rosenfeld, Paul, and Amy L. Culbertson. 1995. "Hispanics in the Military." In *Hispanics in the Workplace*, ed. Stephen B. Knouse, Paul Rosenfeld, and Amy L. Culbertson, 211–230. Newbury Park, CA: Sage Publications.

Ruíz, Vicki L. 1995. "Dead Ends or Gold Mines? Using Missionary Records in Mexican American Women's History." In *Latinos in the United States: History, Law and Perspective*.Vol.2. *Latina Issues: Fragments of Historia (Ella) (Herstory)*, ed. Antoinette Sedillo López, 55–78. New York: Garland Press. Orig. ptd. in *Frontiers* 12(1991): 33–56. University of New Mexico.

―――. 1993. "'Star Struck': Acculturation, Adolescence, and the Mexican American Woman, 1920–1950." In *Building with Our Hands: New Directions in Chicana Studies*, ed. Adela de la Torre and Beatríz M. Pesquera, 109–129. Berkeley: University of California Press.

Russell, Jennifer. 1996. "Gorilla in the Midst: A Conversation with Jennifer Russell." *Women's Review of Books* 13(5): 31–32.

Saldivar-Hull, Sonia. 1991. "Feminism on the Border: From Gender Politics to Geopolitics." In *Criticism in the Borderlands: Studies in Chicano Literature, Culture, and Ideology*, ed. Hector Calderón and Jose David Saldivar, 203–220. Durham, NC: Duke University Press.

Sánchez, Elba Rosario. 1995. "Woman's Word." In *Chicana (W)Rites on Word and Film*. Series in Chicana/Latina Studies, ed. *María Herrera-Sobek and Helena María Viramontes*, 63. Berkeley: Third Woman Press.

Sanchez, Rosaura. 1990. "The History of Chicana: Proposal for a Materialist Perspective." In *Between Borders: Essays of Mexicana/Chicana History*, ed. Adelaida R. del Castillo, 1–29. Encino, CA: Floricanto Press.

Scheman, Naomi. 1993. *Engenderings: Constructions of Knowledge, Authority, and Privilege*. New York: Routledge.

Schor, Naomi. 1989. "This Essentialism Which Is Not One: Coming to Grips with Irigary." *Differences* 1(2): 38–58.

Sedgwick, Eve Kosofsky. 1985. *Between Men: English Literature and Male Homosocial Desire*. New York: Columbia University Press.

Segura, Denise A. 1995a. "Labor Market Stratification: The Chicana Experience." In *Latinos in the United States: History, Law and Perspective*. Vol.2. *Latina Issues: Fragments of Historia (Ella) (Herstory)*, ed. Antoinette Sedillo López, 111–145. New York: Garland Press. Orig. ptd. in *Berkeley Journal of Sociology* 29(1984): 57–91.

―――. 1995b. "Walking on Eggshells: Chicanas in the Labor Force." In *Hispanics in the Workplace*, ed. Stephen B. Knouse, Paul Rosenfeld, and Amy L. Culbertson, 173–193. Newbury Park, CA: Sage Publications.

―――. 1993. "Slipping through the Cracks: Dilemmas in Chicana Education." In *Building with Our Hands: New Directions in Chicana Studies*, ed. Adela de la Torre and Beatríz M. Pesquera, 199–216. Berkeley: University of California Press.

―――. 1986. "Chicanas and Triple Oppression in the Labor Force." In *Chicana Voices: Intersections of Class, Race, and Gender*, ed. Teresa Córdova, Norma Cantú, Gilberto Cardenás, Juan García, and Christine M. Sierra, 47–65. Albuquerque: University of New Mexico Press.

Sierra, Christine Marie. 1986. "The University Setting Reinforces Inequality." In *Chicana Voices: Intersections of Class, Race, and Gender*, ed. Teresa Córdova, Norma Cantú, Gilberto Cardenas, Juan García, and Christine M. Sierra, 5–7. Albuquerque: University of New Mexico Press.

Sosa Riddell, Adaljiza. 1995. "Chicanas and El Movimiento." In *Latinos in the United States: History, Law and Perspective*. Vol.2. *Latina Issues: Fragments of Historia*

(Ella) (Herstory), ed. Antoinette Sedillo López, 401–411. New York and London: Garland Press. Orig. prtd in *Aztlan* 5 (1974): 155–165.

Spivak, Gayatri Chakravorty. 1988. "Can the Subaltern Speak?" In *Marxism and the Interpretation of Culture*, ed. Cary Nelson and Lawrence Grossberg, 271–313. Urbana: University of Illinois Press.

Sternbach, Nancy Saporta. 1989. In *Breaking Boundaries: Latina Writing and Critical Readings*, ed. Asunción Horno-Delgado, Eliana Ortega, Nina M. Scott, and Nancy Saporta Sternbach, 48–61. Amerst: University of Massachusetts Press.

Tatum, Charles M., ed. 1992. *New Chicana/Chicano Writing*. Tucson: University of Arizona Press.

Teng, Jinhua Emma. 1996. "The Construction of the 'Traditional Chinese Woman' in the Western Academy: A Critical Review." *Signs: Journal of Women in Culture and Society* 22(1): 115–151.

Torre, Adela de la. 1993. "Hard Choices and Changing Roles among Mexican Migrant Campesinas." In *Building with Our Hands: New Directions in Chicana Studies*, ed. Adela de la Torre and Beatríz M. Pesquera, 168–180. Berkeley: University of California Press.

Torre, Adela de la, and Beátriz M. Pesquera, eds. 1993. *Building With Our Hands: New Directions in Chicana Studies*. Berkeley: University of California Press.

Torres, Hector A. 1995. "Story, Telling, Voice: Narrative Authority in Ana Castillo's *The Mixquiahuala Letters*." In *Chicana (W)Rites on Word and Film*. Series in Chicana/Latina Studies, ed. María Herrera-Sobek and Helena María Viramontes, 125–145. Berkeley: Third Woman Press.

Trambley, Estela Portillo. 1993. "The Paris Gown." In *Infinite Divisions: An Anthology of Chicana Literature*, ed. Tey Diana Rebolledo and Eliana S. Rivero, 360–368. Tucson: The University of Arizona Press.

———. 1983. *Sor Juana and Other Plays*. Binghamton, NY: Bilingual Review Press.

Valenzuela, Luisa. 1993. "Dirty Words." In *Pleasure in the Word: Erotic Writings by Latin American Women*. ed. Margarita Fernández Olmos and Lizbeth Paravisini Gibert, 126–129. Fredonia, NY: White Pine Press.

Valle, Carmen. 1988. "Diary Entry #1." In *Reclaiming Medusa: Short Stories by Contemporary Puerto Rican Women*, ed. and trans. Diana Vélez, 135–137. San Francisco: Spinsters/Aunt Lute.

Vélez, Diana. 1989. *Cultural Construction of Women by Contemporary Puerto Rican Women Authors: The Psychosocial Development of Puerto Rican Women*, ed. Cynthia García Coll and María de Lourdes Mattei. New York: Praeger.

Velez-I, Carlos G. 1995. "Se me Acabó La Canción: An Ethnography of Non-Consenting Sterilizations Among Mexican Women in Los Angeles." In *Latinos in the United States: History, Law and Perspective*. Vol.2. *Latina Issues: Fragments of Historia (Ella) (Herstory)*, ed. Antoinette Sedillo López, 183–203. New York: Garland Press. Orig. ptd. in Magdalena Mora and Adelaida R. Del Castillo, eds., *Mexican Women in the United States: Struggles Past and Present* (1980): 71–91. Chicano Studies Research Center.

Viramontes, Helena María. 1995. *Under the Feet of Jesus*. New York: Dutton.

———. 1992. "Tears on My Pillow." In *New Chicana/Chicano Writing*, ed. Charles M. Tatum, 110–115. Tucson: The University of Arizona Press.

———. 1989. "'Nopalitos': The Making of Fiction." In *Breaking Boundaries: Latina Writing and Critical Readings*, ed. Asunción Horno-Delgado, Eliana Ortega, Nina M. Scott, and Nancy Saporta Sternbach, 33–38. Amherst: University of Massachusetts Press.

————. 1988. "Miss Clairol." In *Chicana Creativity and Criticism: Charting New Frontiers in American Literature*, ed. María Hererra-Sobek and Helena María Viramontes, 101–05. Houston, TX: Arte Publico Press.

Walters, Suzanna Danuta. 1996. "From Here to Queer: Radical Feminism, Postmodernism, and the Lesbian Menace (Or, Why Can't Woman Be More Like a Fag?)." In "Feminist Theory and Practice," ed. Barbara Christian, et al., Special Issue of *Signs: Journal of Women in Culture and Society* 21(4): 830–869.

West, Cornel. 1993. *Prophetic Reflections: Notes on Race and Power in America*. Monroe, NY: Common Courage Press.

Wheatwind, Marie-Elise. 1993. "Middle Management: Review of *Nepantla: Essays from the Land in the Middle* by Pat Mora." *Women's Review of Books* (10): 11.

Whisman, Vera. 1993. "Identity Crises: Who Is a Lesbian, Anyway?" In *Sisters, Sexperts, Queers*, ed. Arlene Stein, 47–60. New York: Plume Book/Penguin.

Wilson, Anna. 1999. "Present at the Creation." Review of *The Feminist Memoir Project: Voices from Women's Liberation*, ed. Rachel Blau DuPlessis and Ann Snitow. *Women's Review of Books* 16(6): 4

Yarbro-Bejarano, Yvonne. 1994. "Gloria Anzaldúa's *Borderlands/La Frontera*: Cultural Studies, 'Difference,' and the Non-Unitary Subject." *Cultural Critique* 28: 5–28.

————. 1988. "Chicana Literature from a Chicana Feminist Perspective." In *Chicana Creativity and Criticism: Charting New Frontiers in American Literature*, ed. María Hererra-Sobek and Helena María Viramontes, 134–143. Houston: Arte Publico Press.

Zamora, Bernice. 1995. "Theatre." In *Chicana (W)Rites on Word and Film*. Series in Chicana/Latina Studies, ed. *María Herrera-Sobek and Helena María Viramonese*, 37. Berkeley: Third Woman Press.

————. 1993. "Pueblo, 1950." In *Infinite Divisions: An Anthology of Chicana Literature*, ed. Tey Diana Rebolledo and Eliana S. Olivero, 315. Tucson: University of Arizona Press

Zamora, Margarita. 1991. "Abreast of Columbus: Gender and Discovery." *Cultural Critique* 16: 127–150.

Zavala, Iris M. *Colonialism and Culture: Hispanic Modernisms and the Social Imaginary*. Bloomington: Indiana University Press.

Zinn, Maxine Baca. 1995. "Political Familism: Toward Sex Role Equality in Chicano Families." In *Latinos in the United States: History, Law and Perspective*. Vol.2. *Latina Issues: Fragments of Historia (Ella) (Herstory)*, ed. Antoinette Sedillo López, 237–250. New York: Garland Press. Orig. ptd. in *Aztlan* 6(1975): 3–26.

Index

About the Author

PHILLIPA KAFKA is Professor Emerita of English and former Director of Women's Studies, Kean University. Her previous books include *(Un)Doing the Missionary Position: Gender Asymmetry in Contemporary Asian American Women's Writing* (Greenwood, 1997), and *The Great White Way: African American Women Writers and American Success Mythology* (1993).